Violent cri_____our society tha_____ly another par_____e police are of_____It's too late, many pe_____ing steps to provide their own protection: They are arming themselves with guns.

This book does not suggest that everyone should buy a gun for protection. Many people who already have guns would probably be better off without them. On the other hand, there are many people who have avoided firearms who, with the proper instruction, could safely keep one. The pros and cons of gun ownership are discussed in considerable detail, but in the end you will have to decide for yourself whether you'll be better off with or without a gun.

Also by the author:

SURVIVE THE COMING NUCLEAR WAR: How to
Do It (with Robert L. Cruit, M.D.)

How to
Defend Yourself *Legally* with a Firearm

INTRUDER IN YOUR HOME

Ronald L. Cruit

STEIN AND DAY/*Publishers*/New York

Author's Note

The legal information contained herein is the latest updated information that was received from the legal sources as of May 15, 1984.

FIRST STEIN AND DAY PAPERBACK EDITION 1984
Intruder in Your Home was first published in
hardcover by Stein and Day/*Publishers* in 1983.
Copyright © 1983 ,**1984**, by Ronald L. Cruit
All rights reserved, Stein and Day, Incorporated
Designed by L. A. Ditizio
Printed in the United States of America
STEIN AND DAY/*Publishers*
Scarborough House
Briarcliff Manor, New York 10510
ISBN 0-8128-8091-**9**

Okay, Su,
this one's to you

CONTENTS

INTRUDER IN YOUR HOME

1.

Intruder in Your Home

"Crime is so far out of hand, we can't protect the average citizen. He must protect himself."
—former chief, Los Angeles Police Department

You're sleeping soundly when a noise from the living room wakens you. Was it a dream? No, there it is again—someone is in your home. Heart pounding wildly, you slip the loaded pistol from your bedside drawer and move cautiously down the hall. An imposing figure with a small flashlight is going through your desk drawers. You flip on the light and carefully aim your .38 revolver at the large, intimidating man who jerks around to face you. Although he appears to be unarmed, he's still very frightening.

He has a handful of jewelry along with some money he's found in the kitchen. "Okay, just freeze right there," you command in a stern, surprisingly calm voice. But, unexpectedly, the man blatantly ignores you. He turns to the bookcase, removes your expensive camera, and then begins to move toward the open back door.

"Stop right where you are, or I'll shoot," you command again.

The man stops and fixes you with a look of pure hatred. With a slurred growl he says, "I'll come back when you ain't hidin' behind a gun and I'll kill you." To add emphasis to his threat, he pulls a knife from his pocket and utters several profanities before continuing to move toward the door.

Believing every word the man has said, you lower your gun slightly, so that your sights are centered on his leg. Then, when he's about five feet from the door, you fire one shot, right on target. The intruder falls to the floor, well inside your home, and obeys your instructions to remain still while you phone the police.

You will later learn that the man has a long record of burglary and violent crime, including rape and attempted murder. You'll probably be considered a hero, commended by the authorities, right? Wrong. In most states you would be charged with assault with a deadly weapon and would be in much more trouble than the intruder. And then, to add insult to injury, the intruder can turn around and file a civil lawsuit against you for damages, and he can probably collect.

Most decent, law-abiding people wouldn't consider such an outcome to be just. Maybe it is and maybe it isn't, but this book isn't going to tell you about justice—it's going to tell you about the law. And if you have a gun or have ever considered the purchase of one, you had better fully understand your state's laws concerning self-defense.

Don't get the impression that the example just given is some hypothetical scenario that could never really happen. A lot of honest, well-meaning people have gone to prison or been sued for everything they owned, because they didn't understand the laws of self-defense. As is so often the case, many of these laws seem to be designed to protect the criminal rather than the victim.

The primary emphasis of this book is to tell you how to use a gun for protection in your home without finding yourself under arrest for murder, manslaughter, or assault with a deadly weapon. But this book is much more than that. It also attempts to make you fully aware of the serious responsibilities that you incur when you decide to keep a gun in your home; safety must never be taken for granted, no matter how experienced you are.

A gun should be used only as a last resort. Your first line of defense against violent crime must be strong and secure doors, windows, and locks. A burglar alarm system or a dog should then be considered as a second line of defense. And finally, common sense and awareness are also required if you wish to keep criminals out of your home and away from you.

Violent Crime—Out of Control

The latest FBI figures show that violent crime—murder, rape, robbery, and assault—has once again reached record levels. Murder is up by 10 percent, rape soared 13 percent, robbery is up 11 percent, aggravated assault increased 9 percent, and burglary rose 5 percent. And these figures must be viewed with the realization that perhaps one-half of all violent crimes and burglaries are never reported. Rape is probably the clearest example of this, with close to 90 percent of such incidents going unreported.

Contributing to this crime wave are the cuts that many cities and localities have been forced to make in their police departments. High rates of inflation coupled with increasing citizen resistance to higher taxes have eaten deeply into the funds available for police protection. A reduction of several hundred patrolmen in a single police department is not uncommon.

At one time, residents of the suburbs, smaller towns, and rural areas could feel secure in the knowledge that this sort of crime was not their problem—no more. This crime epidemic has now spread into these heretofore "safe" areas as well. In fact, over the past few years, some of the sharpest increases in violent crime have occurred in these traditionally peaceful communities.

Violent crime is now so common in our society that it is often accepted as simply another part of our lives. Many people, especially the elderly, have become virtual prisoners in their own homes, but they are no longer safe even there. Studies of rape have shown that this crime is just as likely to occur in the victim's home as anywhere else. In fact, one study found that most of the women were attacked in their own beds.

Aware that the police are often unable to help until it's too late, many people are taking steps to provide their own protection: They are arming themselves with guns. A recent survey found that more than half of the people in America keep a gun at home for protection, and in some parts of the country that figure runs as high as 70 percent.

No one knows exactly how many guns are in civilian hands. A study completed in 1968 estimated that there were 103 million civilian-owned firearms of all types, with handguns comprising 28 million of that total. Sales of guns have soared since that time, probably doubling those figures. The number of handguns in circulation is now estimated to be at least 55 million. Over the past decade an average of 2.5 million handguns have been sold each year. More than 40,000 handguns were purchased in the city of Miami alone in 1981. The figures on handguns are significant because there are virtually only two things you can do with this type of firearm: You can shoot targets, or you can shoot people.

This book does not suggest that everyone should buy a gun for protection. Many people who already have guns would probably be better off without them. On the other hand, there are many people who have avoided firearms who, with the proper instruction, could safely keep one. The pros and cons of gun ownership will be discussed in considerable detail, but in the end you will have to decide for yourself whether you'll be better off with or without a gun.

The Violent Criminal—Who/What Is He?

There's no clear-cut, simple answer to this question. The generalities we use when attempting to determine what type of person we are concerned with are just that—generalities that aren't going to cover every case. We can safely say, however, that the intruder will probably be a male; only about 5 percent are female. And don't be surprised if he's young, just barely into his teens. About half of all burglaries are committed by kids seventeen and younger.

The more violent crimes—rape, murder, aggravated assault, and robbery—are not as often committed by younger people, although they are involved in a substantial percentage of these as well. Over 60 percent of all reported rapes were committed by men twenty-five and younger; 14 percent by those seventeen and younger according to the 1980 F.B.I. "Uniform Crime Reports." The seventeen-and-under age group was also responsible for about 15 percent of the assaults and 7 percent of all murders.

What can be drawn from this is that the intruder who breaks into your home may be of any age, but don't underestimate him if he seems to be just a kid. That kid is fully capable of killing you, and he may be very willing to do so.

A fact that has emerged clearly in recent years is that the majority of intruders are drug addicts. In some cities the police estimate that 85 percent of all burglaries are committed by addicts. The average heroin addict needs almost a hundred dollars a day to support his habit, but such a person is unlikely to have any sort of steady income. As a result, you can guess where he is going to get the money for his drugs. An addict is likely to be either high on drugs or desperately in need of another fix.

This means that an addict often will be irrational, extremely dangerous, and totally unpredictable.

The professional burglar is often a master of his "craft" and enters a home solely to steal something of value. He wants to avoid people at all costs. This sort of intruder is usually rational and is not inherently dangerous unless cornered or attacked. (One could make the same observation of most wild animals.) But this person is the least likely of any of the criminal types to turn up at the average home. He won't waste his time on penny ante goods. He is much more likely to strike where he knows in advance that there are plenty of valuables such as jewelry, furs, or cash.

You can count on an intruder, whatever type he is, to be nervous. If he is young he will probably be very quick and inclined to react before thinking. Although most intruders may only be in your home for the purpose of stealing something, there are very few who, when threatened, will not resort to violence in an instant.

There are also the other sorts of intruders whom we read about all too often: the sexually disturbed, the "psychos," the thrill killers, and the maniacs. Perhaps they aren't typical intruders, but because so many of them aren't able to function normally in society, they often make a living by stealing. If they happen to find someone whom they can kill or rape at the same time, then, they feel, so much the better.

This all underscores the point that all burglars are not the nice "gentlemanly" types so often shown on TV. There have been many instances of people being beaten and tortured in order to force them to reveal the location of real or imagined valuables.

What all of this means for the average person attempting to protect himself or herself is that we must assume the worst. If an intruder breaks into your home, don't just lie there in bed thinking that he will leave as soon as he has found something to steal. And don't assume that the person you hear in the middle of the night will quickly run away if you make a little noise. He may, but you can't be sure.

You have to go on a worst case assumption. When you hear someone breaking in, you must assume that this is a violent criminal who will act irrationally and will rape or kill if given the chance. If you respond in this manner, you will be ready for whatever comes, and, hopefully, the intruder will turn out to be only a simple burglar who will be easily frightened away.

2.

A Gun in the Home—Is It for You?

The question of whether to keep a gun in your home is complex indeed, and no two people have quite the same set of circumstances to take into consideration. This book can't tell you if you should keep a gun or not; you'll have to make that decision yourself. Of course, there will be some situations that yield simple answers. If you are an alcoholic with suicidal tendencies, or if your spouse has a violent temper and a history of attempted murder, then you should not have a gun in your home. On the other hand, if you live alone, are quite stable, don't drink or use drugs, and never have any children or other visitors around, you should be able to keep a gun safely. The problem is that about 95 percent of us fall between these two extremes.

One basic fact that you should be aware of, whether you have a gun or not, is that an intruder, whether a burglar, rapist, drug addict, or psycho, can get into your home if he wants to badly enough. No matter how strong your doors and locks may be, if you think that no one can get through, you are just burying your head in the sand. You may look at your doors and windows and think that they are impenetrable, but you aren't looking at them as an intruder would. Your expensive "pickproof" locks and solid doors will only slow down a determined man with a crowbar—they won't stop him. He'll just rip your door frame apart, bypassing all of your protective measures. Granted, this may take more than a little time and effort and make a fair amount of noise, so strong doors and locks are definitely a deterrent to a criminal. But you may be contending with an intruder who either doesn't care about the noise or who thinks that no one will hear it.

If an intruder were to break into your home, what would you do? Call the police? Unless you live next door to a police station, an intruder would probably have more than enough time to do what he's there for and leave before help ever arrived. This is certainly no reflection on the police; they usually do an excellent job with what they have. But once a criminal is inside your home, he needs very little time to rape or kill. With rare exceptions the police just aren't going to be able to respond that quickly. In fact, every once in a while one hears of an incident in which the police never responded to a call for help at all; the message got lost or the wrong address was passed along to the investigating officers.

One way to delay an intruder is to have an internal security room, usually a bedroom, with strong locks on the door. Although this is an excellent tack, you still face the same problem. If an intruder was able to get through your exterior doors, he probably will be able to get through the door of your security room as well, and once he's inside your home, any further noise he has to make won't be as much of a deterrent to him. As a result, you'll still have to pray that the police get to you before your assailant does.

The majority of the criminals who would break into your home are burglars, and the vast majority of these types are there only to steal something; they don't want to have anything to do with you. If burglars were all you had to be concerned with, you could probably forget about keeping a gun; but they aren't. You have to consider a gun because of the rapists, the drug addicts, the murderers, and the other assorted nuts who are running around. And if you don't believe that there are plenty of these types loose, just read a newspaper.

The best way to decide whether you'll be better off with or without a gun is to evaluate the following topics as they apply to your own situation. Though these are significant considerations, they are by no means the only factors you may need to take into account. You may have other circumstances not mentioned here that will influence your decision.

Suicide

Thousands of people commit suicide with a gun each year. Although there's no way of knowing if all of these people would have taken their lives by other means if a gun had been unavailable, it is reasonable to assume that some of them would not have done so. The problem with a gun is that it is so instantly final. If a person takes a drug overdose or some sort of poison, he often still has time to change his mind and call for help, or perhaps someone will find him before it's too late; many suicide attempts are actually a cry for help. But with a gun there is rarely any turning back once the trigger is pulled.

Stop for a moment and consider all of the people who would have access to a gun in your home. Family, friends, visitors, yourself. Do any of these people have a history of threatened or attempted suicide or problems with depression or extreme mood changes? If so, you now have to decide whether or not you could keep a gun away from such a person.

In order for someone to have access to your gun, you don't actually have to allow that person to use it. If someone knows that you have a gun and he can get to it, then that person has access to your gun.

Alcohol and Drugs

Alcohol or drugs mix no better with guns than with driving. You certainly shouldn't keep a gun where someone with a drinking or drug problem may be able to get to it. Such a person needn't be a recognized problem drinker or an addict to create a hazard for both himself and others. Quite a few people are killed each year as a result of horseplay or clowning around with firearms, and 52 percent of all murderers act under the influence of liquor or drugs.

This isn't to say that anyone who occasionally has a cocktail or even drinks a little too much would automatically do something dangerous with a gun. Different people react differently to drugs and alcohol. Some become sleepy and passive, while others may become overly aggressive and violent. Many people wouldn't dare touch their guns when they've had too much to drink, because they have such a deep, basic respect for the consequences of being careless with firearms.

Of course, one problem with a person who abuses alcohol or drugs is that he is often the last to admit, even to himself, that he has such a problem. As a result, in many cases the very people who are most dangerous around a gun are the people who are incapable of coming to such a rational conclusion. A spouse, friend, or relative should carefully attempt to steer such a person in the right direction on this matter.

Children

Children under the age of fifteen suffer approximately one-third of the deaths caused by guns in the home. You must consider this problem if you have children or if youngsters ever come to visit, however seldom. Assuming that a child will be unable to find and fire a gun is a dangerous risk. Most children are much more intelligent and capable than we give them credit for; there are numerous instances of mere toddlers managing to fire a gun.

One often suggested solution is that you store your firearm and ammunition in separate places, but this negates the reason for keeping a gun at home in the first place. But there's no denying that the chances of an accident are greatly reduced that way. A firearm should either be kept so that it is readily available for use or it should be stored in a safe, secure place apart from the ammunition. There is no reason to keep a gun in any state other than these two extremes.

When a gun is kept for self-defense, it should be readily accessible from your bed. Typical storage places are in bedside tables, headboards, and under the bed. Even though you may keep it loaded, if your gun is locked up in the back of a closet somewhere, it won't do you much good if you should ever need it quickly.

There are several things you can do to keep your gun readily accessible to you but not to your children. What you choose to do will, of course, depend to a large extent on the age of your children.

A friend of mine has two kids in the toddler stage. For that reason, the pistol that he keeps in his bedside drawer is a .45 automatic. He keeps a loaded clip in the gun but no bullet in the chamber. If he ever needs it, he can pull the gun out of the drawer, snap the slide back in an instant, and be fully prepared to fire. But it is so hard to pull the slide back on this gun and get a cartridge into the firing chamber that his kids won't be able to move it until they are at least ten years old, though this will vary from child to child. In fact, his wife, a lady of average size and build, can just barely manage it herself.

Later chapters will discuss the pros and cons of the various types of firearms. While the automatic has some of both, in this case the safety advantages of the .45 far outweigh any possible disadvantages.

Another common recommendation when children are a concern is that you keep your gun in a locked drawer, but this brings up the problem of where to keep the key. Hiding it poses another risk: Kids love nothing more than a game of hide and seek and are quite good at it from an early age. This approach may present the children with a real challenge—one they can't resist.

An even less promising solution is to put a combination lock on a gun drawer, but then you'll have a real problem getting the drawer open in the middle of a dark night when you can't safely turn on a light. One way to cope with that drawback is to use a combination lock of the sort that has several single-digit wheels rather than one with a single left-right rotating dial. As long as you can feel the numbers click into position, you can set each digit wheel one number away from the proper combination; then you'll be able to open the drawer in the dark. You may elect to unlock the drawer every night when you go to bed, but the danger of simply leaving such a drawer unlocked all night is that you may forget to relock it the next morning, or your kids may even wander in while you're still asleep.

One lady devised her own solution: She keeps the key to her gun drawer on a necklace and sleeps with it. Then, when she gets up in the morning, she places the key on a high closet shelf out of the reach of her small children. When her children are a bit older, she plans to move the

Fig. 2-1. A pistol with a trigger lock in place

key from the shelf to a jewelry box or drawer with a combination lock. This sounds like a rather intricate scheme, but it works.

Trigger locks are yet another widely used method of safely storing a gun, but these aren't foolproof either. Many guns, automatics as well as revolvers, can still be fired with a trigger lock in place simply by pulling the hammer back and letting it fall. You can try leaving an empty chamber beneath the hammer, but this will only lessen the danger; it won't eliminate all risk. The cylinder of a revolver can normally be turned once the hammer has been pulled back just a little, so a loaded chamber could easily be moved into firing position by a child who is playing with it. A trigger lock can provide good security when used on a hammerless gun, but again, what do you do with the key to the lock?

Placing a gun or a key high beyond a child's reach is often a good idea, but you should never underestimate youngsters. Kids are very industrious when it comes to stacking up boxes and chairs. Whatever system you devise, you must stay well ahead of your children. Don't wait until your kids have grown enough to be able to get to the gun before you move it; you should revise your safety precautions well in advance of that time. To do otherwise is to invite disaster.

You may be fortunate enough to have very well-behaved young children who listen to you and whom you may be tempted to believe will obey your instructions to leave your gun alone. You should understand your children well enough to know if they are truly sincere and can be trusted. But even if you do have obedient children, don't trust them an inch when it comes to a gun. No matter how well-behaved your children may be, they are children, and part of being a child is disobeying occasionally, however slightly. They all do it, and yours are no exception.

Many people feel that once a child is mature enough and responsible enough he should be taught to use and respect a gun. It will then cease to be a mystical, alluring object of curiosity. Well, sometimes this theory works and sometimes it doesn't; it just depends on the child. Age is certainly not a completely valid measure of whether a child is mature and responsible enough to have access to a gun. In fact, the fifteen- to twenty-four-year-old age group has the highest accidental death rate from firearms.

It's very hard to predict exactly how a child will react to a gun if one is available. Even at a very early age, most children have been exposed to enough television (some of the most violent shows are cartoons) to know exactly what a gun does, and toy guns tend to amplify the fascination with firearms even further. And even though your children may be trustworthy around guns, you can't be sure what will happen when other children are around. There is often a tendency to show off to friends, or the friends may initiate the actions with your child's passive consent.

Even bullets by themselves can be dangerous and should be kept away from children. A blow from a rock or a hammer can set off a bullet just as surely as if it had been fired from a gun. Likewise, if shells or bullets are tossed into a fireplace or trash compactor, they can discharge.

Thus far the discussion has pertained to children who are well-behaved, but what about those who run wild with little or no parental control? There are many homes in which the parents are unable, or unwilling, to control their children. These kids tend to drive other people crazy, while their parents seem to be unaware that anything is going on. The problem in a situation of this sort is not so much the children as the parents. And, as with the problem drinker, such a parent will be the last to realize, or to admit, that a problem exists. In this case, neither the children nor the parents are responsible enough to have access to a gun.

Being Willing and Able

Before you decide to keep a gun in your home, you must be prepared to kill an intruder if necessary. If you don't believe that you can actually bring yourself to shoot someone, then you have no business ever getting a gun in the first place. A gun is not to be used in an attempt to bluff or scare someone; you should never point a gun at anyone unless you are fully prepared to kill him.

This does not mean that you have to kill an unarmed intruder who is passively backing out the door away from you. What it means is that you should not have any hesitation about pulling the trigger if you are actually in danger from such a person.

If you were to point a gun at someone, without the will to use it, you would be running the risk of that person killing you, possibly with your own gun. Along the same lines, if you are unwilling to do anything other than attempt to wound an assailant, you may miss, or the wound may actually provoke an attack.

Keep in mind that every dangerous intruder isn't going to be a huge scary brute. As already noted, half of all burglaries are committed by kids under eighteen years of age. This includes an increasing percentage of kids around the ages of thirteen and fourteen who are involved in much more than just simple burglary; young teenagers are accounting for more and more violent crimes such as assault, rape, and murder. A five-foot-tall fourteen-year-old with a knife can be just as dangerous as a professional criminal, and perhaps even more so. The kid is more likely to be nervous and act impulsively or irrationally than is an experienced professional. Of course, even many adult criminals are dangerously unpredictable, but you must understand that you will have to be fully prepared to shoot a kid if your life is in danger.

Along with being willing to use your firearm, you must also be "able" to use it effectively. Simply reading a book on shooting isn't sufficient. You will have to get out and do enough shooting with your gun so that you feel comfortable with it. A person who is afraid of his or her gun is not going to be able to use it safely in a stressful situation, and to say that being attacked by a criminal is stressful is an understatement. Anyone who is inexperienced with guns should go to a shooting range where formal instruction is available; don't just go out into a field and shoot at a few cans. Someone who is experienced with firearms may be able to familiarize himself with a new gun without the assistance of an instructor, but a beginner must not.

This familiarization or training should be more than just a "one-shot affair." Some people feel comfortable and confident with a gun after one session on the firing range; others need another period or two. You are not going to be an expert marksman after a few sessions; becoming a true expert with a handgun takes a tremendous amount of patient practice. But then you aren't concerned with hitting a small target fifty feet away. You only have to be able to hit a man at the distances encountered inside your own home.

Once you've achieved a satisfactory level of proficiency, it's just like anything else; you'll have to practice occasionally in order to maintain both that proficiency and your confidence. You should try to get out to the shooting range at least once a year; that's the absolute minimum. Someone with considerable experience with guns may be able to get away with that amount of practice, but less experienced people will need to sharpen their skills more often.

If you find that you're so rusty when you practice that you fumble around and are uncomfortable with the gun, then you aren't practicing often enough. Discover the schedule that works best for you and stick to it. Most people find that target shooting is actually pleasant; making regular trips to the range need not seem like some drudgery that you have to force yourself through.

Temperament

This should be obvious, but if you or someone in your family has a hot temper that leads to rather violent reactions, you should not keep a gun around. Most murder victims are killed by someone they know. The exact figures vary, but the single greatest cause of murder is the domestic argument—family members killing one another.

Murder is usually a crime of passion. While that can't be blamed on the gun, it is true that having a firearm handy can turn a heated argument into a murder more quickly and effectively than can a knife or a club. The gun is not the sole cause of the problem, but it does contribute to the risks.

This is not to say that everyone with any sort of temper is automatically dangerous around firearms. Many people have quick, hot tempers but are never inclined toward violence. You should know the members of your own family well enough to decide whether they would be dangerous or not.

Women and Firearms

Though much has been done over the past few years to dispel the myth of females who are helpless and fainting in the face of physical violence, many of the old stereotypes still exist. Women are often advised against attempting to defend themselves with firearms, because it is presumed that they are incapable of doing so safely. Guns traditionally have been looked upon as something to be handled by males only, and a great many women still tend to feel this way.

Yet no such conclusion could be further from the truth. A firearm very effectively equalizes the sexes in a confrontation. Numerous shooting instructors will attest to the fact that a woman is just as capable of mastering and effectively using a gun as is a man. There probably are some exceptions, but those pertain mainly to the handling of very large, heavy weapons. Such firearms don't concern us in a discussion of self-defense in the home, so for all practical purposes there is no reason that a woman can't handle a gun just as well or even better than a man.

Some women may feel that the weight and kick of a shotgun are a little hard to adjust to, so they may prefer to use a handgun. On the other hand, many women would rather use a shotgun, since it requires far less skill to hit what you are shooting at. With the wide variety of firearms available, no one should have any trouble finding one that suits his or her own personal needs.

Many folks who are against guns in the home have advised women not to carry firearms, suggesting that the weapons could be taken away and used against them. But after telling women not to use a gun, these same people often then suggest all sorts of tips on how to kick and scratch and use makeshift weapons such as bobby pins and nail files.

If an assailant were to take a gun away from a woman, why would he then kill her with it unless he was planning to kill her in the first place? In most cases a man who attacks a woman has enough physical advantage to be able to kill her, if he is so inclined, without having to use her gun to do so. On the other hand, if a woman were to poke an attacker in the eye with a bobby pin, there is a good chance that he would be enraged and retaliate violently.

Just because a woman has a gun doesn't mean that she has to try to use it if doing so will place her in more danger. That is the same reasoning that should be applied to the use of any sort of resistance. But how in the world is an attacker going to take a woman's gun away from her? If he tries, she can simply shoot him. Actually, it's highly unlikely that an intruder will attempt to take a gun away from a woman when it's being pointed at him. An assailant in such a position will probably not agree that the "helpless" woman is incapable of using the thing effectively.

Dreamers and Sleepwalkers

My dreams sometimes carry over into action, so I speak from experience. On a couple of occasions I've wakened in the middle of the night thinking that I had heard a noise somewhere in the house. My wife woke to find me sitting up in bed holding my gun. When you find yourself in that half-awake half-dream world, you often believe that you are thinking and behaving perfectly rationally, but then when you think back on it the next morning, you realize that what you were thinking or doing made no sense at all. After I pulled this stunt a couple of times, we decided to leave the gun on my wife's side of the bed. It's still readily available, but I can't pick it up and wave it around while I'm half-asleep.

Some of you who read about my dreaming may think that I'm somewhat paranoid. We live in a quiet, middle class suburb where, it is said, "nothing ever happens." Yet, recently, one of our neighbors was forced to go to the bank where he works and pick up a large amount of money for two shot-gun wielding criminals who were holding his wife and children hostage. Preparing for the worst is not paranoia. More and more such prudence is the mark of a realist.

One of my friends has a dreaming problem similar to mine, but he lives alone, so he can't put someone else in charge of the gun. He solved his problem by placing his pistol in a zip-up case in his bedside table. He says that by the time he could get the gun out of the case, he would be fully awake, so he won't end up waving around a loaded gun while half-asleep.

Someone who is in the habit of sleepwalking can be even more dangerous around a gun. Such a person can easily pick up the gun, walk to a window, and shoot through it. If you have a sleepwalker in your home, you should restrict his access to the gun, at least during the night.

Alternative Defenses

You may want to consider some alternatives to keeping a gun for defense. Small spray cans of tear gas or Mace that can be carried in a purse or a pocket are very popular, but there are a couple of problems associated with the use of these devices. First, you may only enrage your assailant, not disable him. Some of these gadgets are so small that the amount of gas they contain won't completely stop an attacker even if you spray him directly in the face at short range. The owner of a Dallas pawn shop is an excellent recent example of that. He was unexpectedly sprayed right in the face with a can of Mace but still was able to pull out his .357 magnum and shoot his assailant twice, critically wounding him. The claims that the makers of these devices make are sometimes greatly overstated.

If you do decide to depend on one of these sprays, you will have to be fairly close to your attacker before using it, and he may easily grab your arm and turn it against you. The sight of you holding one of these things is no guarantee that the criminal won't go ahead and attack you anyway, while a gun will almost always cause an assailant to stop and think twice.

Tear gas shells are available for many handguns and shotguns, but they are of no practical benefit unless you have to control a riot. Such devices are often used by the police, but they are virtually useless for a person confronted by a single assailant.

Another disadvantage of Mace or tear gas is that many of the legal restrictions and problems that apply to firearms also apply to them. For example, if you spray a suspicious-looking character in the face when you aren't actually in danger, causing him to fall through a plate glass window and bleed to death, you may find yourself charged with manslaughter. And if the deceased had a family, you will most likely be sued for everything you own as well.

Furthermore, these sprays are illegal in some states, even though they may be readily available in many stores. This sort of device may be better than nothing if you are attacked outside your home, but for defense inside your home, it is sadly lacking compared with a gun.

Another alternative to a gun is a knife, but unless you are an experienced street fighter with numerous knife fights to your credit, you had better forget this option. This is an excellent way to get yourself killed. It forces you into close hand-to-hand combat, and you can easily end up being stabbed with your own knife. In fact, rather than scaring your assailant off when you pull your knife, you may find yourself being attacked with one. Other weapons of this type such as hatpins, bobby pins, or nail files are also good ways to get yourself killed. If you are already in life-threatening danger, you may have little to lose by using such a weapon, but you should think twice before using anything like this against an armed or more powerful attacker.

A popular recommendation in many self-defense manuals is that you resort to hand-to-hand combat: kicks, gouges, and punches to critical points on an assailant's body. This is another good way to get yourself killed. It takes a tremendous amount of training and practice to become proficient at fighting someone larger than you or someone armed with a knife. If you poke someone in the eye or kick him in the groin or break his finger, you may find out very quickly that the move wasn't such a good idea after all. An action of that sort may turn a burglar or rapist into a murderer.

This isn't to say that such actions haven't helped people at times, but you shouldn't be misled into thinking that you can effectively defend yourself against a larger assailant simply by reading a book on hand-to-hand combat.

Accidents

In general, there are three situations that account for almost all of the accidental firearm deaths that occur in the home: The gun or ammunition is defective; someone shoots an innocent person thinking that he is an intruder; someone shoots himself or someone else while handling a gun.

The first cause is relatively rare and usually involves someone breaking a safety rule at the same time. An example of this is the safety failing on a loaded gun when it is being pointed at someone. Accidents of this type are extremely rare when proper safety procedures are followed with quality firearms and ammunition.

Much more common is the case of someone waking up in the middle of the night and mistaking a member of the family for an intruder. One man shot his daughter as she stood in the doorway letting the dog out, and on several occasions family members have been shot when they unexpectedly returned home late at night. Such incidents often involve extenuating circumstances such as darkness and the shooter still being half-asleep.

If you keep a gun at home, you should make the dangers of coming home unexpectedly very clear to all members of your family. It is best to call first or at least ring the doorbell rather than just barge in, or, what is perhaps worse, trying to tiptoe in quietly.

Even though you may be positive that an intruder is not a member of your family, it may be a neighborhood kid simply pulling an innocent prank. As a result, you should be very sure than an assumed intruder is actually endangering you before you resort to shooting.

The last situation, a gun that accidentally discharges while someone is handling it, is responsible for most in-home firearm accidents. Studies have shown that a few specific activities account for most of these accidents: cleaning, loading, playing with, and examining or demonstrating the firearm head the list. Other activities that consistently turn up, though not as often, are target shooting, Russian Roulette, and scuffling for possession of the gun.

Males are by far the most common victims of such accidents, since they tend to be much more involved with firearms than are females. Most of these sorts of accidents occur on weekends; that stands to reason, since that's when people have the most time for recreational activities which involve shooting.

Strangely enough, though, people who are experienced with guns are more likely to suffer such an accident than those with little or no experience. This can probably be explained by the fact that an inexperienced person may be overly cautious around a gun, while someone who is more experienced may become a little careless without realizing it. Also, someone who is inexperienced with guns is rarely around them and therefore has little chance of being involved in an accident with one.

Although firearms rank low on the list of all causes of accidental deaths, you must still give very careful consideration to that possibility when deciding whether or not to keep a gun. If you do have a gun, it is vital that you understand the causes of these accidents and take steps to avoid them yourself. Later chapters will consider the safety procedures that must be followed when using various types of firearms.

Is Your Gun More Likely to Help or Hurt You?

If there were a simple answer to this question, it would be much easier to decide if you should have a gun in your home, but unfortunately there is no clear-cut, uncontroversial answer. Much has been written on this subject, but it has, in most cases, been slanted by the personal viewpoint of the writer. When anti-gun advocates look at the subject, they invariably decide that a gun is far more likely to injure you or a member of your family than it is an assailant.

One such article, published several years ago in a major magazine, contended that keeping a gun in the home was much more hazardous than any possible protection it might provide. The author's findings were based on his unsupported assertion that 27,000 people had been accidentally killed by firearms that year. But his figures were wildly incorrect. According to the National Safety Council, 2,400 people had died as a result of firearm accidents that year, and that included hunting accidents, not just in-home accidents. We can mourn those 2,400, but they are less than one-tenth the number erroneously cited to support the anti-gun conclusions.

Conversely, the people on the other side of the issue are often guilty of using only the figures that tend to uphold their viewpoint. As a result, much of what has been written on this subject merely attempts to "shoot holes" in what the opposing side has previously written or said. The advocates of keeping a gun in the home often try to show how safe they believe firearms really are by pointing out that more people die each year from other accidental causes, such as lightning or choking. Well, that may be so, but it has nothing to do with whether you are safer with or without a firearm. All of these charges and countercharges only further cloud the issue.

We know that guns often are used against friends or family members, and we know that many of these murders would occur anyway, but how can we determine how much the gun truly contributes to the problem? The same question arises concerning suicides by the use of firearms. These show up in the statistical category of "gun injury of family members," but as we've already noted, many of these deaths would have occurred even without a gun.

I've recently heard of someone who is in the middle of a messy divorce. Her husband has threatened to kill her, so she presently has a restraining order against him. Since the lady now lives alone and is a very stable person, a friend recommended that she keep a gun at home for her protection. Now, if her husband were to come to her home and attack her, as he has threatened, and she were to shoot him in self-defense, it would be recorded as a gun being used against a family member. The conclusion one might draw from simply looking at the category under which the police report would be filed is that having a gun is not advisable in her case, since it would have been used against a family member rather than against a person classified as a criminal.

This is exactly the sort of incident that occurs over and over again, creating statistics that are often misleading. This is certainly not to imply that all "family shootings" are justifiable, but some are.

A widely publicized and often quoted study conducted several years ago concluded that a gun kept in the home is six times as likely to be used against family or friends than against a criminal. But the study included all suicides and family murders; the figure isn't valid and doesn't tell us how dangerous it really is to have a gun.

What about the other side of the equation? Much has been written about how likely your gun is to be used against you or your family, but how likely are you to use it successfully against a criminal assailant? Again, that's not an easy question. There are plenty of available statistics concerning firearm deaths in general, but very little accurate information that tells how many people have effectively defended themselves with firearms. The highly regarded "Nova" series on PBS television recently presented a show entitled, "The Science of Murder." This program estimated that 4 to 8 million Americans have successfully used a gun for self-defense.

A study conducted in Chicago found that over the past few years private citizens had killed nearly three times as many criminals as had the police. This is especially significant in light of the fact that during that period, out of the country's five largest cities, the Chicago police department had killed the most criminals.[1]

Probably the best attempt to analyze the success or failure of individuals defending themselves with guns was undertaken by Don B. Kates, an attorney and professor of criminology at St. Louis University. Professor Kates had his students search through thirty daily newspapers over an eighteen-month period for any stories about people who had, successfully or unsuccessfully, attempted to defend themselves with a gun. Almost 300 incidents were found during this period; some interesting patterns emerged once the data was analyzed. It turned out that the success rate of private citizens in defending themselves against criminals was about the same as that achieved by the police or armed security guards.

Professor Kates defined success as killing, wounding, or chasing the criminal away. The citizens were successful in 84 percent of the incidents, while 6.5 percent of the citizens were killed and 11.3 percent were wounded. When Kates looked at the figures for police and uniformed security guards, he found that 73.3 percent were successful, 6 percent were killed, and 15.1 percent were wounded. It's somewhat surprising that the private citizens were slightly more successful in defending themselves than the police, but that is probably due to the fact that a criminal expects a police officer to have a gun, while it is quite often a complete surprise when a private citizen turns out to be armed.[2]

Those who are determined to "prove" that keeping a gun is dangerous are likely to point to these findings and say, "Look, 16 percent of those people were killed or wounded. That means that having a gun is dangerous." That's simply not so. Remember, this was a study of people who were confronted by criminals who were so threatening that the potential victims were compelled to defend themselves. It is valid to ask how many of these people would have been killed, wounded, or raped if they had not been able to protect themselves with a firearm.

Professor Kates admits that his study is certainly not a precisely controlled analysis of all such events, because many of the people who successfully use a gun to chase away a criminal don't report the incident to the newspapers. In fact, many of these incidents are never even reported to the police. Often the defender has the gun illegally, or he just doesn't believe that the police are going to be able to do anything once the criminal has gone. On the other hand, if a criminal kills or wounds his victim, this event will almost always be publicly recorded, with the result that that statistic seems to reinforce the anti-gun point of view.

Those who feel that armed defense is useless often base their belief on statistics that show how few criminals are killed by citizens each year. They point out that most criminals who break into homes are burglars, and very few of them are ever killed by citizens. That's a true statement; it is also somewhat misleading. The reason that so few burglars are shot is that most of them try to break into a home when no one is there.

Only a small percentage of the people who successfully defend themselves with a firearm actually kill a criminal. As it turns out, the assailant is much more likely to be wounded than killed outright. And while some surrender, probably many more intruders who are confronted with a gun are chased off without a shot ever being fired. If you were to point your gun at an intruder in your home and he turned and ran, you would justifiably feel that you had been successful in defending yourself, even though you hadn't killed anyone.

How about the police? What do they say? They are the people who are involved in such incidents day after day. Those opposed to guns in the home are fond of quoting police chiefs who feel the same way they do. But that is hardly the universal police attitude, as is attested by the fact that many police departments have set up programs to train private citizens to use guns to protect themselves. And many of these programs are combat shooting courses, not just little classes on gun safety.

One of the clearest examples of this is the program set up by the Orlando, Florida, police department in 1966. More than 6,000 women went through this well-publicized program. The result? While rape was rising dramatically throughout the rest of the country, it dropped 90 percent in Orlando in 1968. Assaults and burglaries decreased significantly as well—close to 25 percent. In fact, Orlando was the only city of greater than 100,000 population to report a decrease in violent crime.[3]

A similar program in New Orleans was set up first for pharmacists and was then expanded to include grocers. Pharmacy robberies there dropped from an average of three a week to three in six months. The experts admit that the publicity surrounding such programs is probably as responsible for the decrease in criminal activity as anything else. Obviously, an individual who arms himself without a criminal's knowledge still has as high a chance as ever of being attacked.

Surveys and interviews with convicted criminals have turned up some revealing sentiments. Criminals go out of their way to avoid confrontations with armed citizens, and they are strongly in favor of gun control. Many of the criminals admitted that they would attempt to break in and steal a gun from a home if they knew that one was there, but they confessed that they would certainly not attempt to do so when the owner was home. In fact, some told of planning a crime and then canceling their plans when they learned that the intended victim was armed.[4]

A final problem with statistics and theories concerning firearms is that they are derived from large groups of people, often entire populations. This means that they may be largely irrelevant when applied to individual situations. You aren't concerned with how many people out of a million will be killed by a gun. You want to be able to evaluate the risk that you may be killed by one.

You should already have a fairly accurate idea if your personal situation is conducive to safely keeping a gun at home. Concerns about suicide, alcohol and drugs, children, being willing and able to use your gun, temperament, and dreamers and sleepwalkers have already been discussed. How many of the people who are involved in firearm deaths at home should have been the subject of these concerns? There's no way to know for sure, but it's likely that one or more of these factors are involved in a majority of such deaths. If we could eliminate every one of these potential problems, the in-home death rate from firearms probably would drop dramatically.

Although we can't do that with an entire population, we can do it on an individual basis. That is, you can analyze your own situation to decide if any of the potential danger areas may affect you. If so, you either should take steps to change the situation, or you should think twice about keeping a gun in your home.

3.

Doors, Windows, and Locks

Your first line of defense against an intruder, whether you have a firearm or not, must be secure doors, windows, and locks. At the very least this first line of defense should be adequate to slow down an intruder and cause him to make enough noise to alert you.

Many people who rent an apartment or house have no desire to make improvements to someone else's property. That's understandable, but such an attitude can be very dangerous. Many of the improvements and devices that will be recommended in this chapter can be taken with you when you move, and some of the more permanent improvements can be made at little or no cost.

Doors

Although exterior doors offer much more security when constructed either of metal or solid wood, most people don't want a plain solid door, especially at the front entrance, because it isn't stylish. Glass panes or recessed wooden panels are much more attractive. But the problem is that doors with windows or recessed decorative panels invite intruders. If you must have such amenities, however, you can still have a strong, secure door. Some wooden doors with recessed panels also incorporate an interior sheet of metal, and the exterior surface of a solid wooden door can incorporate moldings that will impart a paneled appearance. And having a metal door doesn't mean that your home has to look like Fort Knox. Many doors that are primarily of metal construction are available with a wooden veneer.

Recessed wooden panels are undesirable because they present a weak spot that an intruder can easily attack. Most are so thin that almost anyone can kick one in with little effort.

A further drawback of many wooden doors is that they may appear to be solid when they are not. Many apartment buildings are especially lax in this regard. They employ hollow wooden doors that an intruder can put his foot right through and then reach inside and unlock.

A double-keyed deadbolt lock will make a hollow door more secure, but as long as an intruder doesn't care about the noise, he can continue to beat or kick the door until he can step through. Though that will make some noise, that task does not require a prohibitive amount of time or effort.

If you have hollow wooden doors, you needn't automatically throw them away, though. The strength of such a door can be increased considerably by the addition of a sheet of ¼- or ½-inch plywood. Simply glue this sheet onto the inside of the door with one of the putty-like adhesives such as Liquid Nails. A little molding can then be added to the edges of the plywood, so that the finished product has a professional appearance.

Glass panels also present a serious problem, though it, too, can be solved. The danger, of course, is that an intruder will simply break the glass, reach in, and open the door. A small section of glass can be broken out with very little noise, so don't count on hearing someone who attempts this, especially if you are asleep. For the criminal who doesn't want to take a chance by breaking the glass, a glass cutter and a suction cup can be bought very inexpensively at any hardware store. Then, just as in the movies, the intruder attaches the suction cup, etches out a small section of glass, gives it a slight tap, and removes it. This can be done in a matter of seconds, and you would have trouble hearing anything even if you were standing in the room at the time.

The best thing to do about a door with a glass panel is replace the standard glass with tempered or plastic glass. There are several different brands available, all having nearly the same characteristics. This kind of glass is very hard to cut or break, and some is so strong that it can withstand the force of a brick being slammed against it. When it does break, the pieces are usually small and dull; the same effect you get when the windshield of a car is broken. Prices vary quite a bit, but such glass is generally more expensive than standard window glass.

Some of these materials come only in large thick sheets, so it may be difficult to find a suitable replacement for one small pane of glass. There are other substitutes available, such as glass with wire mesh in it, but these are not very desirable for home use. Ask your local glass dealers for their recommendations.

Door Hinges

In most cases, standard door hinges do not compromise your security, since they are fairly well concealed when the door is closed. And since most exterior doors open inward rather than outward, most hinge pins are located inside. But if your door opens outward, take a good look at the exposed pins. If they are removable, a criminal can easily and silently pop them out. Then, even if it is securely locked, he can pull the door right out of the frame—also with little or no noise. The installation of nonremovable hinge pins will effectively and cheaply take care of this problem.

Door Frames

You may have a solid door equipped with good locks, but if you haven't taken steps to ensure that the door frame is adequate, your precautions may be useless. One of the most common ways for an intruder to get through a door is to use a crowbar or large screwdriver to pry or break the door away from its frame. These tools can rip iron grating loose, so you can imagine their effect on an average wooden door with a cracked or rotted frame.

The first thing to check is how well the door fits against the jamb. (See Figure 3-1.) If there's a gap, especially where the lock fits into the jamb, it will be much easier for someone to insert a tool and get enough leverage to break the door open. This technique can cause the jamb and door to be pried far enough apart for the lock to slip out, for the jamb to be broken, or for the lock itself to be broken.

When a door opens outward, this gap is especially critical. If the door opens inward there will be, or should be, a piece of stop molding that the door closes against. If this piece of wood is rotted, cracked, or just insubstantial in the first place, it can be removed quite easily, giving the

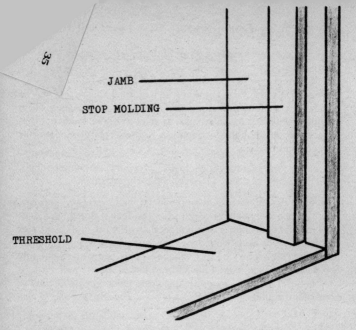

Fig. 3-1. Door jamb, stop molding, and threshold

criminal a good opportunity to wedge his tool between the door and the jamb.

The existence of a gap also means that less of your lock is inserted into the jamb. If you've a deadbolt that extends three-quarter-inch, but there is a one-half-inch gap between the door and the jamb, you only have one-quarter-inch of the bolt engaged. It won't take much force with a crowbar to pull the bolt out of place.

Several things can be done to lessen an undesirable gap. One solution is to install a larger door, though that is a rather expensive fix. On the other hand, if the door is a weak, hollow wooden thing, replacing it can solve two problems at one time. An easier solution is to add a strip of wood to the jamb. Smear it with Liquid Nails or a similar product and nail it on. You may not be able to find a piece of wood of the precise thickness you need at a builder's supply store, so try a cabinet shop or woodworking shop. They should have the tools required to quickly and cheaply cut for you exactly what you need.

If most or all of the jamb is weakened by rot or cracking, remove the entire piece of wood and replace it. In this case simply adding a thin strip of new wood over the old is inadvisable, since the screws for the strike plate need plenty of sturdy wood in order to get a good grip. Whenever you add or replace a piece of wood, you should get a solid piece of hardwood rather than a softwood such as pine. Screws hold much better in oak, and a hardwood will also be less susceptible to attack by burglar tools.

Finally, check all the screws in both the door and the jamb. As time passes, screws tend to loosen and wriggle around enough to enlarge their holes, leaving them easy to pull out. Whether they are in the hinges or the locks, loose screws make the intruder's job even simpler.

If a screw seems to be a little too small for its hole, you can use either a larger screw or fill the hole with putty. The screw can then be put back into the same spot again, but make sure that it is long enough to get a truly secure grip in the wood. Even though a short screw may seem to be in the wood securely, it usually won't provide as much protection as will a longer one.

Garage Door

When you're analyzing the security of your home it's easy to overlook the garage door. If an intruder can get into your garage, he practically has a ticket into your home. Once he's inside the garage, he can work with little or no fear of visual detection, and he can also afford to make more noise.

Though the criminal is likely to have his own tools, most garages contain tools that will further assist him in getting into the house. Even if the door from the garage into your house is too secure for a house-breaker to get through, he can still cut an opening in the wall large enough to step through. Do you find that possibility far-fetched? Stop and take a look at your garage wall. Chances are, it consists of two pieces of drywall or paneling with a little bit of insulation between them. All it takes to cut through drywall is a pocket knife, and most paneling isn't much stronger.

Even if a criminal isn't able to get into your home once he's inside the garage, he can still steal whatever you have stored there. Or worse, he can wait for you. Rapists have used this technique to catch their victims completely unaware.

Garage door locks are usually very cheap and easily broken; a lock-smith should be able to supply you with something more substantial. If your garage door has a lock on one side, as many do, an intruder can

pry up the other end far enough to slip under. Another disadvan-
~ to a side lock is that it usually consists of a slide bolt and a padlock.
Although most padlocks appear to be quite strong, many can be cut
rather easily with a hacksaw. And even if your padlock can't be cut, the
bolt almost always can be. You will be very wise to relocate this sort of
lock to the inside of the door. You would then have to go through the
house in order to unlock the garage, but the added security is well worth
the slight inconvenience it will cause.

Storm Doors

Storm doors should not be considered to be an effective deterrent to
an intruder. Most metal storm doors are made of thin aluminum and can
literally be jerked right out of their frames. Even the more substantial
models can usually be pried open with a regular screwdriver. Besides
that, storm doors normally have glass panels that can be cut or broken if
the intruder can't get the door open any other way.

Virtually all of these doors have a lock of some sort, and you should
use it. Though it offers no real protection, it will slow the intruder down
just a little and perhaps cause enough noise so that you or a neighbor will
be alerted.

Screen Doors

Screen doors are in the same category as storm doors, in that they may
slow down a criminal and cause the intruder to make a little noise, but
they offer no real security. The main disadvantage of a screen door is that
the screen material can be cut by a knife with little more noise or effort
than it would take to cut a piece of cardboard. Still, if it has a lock, use it.

Sliding Glass Doors

This type of door presents special problems—not to an intruder, but
to the occupants. The first drawback, of course, is that the door is all
glass. As a result you should seriously consider one of the alternative
types of glass that have already been mentioned.

Another major disadvantage of a sliding door is that it often can be
jiggled and lifted right up out of its tracks, even when locked. A very
simple and effective means of avoiding this is to insert three screws,
evenly spaced, into the top track of the door. These should be screwed in

just far enough to allow the top of the door to clear them. The screws will then be concealed by the door when it is closed, thus preventing anyone from lifting the door or removing the screws.

Probably the most common way that people attempt to protect a sliding door is to lay a piece of wood such as a broom handle into the bottom track. But if the door has no screws in the overhead track, an intruder can use a screwdriver to lift the corner of the door up over such an obstruction. Even when screws are in place, a criminal may be able to remove the wood by forcing a screwdriver between the two door frames. Be aware that the use of a broom handle may be providing only false security.

A better way to secure a sliding door is to drill a hole through the two frames where they overlap and insert a pin or a nail. By drilling the hole at a slight downward angle, no amount of jiggling the door will cause the pin to fall back out.

The locks on most sliding doors are almost useless. Many can be undone simply by jiggling the door, while others will yield quickly to a standard screwdriver. The most secure type of lock for a sliding door is a track lock. Several models are available that are fairly inexpensive but very effective. Most screw or clamp onto the track, and, when engaged, keep the door from being moved. It's even better to spend just a little more to get a track lock with a key lock on it. Once installed, even if someone were to break or cut the glass, he wouldn't be able to open the door. The intruder would be forced to break or cut all of the glass out of his way to crawl through the frame.

Another device that will very effectively protect a sliding glass door is a charlie bar. This is a metal bar mounted parallel to the floor about halfway up the door. A bar that is mounted in the middle of the door is much harder for an intruder to reach than one at the bottom. The addition of a lock to a charlie bar creates a very secure arrangement.

French/Double Doors

This hybrid door creates all sorts of security problems for residents. Since these doors contain numerous glass panels, a double cylinder deadbolt lock is a necessity, but the particular problem inherent in these doors is that they close and lock into each other rather than into a secure door jamb. Thus, unless proper precautions have been taken, an intruder can push against the doors where they meet, causing each door to give a little and then pop right open with little warning noise.

Double doors also have a crack where they meet that is usually covered by a small piece of metal or wood. This piece easily can be pried off allowing the intruder to slip a knife or screwdriver in through the crack to jimmy a standard lock.

The best thing to do with double doors is to secure one of the pair so that it is tightly closed and cannot be opened. Once one of the doors has been fixed in place, the remaining door will then have a more secure jamb, as it were, to lock into. Ninety-five percent of such doors are just for show, so you probably don't need both of them to open at the same time anyway.

There are several ways to secure such a door. Recessed bolts can be mortised into the top and bottom edges, so that they will secure the door to the upper frame and the floor. When the second door is closed, these locks are no longer exposed.

Another way to achieve the same effect is by the use of slide bolts mounted on the door's interior surface, both at the top and the bottom. This requires less work than installing recessed bolts, but they do show, and if you have breakable glass in the doors, these bolts would not guarantee much security.

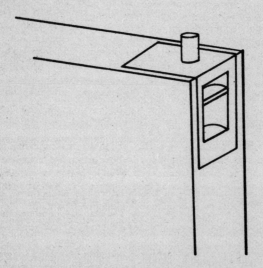

Fig. 3-2. Recessed bolts at the top and bottom will help secure a double door.

Actually, neither the recessed nor the slide bolts will keep the first door permanently closed. You can easily open it again if you ever have to. A more permanent (and probably more secure) arrangement is to nail or screw that door into place.

Self-Latching Door Locks

The most common door lock is a self-latching device that snaps into place when the door is pushed shut. The door is then locked or unlocked from the inside by simply pushing a button or turning a knob. This sort of lock provides minimum protection at best, and should be considered no more than a first step at securing a door. This model has several drawbacks that make it unwise to rely upon it as your only lock. This is the easiest kind of lock to get past; even children can often bypass it. The only intruder who will be stopped by one of these is one who is looking for an unlocked door.

First of all, the curved surface of the bolt that allows it to slide over and then snap into the strike plate also allows an intruder to use a knife, screwdriver, credit card, or anything flat to push it back, thereby opening the door. This is commonly referred to as "loiding" in criminal circles, because celluloid cards are so often used. The intruder simply slides his tool between the door and the jamb and slides the bolt back out of its hole. It makes no difference whether the door is locked or not.

Sometimes the stop molding will prevent a criminal from inserting his loiding tool, but there are other ways to get past this sort of lock. Many can be broken by a strong man who simply grasps the knob and twists it hard. If that doesn't do it, a screwdriver can be jammed into the keyhole and twisted, producing the same effect. If the lock still refuses to give, a pipewrench can be clamped onto the handle. One good twist will then finish off all but the very best of this sort of lock.

There is a vast difference in the quality, and therefore the security, of locks of this design. Some will yield to the above mentioned techniques much sooner and more easily than others. Most locks that are installed in apartments and new homes are of the cheaper variety. And why not? They look just like the better ones to anyone but an expert, and it certainly saves the builder a lot of money. The best way, and often the only way, to tell if a lock is adequate is to take it to a locksmith and ask his opinion.

Many of these locks are made with a second piece of metal, a trigger guard, alongside the sliding bolt. The purpose of this is to make it harder to loid the lock. Note that this only makes it harder, not impossible. As one locksmith commented, "All this sort of lock really does is keep the wind from blowing the door open."

There is one advantage to this sort of self-latching lock, and that is the fact that it is self-latching. When you come home and slam the door behind you, it pops into place right away and you can then quickly lock it with a twist of a knob or the push of a button. That means that there is less chance that someone can push through the door behind you before you're able to secure it. That can provide the time you need to trip a second, more sturdy lock.

Deadbolt Locks

You should have a deadbolt on any exterior door. A deadbolt can't be loided because it doesn't have a curved, self-latching bolt. Instead, it has a squared-off bolt that must be moved into place by turning a knob or a key after the door has been closed. This sort of lock should be used in addition to the standard self-latching model. If you have a hollow door, a door with recessed panels, or a door with a window in or near it, you should use a double cylinder deadbolt. A double cylinder lock can only

Fig. 3-3. Double cylinder deadbolt lock on a door with a window

be locked or unlocked by a key, no matter which side of the door you are on. Thus, if an intruder is able to stick his hand in through a hole or a broken window, he still won't be able to unlock the door.

A single cylinder deadbolt is acceptable when you have a solid door with no windows nearby. This model has a key lock on the outside and a simple turn knob on the inside.

Double cylinder locks can present safety hazards, however, when doors are needed for fire exits. Authorities in some areas have gone so far as to declare such locks illegal. When using a deadbolt lock, you should leave a key near the door. Don't leave it in the lock, though, since this would defeat the purpose of having a double cylinder deadbolt in the first place. You want the key to be readily accessible to you, but not to an intruder who could reach through a hole with a long piece of wire. It's best to have it lying on a nearby table or shelf, so that it's easily seen by anyone inside the house, but not visible to someone outside.

Double cylinder locks can be especially hazardous for children and visitors. Make it a point to give all overnight guests a tour of your house, showing them how to open all of the doors and windows that have special locks or hardware. You may get some amused smiles, but if your guests find themselves trapped in a bedroom with the house on fire, they'll be thankful you made the effort.

You should also teach your children who are old enough how to get out of all the doors and windows. And make sure that the keys to any deadbolt locks are not kept out of their reach if they are old enough to use them.

As with any type of lock, some deadbolts are more secure than others. Be sure to check that the bolt is long enough; the longer it is the more secure it is. It should be at least ¾-inch long, preferably a full inch.

One deadbolt lock that is not as attractive as the standard models, but which some authorities say can be more secure, is the vertical deadbolt. It is mounted on the inside surface of the door rather than being mortised into the door's edge. When it is locked, the bolt, or bolts, move vertically into a plate installed on the door facing.

Be wary of locks that are touted as being pickproof. Locksmiths will tell you that there is no such thing as a pickproof lock. Some are harder to pick than others, but unless you are guarding a fortune in jewels from master thieves, you needn't *overly* concern yourself about that quality. Very few home locks are actually picked anyway. As already noted, there are too many other ways to get by a lock without having to worry about picking it. Virtually the only locks that are ever picked are ones that are well worn and almost useless.

Even a deadbolt lock won't stop a determined, persistent intruder, but it will slow him down and force him to make enough noise, assuming the door and frame are secure, that he may decide that it isn't worth the trouble and risk. And, indeed, slowing a criminal down and forcing him to make noise are exactly what your security measures should be designed to accomplish.

Chain Locks

The chain lock is commonly used, but it should not be employed instead of a deadbolt. It is nevertheless a good addition to a door which already has a deadbolt. Although this lock allows a door to be opened just far enough for you to see who is outside, it shouldn't be used for that purpose. Instead, you should use a door viewer to see who's outside before you actually open up. No matter how good your lock is and how well it is installed, an intruder can still reach through with a pair of bolt cutters and snip the chain in a matter of seconds.

As with other locks that have been discussed, the most widely used chain locks, usually found in apartments, are cheap, weak, and almost worthless. When evaluating a possible purchase, check the construction of the links in the chain. The links of the cheaper models employ metal that is merely bent around so that the ends touch. This type does not provide nearly the security that you get when the ends of the links are actually welded together.

Chain locks can often be opened by someone outside the door with a piece of wire. For this reason, you should get one that has a key lock on it. Although you may not bother to use this additional lock while you are out, it will keep anyone from quietly unlatching the chain while you are at home.

If you have a standard slide chain without a key lock, it's important that you mount it so that there is as little slack chain as possible. When the door is shut, you should just barely be able to slip the chain into the slide. Otherwise, you'll make an intruder's job very easy.

The biggest disadvantage of this type of lock is that a strong man can usually break it loose by smashing against the door. You can't expect even a quality chain lock to keep a heavy, determined intruder out for long, but once again, a good one should slow him down and will force him to make enough noise to warn you.

As with other locks, one of the most common weaknesses of a chain lock is in the installation. This lock in particular needs to have long screws set securely into solid wood or metal. The only way to determine if your lock is as secure as it should be is to try to break it in. Get outside the door with the chain on and throw your weight against it. If you are hesitant to do this because you don't want to damage the lock or the door, you have just answered the question of whether your lock is secure enough.

Now don't get carried away with this test, though, because unless you have a metal frame and door, you will probably be able to break in after a while if you are large enough. The test is just to see if it will withstand a few fairly good jolts without coming apart right away.

It's also a good idea to keep a rubber wedge-shaped doorstop by the door. Then, if you must open the door a crack to speak to someone you aren't sure about, you can stick this under the door as you do so. You now will have not only the chain lock holding the door but the rubber wedge as well. If an assailant begins to throw his weight against the door, the rubber stop should absorb part of the force, taking part of the load off the chain lock.

Fox Police Lock

This is probably the most secure lock that you can get for a door. It sticks out into the room a little and isn't very attractive, but if you live in a high crime area, it will probably look beautiful. One advantage of this lock is that it doesn't matter if your door jamb is rotted and weak and the door no longer fits properly. If someone outside is attempting to break the door in, the force is being exerted against the bar itself, rather than against a few screws set into the door frame.

The bar can also be used when you are away from home. When you return you can unlock the bar with a key, and it will then slide over far enough for the door to be opened about halfway.

Padlocks

Most low quality padlocks can be cut with a hacksaw or a bolt cutter in just a minute or so without making much noise at all. You can prevent this, however, by spending just a little more money and getting one that has a hardened steel clasp. This type will withstand a hacksaw quite well.

Many padlocks have a key number stamped on the case. This should be filed off in order to keep a criminal from simply reading the number and then getting a key made. But, before you rub out this number, make sure that you record it somewhere in case you lose the key.

Locksmiths

The legal requirements covering the professional quality and personal character of locksmiths vary widely from one area to another; many jurisdictions impose no requirements worth mentioning. Although most locksmiths are hard-working, honest people, there are bound to be a few who are willing to take advantage of you. After all, they can end up with your name, address, and keys to all your locks. If you don't know of a reputable locksmith, check with your local police department. They frequently need the services of a locksmith themselves and should be able to recommend someone to you.

The main reason for going to a locksmith, no matter what type of lock you want, is that he'll be able to tell you exactly what you're getting. Since cheap locks tend to look just like quality ones, you really have little idea what you have if you buy a lock from anyone other than a locksmith. You'll often find that you can spend just a little more money and get a lot more quality, and therefore a lot more security.

Windows

Windows often present an intruder with the quickest route into a home. Most people never give their windows a second thought, because they themselves do not use them as entrances or exits except in an unusual situation. But when a criminal looks at your house, a window is just as inviting an entrance as a door, and often more so because windows are rarely as secure as doors.

The biggest problem with windows is that, of course, they are made of glass. The same recommendations that were applied to window panes in doors also hold true for standard windows. The best thing you can do is replace the glass with tempered or plastic glass.

Another good way to keep someone from breaking in through your windows is to install exterior metal gratings. These come in various sizes and styles; some are set into the brick or mortar around the window, others are attached with screws or nails. It isn't a very good idea to depend on nails, even mortar nails, because they often can be pulled out rather easily. Gratings should be set into mortar or brick or they should be attached with one-way screws. These are screws that can be screwed in but can't be screwed back out.

While such grilles can provide excellent protection, they can also be dangerous. If a nonremovable grating is installed over a window that would be needed as an exit in case of fire, you have created a potential deathtrap. That has happened often with bedroom windows.

Most bedrooms have an interior door and a window or two. At least one of these windows must be kept available as a means of escape. If your bedroom also happens to have a door that opens to the outside, then you probably won't need the windows for emergency exits, but such a design is somewhat unusual.

Even though a window may be needed as an emergency exit, you can still put a protective grating on it. There are several different models that allow you to unlock the grating and swing it out away from the window. Some sort of lock is often used on the swing-out designs, but as with any keyed lock on the inside of a door or window, make sure that you keep the key readily available.

Don't be fooled into thinking that window screens or storm windows give you any measure of protection just because it is hard for you to get the things off and on. These offer no more security than do screen doors or storm doors.

Not every intruder who happens along will attempt to cut or break a window. All you need in order to stop many criminals is a good strong lock. But the standard locks on most double hung or sliding windows are neither good nor strong. A screwdriver can often be forced between the two windows and then the lock can be unhooked, knocked loose, or simply broken off. Another sure-fire technique is to shoot a small hole in the glass with a BB gun. An ice pick is then inserted through the hole and used to unfasten the lock. The procedure is very quick and surprisingly quiet.

For maximum protection, key locks should be used on windows; don't depend on locks that simply turn and slide into place. Key locks are readily available at any key shop and many hardware stores; their prices are generally between four and six dollars. This type of lock will stop the criminal who isn't going to break or cut the glass. Many of these locks can be mounted so that the window can be locked closed or locked open a few inches to provide ventilation.

If you've a window that is never opened and isn't needed as a fire exit, you can save a little money by simply nailing or screwing it shut. An intruder can still get in through a window that he can't get open, but it will take him longer, he will make more noise, and he will run the risk of cutting himself. Even when a window consists of several small panes, the wooden or metal strips between them can be chopped, sawed, or knocked out to create an opening large enough to crawl through. But the attendant noise will probably give anyone inside the home plenty of warning.

Sliding windows (those that slide horizontally like a sliding glass door) present the same problems as do sliding doors. Since they can be lifted out of their tracks like a sliding door, they should have screws put into the upper track. The other techniques for safeguarding a sliding door should also be applied to a sliding window. Keep in mind, though, that many of these techniques are of little value when an intruder is willing to break or cut the glass.

A window air conditioner can be an irresistible invitation to an intruder unless you take precautions. The unit should be securely attached to the inside of the house, not just to the outside. If your unit is supported only by angle irons screwed into the outside wall, an intruder can remove it quickly and quietly. And finally, the window holding an air conditioner should either be secured by a keyed lock or fixed into place with nails or screws.

Transoms are not as common as they once were, but if you have one, you should secure it just as you would a normal window. Don't be deceived by the fact that it appears to be way up out of reach. And even if your transom is too small for anyone to crawl through, it can still allow an intruder to reach inside with a tool and unlock the door.

Security Room

A security room can usually be set up with little money or effort and can provide excellent protection when used in conjunction with the security measures that have already been presented. This is a room to which you can retreat if an intruder breaks in or is about to. Even though you may have a firearm, you shouldn't plan to stand in the middle of your living room and shoot it out with a criminal. In most cases you will be much safer if you withdraw to a security room.

A logical choice for this purpose is your bedroom. After all, this is where you are most likely to be if an intruder breaks in during the night. You are also likely to have a telephone in your bedroom—every security room should have one.

Such a room should also have an outside entrance, window or door, so you can escape from it if you have to. If the room is on an upper floor, have an emergency ladder readily available. A rope ladder will usually fulfill this need quite well, since they are relatively inexpensive and can be easily stored beneath a bed.

Examine the door to your security room with the same considerations that are applied to an exterior door. Since most interior doors are hollow and weak, you should probably replace it or strengthen it by the addition of a sheet of plywood.

The locks on this door must be secure, but they don't have to be exactly like those on an exterior door. For example, you'll have no need for a chain lock or a double cylinder deadbolt. Whatever lock you put on this door, however, make sure that it is not only secure, but can also be engaged very quickly. You may have just a few seconds to get the door closed and locked before an assailant reaches you.

You may also consider having a security hall. If all of your bedrooms are down one central hall and separate from the rest of the house, you can make the hall door into the security door. When children are in other bedrooms, it may be more practical to jump up and lock the hall door rather than try to waken everyone and herd them back into your bedroom. Alternatively, you can set up a child's bedroom as the security room. That, too, will probably be quicker than trying to get everyone back to your bedroom.

You may even consider installing a metal roll-up door on your security room. These roll up and down like a window shade and will withstand virtually anything short of a blowtorch.

4.

Security through Common Sense

The tricks, scams, and ruses perpetrated by criminals are almost unlimited in number and scope. What this chapter addresses are the things that you can do to avoid these plots to circumvent your security efforts. Above all, you should be aware, alert, and use your common sense. Many violent crimes are committed after the victim has willingly opened the door to the criminal or unwittingly informed him that there are valuables in the home worth stealing. Some of these precautions seem almost too obvious to bother mentioning, but time after time people usher criminals into their homes just because they fail to think.

Many of the techniques employed by criminals are designed to find out when you are away from home. It is much easier for an intruder to break into your home when you are out, since he can afford to make more noise. A serious danger to you if an intruder strikes while you are away is that you may return and walk in on him unexpectedly, thus triggering a violent attack. Or, a criminal may break in while you are away purely for the purpose of waiting there for you.

Keys

Everybody knows this, or should, but many people still persist in doing it: Don't hide a house key outside near your door. The most common hiding places are over the door, under a flower pot, in the mailbox, or under the doormat. You may have a more original or unique hiding place, but chances are, a burglar has already seen or thought of it. Remember, you are attempting to hide your key from someone who makes his living finding keys. The average burglar has seen hundreds of different hiding places; it is very unlikely that you will be able to come up with one that no one else ever has.

One exception to this rule is to bury a key in a jar out in the middle of your yard somewhere. Unless the criminal had seen you bury it, he'll have to dig up your entire yard to find it, and he isn't going to go to all that trouble when he isn't even sure if one is out there. If you decide to do this, bury it on a day when you're doing some gardening or lawn work, so you won't draw the attention of passers-by. Don't try to put up any sort of marker, just remember that you buried it two paces from the water meter back toward the house or something of that sort. This key, of course, provides the means for you to get into your home if you're accidentally locked out; it's not something to be used every time you come home.

Not only should you not hide a house key outside your door, you shouldn't try to hide one in your car. A car in particular has a limited number of places in which to hide a key, and once again, the criminals know them all much better than you do. The first thing they will look for is one of those small magnetic boxes that are designed to hold a key; those things must have been invented by a thief.

Rather than try to hide a house key somewhere, it is much wiser to give a copy to a neighbor for safekeeping. But make sure that you have more than a mere acquaintanceship with your neighbor, and that he is trustworthy. Unless you know otherwise, that nice old gentleman to whom you give your key may turn out to be a retired rapist and murderer. Why not? What happens to criminals when they get old? They don't all go to jail for life, that's for sure!

If you do give a key to a neighbor, don't then leave a note on your door telling someone to pick up the key from next door and come on in. This tells anyone who is passing by that you are not at home and invites the uninvited.

While it is often much easier to leave a key with various service people such as the milkman, delivery boy, or meter reader, you should not do so unless it's absolutely necessary. And even then you should try to find an alternative. Though the person you give it to may be thoroughly honest, you don't know how many other people will also have access to your key.

Many homes have the gas or electric meters located inside, so that a reader has to have access, either by having a key or by the residents letting him in. Neither is a good idea. It's much better to have the meters relocated outside your home, so that no one has to come inside to check them. Another thing you might try, if it isn't practical to move the meters, is to arrange to have readings taken annually, or at least quarterly. Many utility companies will agree if you request it.

Building or apartment managers constitute another problem; these people usually require you to leave a key with them. Although such people can be very forceful in demanding a key, the law doesn't always support their demands. In many states an apartment manager cannot legally force you to give him a key. He may not even realize this himself, since most people are hesitant to push the issue. If you do have to give the manager a key, you should have your own deadbolts installed and lock them only when you are at home. This will allow the manager to have access while you are gone, but provides you with added security when you're at home.

An alternative means of giving the manager access to your apartment is to give a copy of your key to a neighbor and tell the manager to see the neighbor if he must get in. The main objection to leaving a key with the manager is not that he is dishonest, though he could be, but rather that other people may have access to it. There have been numerous cases of burglars breaking into a manager's office and making off with hundreds of keys. They then have access to every apartment in the building or complex. You may not even be told about such a theft, since the apartment owner would then be forced to change the keys for every single apartment.

If you ever lose your keys or think that someone else may have had access to them, you should immediately have your locks rekeyed. You needn't actually change all of the locks; rekeying is much simpler and cheaper and will just as effectively prevent your old key from opening the lock.

You should also have the locks rekeyed every time you move. Although the previous owner or occupant may have been honest, you face the familiar problem that you have no idea who else may have had access to the keys. In fact, some criminals specialize in getting keys to homes that are for sale or apartments that are for rent. They will burglarize a real estate office or may even pretend to be interested in purchasing a home in order to gain access to a key. Then after the new residents move in, so does the intruder.

The same problems apply to a brand-new house or apartment when you are the first occupant. While the property was under construction, everybody and his mother had access to the keys. Some door locks can be rekeyed once the builder has finished simply by inserting a new, special key. But unless you are absolutely positive that you have such locks on your new home or apartment, you should have them changed or rekeyed.

If you keep your car and house keys on the same key chain, stop and think before leaving them with a parking lot attendant or the neighborhood mechanic. The people at the corner garage may be honest folks with whom you've done business for years, but a new employee or someone just passing by could easily end up with a key to your home.

If your house keys were actually missing when your key chain is returned, it would be obvious that someone had stolen them. But a criminal wouldn't have to take them; he could simply make an impression on the spot and then get a copy made.

Avoid having any sort of identification attached to your keys. This includes your name, address, telephone number, or license number. If you were to loose your keys, this type of information would enable anyone who found them to locate your home very quickly and easily.

Some people think that it's all right to disregard these precautions as long as they are far away from home where no one knows them, but that's not at all prudent. All a dishonest parking lot attendant has to do is make an impression of your house keys and copy down your license plate number. He can then trace the ownership of the car with little effort and come up with your address.

Finally, ladies should be very careful about letting their purses out of their sight, even momentarily. Be especially careful to watch it in the grocery cart and in the changing room at a clothing store. Many criminals specialize in getting keys from these places.

Telephone

Your telephone can be one of your best security devices, but it can also be used against you by a criminal. Your concern should start with your listing in the directory. If you are a single woman, you certainly should not advertise that fact by having your full name listed. It not only tells everyone that you are single, but it also gives a potential rapist your address. You don't have to end up with an unlisted number in order to protect yourself, though. Simply list only your initials and last name.

You should never give out any information to strangers over the phone, no matter whom they may claim to be. If someone calls asking to speak to your husband and you are single, don't correct them. Just say that your husband can't come to the phone and you will be glad to have him return the call. If you are married and your husband isn't at home, you should say the same thing. Never admit to being at home alone. If the call is legitimate, the party will leave a number. A single woman could later return the call and say that her husband wasn't interested in their offer, or she could say that they apparently had the wrong number. If the call isn't legitimate, the person won't leave a valid number.

Occasionally you will receive a call from someone asking, "What number is this?" or "Who is this?" Again, don't ever give out that sort of information. Instead, you should politely ask to whom they wish to speak.

Obscene phone calls are best handled by simply hanging up immediately without saying a word. The caller gets no satisfaction from someone who gives no response or feedback. He probably will quickly find someone more interesting to bother. The exception, however, is if someone has picked you in particular to harass. If you continue to receive such calls, contact both the telephone company and the police.

It is fairly common to get a call from a salesman who will try to make an appointment to come to your home, so that he can give you his sales pitch in person. But before you agree to meet such a person, even in a public place, get his name, company name, address, and telephone number. Then check him out thoroughly. Call information or consult the phone book to make sure that his phone number matches his company name. Then call and make sure that such a person actually works there. It's also advisable to go a step further and check out the company with the Better Business Bureau. Even after all of that, it's a good idea to have a friend there with you at the appointed time.

These telephone techniques for fending off suspect callers should be taught to everyone who answers your phone, including children and babysitters. Someone else may innocently give out information about you and never even think to mention the call.

If you leave a telephone answering machine hooked up when you are away from home, be very careful about what you record as the answering message. Never reveal what time you'll be back, or that you are away for an extended period of time, as when on vacation. This is exactly the sort of information that a criminal wants. And if you really are at home, but just have the recorder on because you don't feel like answering the phone, a message that says that you aren't at home can even invite an assault by a surprised intruder who breaks in thinking you are gone.

Probably the best answer to play on your recorder is something that just says that you can't get to the phone right then. That should keep a potential intruder from learning whether you are at home or not.

It's a very good idea to have a phone in your bedroom, so that you can call for help if you hear an intruder breaking in during the night. Although the police probably won't be able to get there before the assailant can do you harm, if that is his intent, you should still call for assistance if at all possible. One problem, though, is that an intruder can lift the receiver off the phone in another part of your home and dial a number, thereby cutting your lifeline to the outside.

The best way to prevent this is to have your bedroom phone on a completely separate line. Then you can still call out no matter what happens to the rest of your phones. In some areas you can get a price break on a second line when it is to be used only for emergency calls or for very few normal calls each month.

Every phone in your home should have a sticker or a piece of paper attached to it with your police, fire, and emergency medical numbers. If you need the numbers when in your bedroom, they won't be of much use if they're only attached to the phone in the kitchen. Of course, if you must call the police in the middle of the night and you can't safely turn on a light, you won't be able to see the numbers. In that case you should simply dial the operator. She (or he) will quickly connect you with the right number or pass the message along for you.

Many areas have 911 service. This is an emergency number that you can call no matter what kind of emergency help you may need. The operator will instantly connect you with the agency you need.

If you do have occasion to call the police, make sure that you clearly tell them where you live. There have been instances when someone calls the police, says that he needs help, and then hangs up, or just says that he lives on Oak Drive and then slams down the receiver.

You've probably seen plenty of movies in which an assailant has trapped a woman in her home when, suddenly, the phone rings. She answers it, but how can she ask for help with the criminal standing right there? The best way to prepare for this possibility is to have a code word or phrase and give it to the people who most often call you. The phrase may be something simple and unobtrusive such as, "I've got to go, I've got a headache." The intruder will never know that you've passed on a message to call the police.

This can be carried a step further. Although the chances of the phone ringing just when an assailant is attacking you are very small, you may be able to convince an intruder that you must make a call right away, because your neighbor is supposed to be coming over in a few minutes. Then you can call your neighbor or whomever you choose and pass your coded message.

Another scheme that intruders use is to call someone who has advertised an item for sale in the paper. The criminal may be attracted by the fact that the item is expensive—guns, furs, or jewelry for example—or he may just be casing the home when he comes to inspect the items.

If you place your phone number in the paper, for heaven's sake don't have printed, "call after 5:30." You'll have informed every criminal in town when you will be home and when you won't.

Once you begin getting calls from people who are interested in seeing your items for sale, you'll have to be very careful about the information you give out. If someone asks when they can come to see the items, don't tell them that you won't be home all day tomorrow, just tell them that a certain time will or will not be okay. It's also a good idea to receive such visitors in a room that has been cleared of any other attractive valuables.

Another method criminals frequently use to get into a home is to come to the door and ask to use the phone. If this happens to you, don't let the person in. You may offer to make the call for him, however.

Lighting

The first place that should be adequately lighted is the outside of your home. Exterior lights are your best friend and the criminal's worst enemy. Chances are, if your home is well lighted, a criminal will move along to a darker house. You should have every entrance lighted, including windows, for these are just as enticing to an intruder as are your doors.

This doesn't mean that you have to have a 250-watt floodlight on every single door and window. Simple low powered bulbs of 60 watts or so are usually adequate. It's best to have these lights installed high up under the eaves, so an intruder will find it harder to reach up and unscrew the bulbs. If you do use floodlights, aim them so that they don't shine right into your neighbor's bedroom. You must be on good terms with your neighbors if you want them to help you out by reporting any suspect goings-on around your property.

Many people leave the outsides of their homes in total darkness, because they don't want to spend any more money on electricity. Go ahead and spend it; the few cents that it takes to burn a 60-watt bulb each night is cheap insurance. Many people also leave their outside lights off when they're home but turn them on when they're gone. That's a signal that's quickly picked up by any intruder who's paid the slightest amount of attention to the home.

If you want to invite burglars when you leave home for a couple of days, just leave the outside lights burning in the daytime. You can avoid calling attention to your house like that by using photoelectric switches that will automatically turn the lights on when it's dark and off when it's not.

The hall lighting in apartment buildings is sometimes so dim that little can be seen when looking through the door viewer. Apartment building owners are often guilty of putting in smaller and smaller bulbs to cut down on utility costs. Some communities have ordinances specifying minimum lighting standards; check into that if your hall lighting is insufficient. You may also just sneak out there and substitute stronger bulbs.

Take a look at the lighting on your street. If you believe it's inadequate, write to your municipal authorities or to the electric company about getting more installed. Sometimes neighbors don't want more street lights, however, because the light annoys them when they're trying to sleep. If you aren't able to get the street lighting increased, you may be able to get the power company to install a light in your yard. There is usually an installation fee, but it's typically much less than you'd expect. This is a good way to illuminate an entire exterior section of your house that's too dark for good security.

The lights inside your home should be used much as those outside. If you don't normally leave lights burning when you are at home, you may be tipping an intruder if you leave them on when you're away. It's much better to regularly keep certain lights burning. Leaving an inside light on all night may create the appearance that someone is still awake, possibly deterring an intruder. And when you're at home alone, keeping a couple of rooms lighted can give the impression that other people are there with you.

When you're away, use an inexpensive timer inside your home. These gadgets can be programmed to make it look as if you are up watching TV for a while and are then going from room to room turning everything off for bed. Then in the middle of the night, it can even appear that someone is up to go to the bathroom.

A radio is a good security device, too. Before you leave, set the volume so that someone just outside the door will be able to hear it. If you live in an apartment, however, you'll have to be careful that it's not so loud that it bothers your neighbors. If an intruder is snooping around outside your home and hears the radio playing, he isn't going to know if someone is home or not, but it will make him think twice before breaking in.

Another handy little device is a battery-powered light that plugs into the wall. If the power fails for any reason, this light will automatically come on. This can be useful if someone cuts your power lines or if your area suffers a blackout with subsequent looting. Radio Shack and similar retailers sell these for about thirteen dollars.

Probably the best lighting device, also offered by Radio Shack, is a wireless control center that will turn on lights or appliances in other parts of your home at the touch of a button. The control unit costs about forty dollars, and each light or appliance that you want to control (up to sixteen) requires a module that costs about fifteen dollars.

If you hear a strange noise outside, one of these control units will allow you to turn on all of your outside lights from your bed. If you hear a noise inside your home, you can touch a single button and instantly activate every light that's hooked into the system.

You probably have a flashlight around the house somewhere, but is it close to the bed, so that you can easily reach it if you ever need it? Stick one into a bedside drawer and check it every once in a while to make sure that the batteries are still good.

Don't Flaunt It

Use a little common sense and don't flaunt your valuables—whatever they are. Women should be aware that revealing clothing may attract a rapist. Although you may be in a safe place at the time, he may note your license plate number or find out where you live by other means and pay you a visit later.

You should also be very careful about wearing expensive jewelry or furs in public. You are simply a walking advertisement for any criminal who happens to spot you. Many intruders keep an eye out for exactly that sort of person; don't play into their hands.

The same cautions apply to the valuables inside your home. Don't show off your priceless coin collection to every salesman or delivery boy who happens to drop by. Even though the person to whom you are showing off may be honest, he may tell others who are not so honest.

For the same reason, you should be discreet about what you say to any outside service people such as doormen, barbers, or hairdressers. These people, sometimes unwittingly, sometimes not, may pass on information about your possessions or your comings and goings. It's wise to keep quiet about a vacation until you've returned; then you can run out and tell everybody all about it.

Exterior Considerations

Take a look around the outside of your home. Are you helping or hurting yourself? Start at the mailbox. How is your name listed? Ideally, your name shouldn't be on it at all. When you put your name on the box, you're only giving a potential intruder additional information that may help him talk his way into your home. Your mail will be delivered and your visitors will find you if your house or apartment number is plainly displayed. Another reason for having your house numbers clearly marked is so the police or fire department can find you quickly if you ever need them.

A single woman who puts her name on her mailbox should make sure, as with a telephone listing, that she doesn't indicate that she is living alone. Only the initials and last name should be listed. Some women who live alone put a second name on the box to make it seem as if someone else is living there with them. You can even go a step further and have your fictitious roommate listed in the phone book. Then if a potential assailant checks up on the name, it will appear that there really is another person living there, too.

Another tip-off for a criminal is an overflowing mailbox. Don't let your mail pile up when you're away; have a neighbor collect it or have it stopped. If you are in and out a lot and don't find it convenient to do either of these things, get a larger mailbox, so that it won't overflow after a couple of days.

Many homes still have mail slots in the door, though these are seen less frequently nowadays. A disadvantage of this arrangement is that an intruder may be able to look through the slot to see if there's mail on the floor. If there is he may assume that no one is home, encouraging him to force an entrance. Of course, you may simply be taking a nap when you suddenly discover that you have unwanted company. You can avoid issuing that invitation by attaching a couple of pieces of metal to the inside of the door around the slot. The mail can still drop inside, but anyone looking in from the outside will see only the metal obstruction, not the floor and any mail that's accumulated. This addition will also make it more difficult for someone to stick a tool through the slot to work on your door lock.

How is your landscaping? You may think that it looks great, and a housebreaker may agree with you completely. Take a walk around your home and see if your shrubbery can conceal someone at any of your doors or windows. If so, get out your pruning shears and cut back that growth so that an intruder has no place to hide. You may even consider replacing the shrubbery closest to your doors and windows with a variety that has plenty of thorns. That will help to discourage someone from spending much time there.

You may have done an excellent job of securing all of the doors and windows on the first floor and basement of your home, but don't forget about the second floor if you have one. Many criminals specialize in getting in through upper-level windows, because few people bother to protect them adequately. When a ladder is left lying around, a good second story man can be inside a house very quickly. Likewise, don't park your car too close to the house, or it too may serve as a stepping stone to your upper story.

If you've downspouts from rain gutters, you can do something to prevent someone from shimmying up. You can smear a little grease on them, or you can coat them with a paint that is specifically designed to be slippery.

Take another walk around your home to see if you can peek in through any of the windows. Do this at night when the lights inside the house are turned on, so that you'll get the same view that a potential intruder will. Any gaps in curtains or blinds can trigger an attack by someone looking in. Women should be very careful about going around the house unclothed unless they are positive that there are no cracks or gaps that can allow an assailant to get a good view.

While we're on the subject of windows, don't forget your garage. Garage windows should also be covered, either by curtains or by paint. A criminal may be enticed to make his entrance into your home via the garage if there are tempting items, such as tools, in view.

Someone at Your Door

Opening your door to a stranger can be a fatal mistake. The Boston Strangler didn't have to break into homes; he simply talked his victims into opening the door and letting him in. Unfortunately, this sort of thing is not unusual. In case after case, smooth-talking criminals get unsuspecting people to voluntarily open up for them. But don't think that anyone with the finesse to talk his way into your home is necessarily just a high-class burglar who'll do you no harm. Many people bent on violent crime use just such approaches to get to their victims.

The lines these criminals use are so varied that it would take an entire book to cover them. For example, a stranger may appear at your door saying that someone has just hit your car. When you open the door to take a look, you may be attacked. In a similar ploy, a stranger may claim that one of your children playing outside has been injured.

Be very wary of men in uniform, such as exterminators or inspectors, especially those you've not called. Most people look very honest and official when in a uniform, but anyone can get his hands on that sort of clothing with little or no trouble. You should ask to see some form of identification from such a person, and you should then ask him to wait a couple of minutes while you call his company to check him out. Don't let a stranger in just on the basis of an identification card with a name on it. A criminal can get something like that with less effort than it takes to get a uniform.

In order to properly screen someone at your door, you need a viewer if the door is solid, which, ideally, it should be. Make sure that the one you have permits you to see the area on either side of the door as well as straight ahead. Otherwise, someone can hide beside the door and wait for you to open it.

You also should have a chain lock on your door. As previously noted, most of these things are not going to hold back a large man who repeatedly slams his weight against it. A good chain lock will, however, enable you to take a look at any identification that the person may be showing you. If the assailant then tries to break through the chain lock, you should have enough time to retreat to your security room and your gun.

If you're alone when someone comes to your door, you should act as if someone else is there with you. Make some loud remark such as, "I'll get it, Killer." Well, that may be overdoing it a little, but you get the idea.

The safest way to talk to someone at your door is through an indoor-outdoor intercom system. A simple battery-operated system costs you about fifteen dollars at Radio Shack or a similar retailer. With an intercome, you won't even have to go near the door to find out who's there. Many people are embarrassed about displaying their suspicion by cautiously keeping the door shut or the chain lock hooked. An intercom partly solves that problem.

Although it seems too simple to believe, another way a criminal can get into your home is to simply walk in the door behind you. The best way to avoid this sort of trap is to approach the door with your keys out and ready. Don't stand around outside fumbling for them. Then, once you're inside, close the door immediately. If your hands are full, kick it shut; don't take the time to go lay down packages and then come back to the door. Called "push ins" in some parts of the country, this sort of intrusion has become increasingly common in metropolitan apartment buildings. And many of the assailants have been known to torture and kill their robbery victims.

Neighborhood Programs

In many communities, the police have established neighborhood security programs. One type encourages neighbors to be observant and report any strange activity to the police. Although many folks do this without prompting, these programs go a step further by getting citizens actively involved with one another, so that neighbors are more aware when someone isn't at home or shouldn't be having visitors. These programs are called by various names: Neighborhood Watch, Operation Town Watch, Crime Watch, or something similar.

Another program available through local police departments is a system for marking your valuables. These programs are usually called something like Operation Identification. You can buy your own relatively cheap engraving tool for marking your items, or you may be able to borrow one from the police department. You then engrave each item with some sort of identification, such as your driver license or social security number. Check with your local police department to see which number they prefer. Once you've marked your property, or even if you haven't actually done so, you can place a sticker on your door informing potential intruders that you are participating in the program. That is often enough to keep a criminal from wasting his time, since marked goods are much harder to dispose of.

Many police departments also make available specially-trained officers to inspect homes and offer security recommendations. This service is free, and the police will be more than happy to assist you if they can.

The final piece of common sense advice is to lock your doors. Believe it or not, the owners of most burglarized homes left their doors unlocked!

5.

Burglar Alarms

Not too long ago burglar alarm systems were seen only in businesses or the homes of the wealthy. But not any longer. The advent of micro-electronics has brought down the price of even exotic alarm systems far enough for the average person to afford one. You can still spend a lot of money on an alarm system, but you don't have to if you know what you're doing. You can buy a complete perimeter system for an average three bedroom home for under $200, or you can spend well over $5,000.

No burglar alarm system is perfect, no matter how much money you spend on it. A really professional burglar with enough time can get through any alarm system, but that type of criminal doesn't often call on the average home. As long as you don't have any items of great value, you really don't have to worry about the international jewel thief types.

An alarm system can provide worthwhile protection, but it is still only a secondary line of defense. Secure doors, windows, and locks must be your first line of protection. An alarm should warn you of an intrusion, giving you enough time to arm yourself, but it isn't going to scare away every criminal who sets it off. Some psychos and spaced-out drug addicts will pay little or no attention to an alarm system that wakes the entire neighborhood. Even a more rational intruder may simply turn off your alarm, or force you to do so, and then do what he is there for. The criminal may be counting on the fact that your neighbors are used to hearing your alarm go off every once in a while and will therefore think nothing of it.

There are two schools of thought about whether you should place stickers on your doors and windows to advertise that you have an alarm system. Many people feel that an intruder will see such a sign and leave, preferring easier pickings. On the other hand, you've just told the criminal that you have valuables worth stealing. And if the intruder knows anything about alarms, and many do, you have just warned him to be cautious and take steps to avoid setting it off. If the intruder is deranged, such a sign probably won't make any difference.

My own inclination is not to advertise the existence of an alarm system. I'd rather have an intruder set it off as he attempts to break in, rather than give him the chance to bypass it. After all, anyone who'd be scared off by a sticker on the window would certainly be scared away by the sound of the alarm going off. My theory, however, pertains only to a home with a perimeter system. That is, a system that protects each door and window and which sounds as soon as any entrance is opened. If you've no alarm system at all, it's probably a good idea to put up stickers saying that you do.

The burglar alarm business has many rip-off artists. This is not meant as a condemnation of the entire alarm industry, because the vast majority of these people are honest and provide excellent service. But many sellers and installers of equipment don't stand behind their products or work. Since it's very easy to get into this business, the turnover rate is very high. Before you have a system installed or buy components to install one yourself, ask your local police department for recommendations and then investigate the companies thoroughly with the Better Business Bureau. Your best bet is to deal with a company that has been in business for several years and which has a good local reputation.

Many businesses now not only install alarm systems but provide monitoring services as well. After you purchase or lease the alarm system, these companies will typically charge you about twenty dollars a month for their monitoring services. If your alarm goes off and isn't shut off within a specified period of time, the alarm company will call you to see if everything is all right. If it isn't, they will immediately contact the police for you.

Be sure to get several estimates when considering any sort of alarm system. Prices vary greatly for very similar products and services.

Perimeter Alarm Systems

Although it is usually a little more costly and difficult to install, a perimeter system normally provides more security than any of the other systems. The advantage of this system is that as soon as an intruder disturbs a door or a window, the alarm will go off. Many of the interior sonic alarms allow an intruder to get completely inside your home before the alarm will alert you. It is obviously much better to be warned before a criminal has actually gotten inside; you'll have more time to respond.

The most common and most desirable way to protect doors and windows with a perimeter system is by the use of magnetic contacts. Two contacts are used per entrance; one is a simple magnet, the other has a switch inside it. The magnet is normally mounted on the moving door or window itself, while the switch is placed on the door facing or window sill.

Fig. 5-1. Magnetic alarm switch

Some windows or doors are not suited for magnetic switches because of unusual construction, but there is an almost endless array of mechanical switches that can be used on such entrances. These mechanical switches may not be quite as reliable as the magnetic ones, so use them only when you have to.

There are two kinds of perimeter systems: the closed system and the open system. In the open system the switches are normally open until the door or window is disturbed. At that point the switch closes and the alarm goes off. But a drawback of the open system is that if someone cuts one of the wires, or disconnects the wires from the switch, or if a wire simply comes loose on its own, the alarm is bypassed and will not go off.

The more widely used design is the closed system. The magnetic contacts look just like the ones in an open system, but the switch is in the closed position until the door or window is disturbed, and then it opens. The system has a small current of electricity continuously flowing through all of the wiring and switches. This amount is so slight that you don't have to worry about it shocking you or even increasing your electric bill enough to make any difference. But if anything breaks that flow of electricity, whether it's caused by a loose wire, a door or window opening, or a wire being cut, the alarm will go off.

Most alarm systems installed nowadays continue to sound after they've been activated, even if the door or window is immediately closed again. Occasionally one encounters an older, cheaper model that doesn't incorporate this feature. Don't buy an alarm that can be shut off simply by reclosing the door or window, because an intruder can step inside your home, shut the door, and go about his business.

You'll also want to consider whether to have a silent or audible alarm, or both. Many businesses have silent alarms that notify the police department or a security company, but the intruder doesn't realize that he's been detected. This isn't such a good idea for a home, however, because you may not know that someone has broken in, and it may take awhile for the police to get to you. Besides, the purpose of alarms on business establishments is often to catch an intruder; you hope that the one on your home will chase away the criminal.

There's nothing wrong with using a system that employs both a silent and an audible alarm. A silent alarm is often more expensive, because it has to have equipment that will notify the people who are monitoring it. Some systems have automatic telephone dialers that will call the police for you and play a recorded request for aid.

If you have a two story house, don't install the system just on the ground floor and then think that you are perfectly safe. This gives an intruder an additional incentive to break in through the second story. It's already been pointed out that it isn't as hard to get in through your upper-floor windows as you may have believed.

There are two ways to get into and out of your home when you have a perimeter alarm system. One is to have a key operated off-on switch outside by the door. That switch is usually operated by a special alarm key that's very hard to duplicate. Fiddling with still another house key, however, can be a bother.

The second way to get into and out of your home is to have an alarm with a delay option. A system with a delay is much easier to work with than one that requires an external off-on switch. When you are ready to leave home, you can switch the alarm to the delay position. You then have approximately thirty seconds (depending on the system) to leave the house before the system arms itself. Once it is armed, if an entrance is opened, there will be another delay of several seconds before the alarm sounds. When you return home, you therefore have enough time to enter the house and deactivate the system before it goes off.

When you're at home, you'll have the system switched to nondelay or instant alarm, so that it goes off immediately if an intruder opens a door or window. If a burglar breaks into the house while you're away, the alarm won't go off until the delay time period has passed, but if you aren't home, it doesn't matter so much if an intruder has a few free seconds inside.

A criminal isn't likely to know exactly where your control panel is, so he probably won't be able to shut it off right away. Also, many control panels require the use of a key to turn off the alarm. So even if an intruder finds your control box, he won't necessarily be able to deactivate it.

The biggest problem associated with installing a perimeter system is running wires all over the house and trying to conceal them. A professional installation company has the specialized tools and know-how to do a good job of this, and that's where much of the expense comes in. If you're installing a system in a house that's under construction, it's a simple matter to run wiring inside the walls, but this isn't so in an existing home.

One solution to this problem is to use an alarm system which uses small radio transmitters rather than wires to send signals to the central alarm box. You place several transmitters around the house to cover all of your doors and windows.

There are several models of this sort of alarm available; the Pittway First Alert system is a good example. The basic control panel and one door transmitter cost approximately $120, but prices for similar devices vary widely. This unit incorporates a delay feature for leaving and entering the house, and you can hook up an exterior siren in addition to the loud horn that's built into the control box.

If you can run wiring to at least a few of your doors or windows, you can hook several sets of magnetic contacts to one transmitter. Since additional transmitters cost about twenty-eight dollars, if you're able to put several doors or windows on each one, you can save quite a bit of money. The transmitters operate on batteries that last about a year, depending on how often that door or window is opened. The control console even has a low battery light that alerts you to the fact when one of the batteries is beginning to weaken.

The First Alert system also has a backup battery in the control box, so that it will work even if the electricity should fail. A feature that this model does not have, however, is a limit timer. That is, a switch that will automatically turn the alarm off after it has sounded for a certain period of time (perhaps ten to twenty minutes). If you're away for the day, your neighbors may not enjoy listening to your alarm system for twelve hours—or even longer if you're out of town for several days.

There's no real drawback to having a limiter, even if you're at home and an intruder sets off the alarm. After ten or twenty minutes, an intruder will already have been scared away or will have had enough time to do whatever he's there for, so you may as well have the limiter. In fact, in many communities you're required by law to have a limit timer on your alarm system.

A possible disadvantage to a system that uses transmitters is that various electrical disturbances may set it off. You can dial your own frequency code into the control panel, so if you find that your neighbor's garage door opener is giving you false alarms, you can simply dial in a new frequency. A friend of mine has had his system for about two years, and the only false alarms he has encountered have been caused by lightning striking near the house.

The variety of options available for most of these alarm systems would impress James Bond. Pressure mats can be slipped under a carpet or a rug to warn you of an intruder who has gotten past the rest of your system; vibration switches designed to sense breaking glass can be mounted on windows; lights can be activated by the system along with the aural alarm; panic buttons are available that allow you to activate the system from your bed if you hear something suspect.

Single Entrance Alarms

Numerous types of alarms are available that are designed to protect just one door or window without using a central control box. This sort of unit may use magnetic switches, or it may be activated if someone merely touches your doorknob from the outside. Most of these devices are self-contained with a battery for power and a small warning horn that makes plenty of noise.

Many of these units can be immediately turned off by anyone who has opened the entrance and tripped it, but the more expensive models won't stop blaring until you turn them off with a key or punch in a code number on a pushbutton panel. This sort of alarm is excellent for a small apartment, but you may find that if you've very many doors or windows to protect, it's just as economical to get a more sophisticated perimeter system. Shop around before you buy; prices and features vary widely.

Motion Detecting Systems

A number of devices are categorized as motion detecting systems: ultrasonic, nondirectional radar, and infrared beams are the most common. Most of the alarms in this group employ a small box that you place at one end of a room. It sends out a beam that detects any motion in its path and then sets off the alarm.

Depending on the model, this beam may penetrate an interior wall, making it possible to protect more than one room with it. But if it takes two or three units to cover your entire home, you probably will be better off buying a good central perimeter system.

The infrared beam units throw a beam of light across a room. If anything breaks the beam, the unit will sound. You can aim it so that anyone entering a certain door or window will have to cross the beam.

Very sensitive motion detecting systems sometimes react to pets, blowing curtains, or even currents of air from air conditioners or heaters. But these units have been much improved in recent years, and many of these problems have been minimized. The real disadvantage of this type of system is that an intruder usually has to enter your home before it goes off. You can point it directly at a window or door, but then a dog or a falling leaf may set it off. Most such units are very portable, on many the sensitivity is adjustable, and you can easily place one where it will do a good job with a low risk of interference.

As with perimeter systems, many of the motion detectors are available with virtually any additional features you may want—delay functions, limit timers, external sirens, lights, and backup batteries. A backup battery is a good idea, since otherwise an intruder can shut off the alarm simply by unplugging it.

So many different models and brands are available that it's hard to keep up with them all. In fact, the biggest problem you'll encounter when you shop for an alarm system is deciding which one best suits your needs.

Dogs

A dog can be an excellent "alarm system." Although a German shepherd or a Doberman pinscher will afford the most protection against an intruder, a smaller dog with a loud bark can be almost as effective. A barking dog will deter an intruder in a couple of ways. First, the burglar may be afraid that the dog will bite him if he breaks in, and second, the noise the dog makes may alert the occupants of the home or neighbors.

In most people the fear that an unseen dog may attack is magnified in the dark—just when the criminal is most likely to strike. Many people put up "bad dog" signs whether they have a dog or not. This alone is enough to keep away quite a few potential intruders.

But not all criminals are going to be scared off by a dog. An intruder may have seen your dog before and know that he is no real threat. He may also know if you are a helpless woman living alone, so he may not care if the barking dog warns you. As a result, you should not depend on a dog for protection to the extent that you neglect your doors, windows, and locks. A dog can supplement your security, but it's unwise to depend on one completely. Many intruders are armed, and they often don't mind shooting a dog that comes at them.

6.

Handguns

Choosing a handgun for home defense can be a very difficult and confusing task. Although it's simple enough to go out and buy a gun, if you don't know what you're doing, you can very easily end up with a weapon that is totally unsuited to your needs.

No one gun is best suited to everyone. A model that's recommended for one person may be improper, even dangerous, for another. The seemingly endless assortment of handguns can, however, be narrowed considerably so that you can evaluate the remaining models in light of your own personal situation. The two most basic choices you'll have to make are whether to use an automatic or a revolver, and what caliber the gun should be.

Virtually all modern-day handguns are either revolvers or automatics. A revolver has a cylinder that rotates as the trigger is pulled, bringing a new bullet into position to be fired. Automatics are designed so that a new cartridge is automatically introduced into the firing chamber after each shot.

Handguns are usually classified by caliber, a measurement that refers to the inside diameter, or bore, of the barrel. The inside of the barrel contains rifling (small grooves) that imparts a spin to the bullet, increasing its accuracy.

As a general rule, the larger the caliber the more powerful the weapon. The most common calibers are the .22, .25, .32, .357, .38, .44, and .45. Guns that are designated as magnum or special (.38 special, .357 and .44 magnum) have more power than normal, because the ammunition they fire contains an extra charge of powder. A .44 magnum is therefore more powerful than a .45.

Revolvers

Revolvers are available in numerous calibers, the most common are the .22, .32, .38, .38 special, .357 magnum, and .44 magnum. The choice of which revolver to buy is basically very simple. The smaller calibers such as the .22 and .32 are too small to be depended upon for self-defense. Although these weapons are indeed deadly if they strike a vital spot, even at long distances, you have to hit an assailant in one of those spots in order to have a chance of stopping him.

There are numerous cases of criminals being shot in vital spots with low caliber bullets but living long enough to kill their victims. In one instance a woman emptied a .22 revolver into her attacker as he came through a window at her, but he still managed to stab her to death. Anger, fear, panic, and adrenalin can all combine to temporarily give an assailant almost super-human strength.

At the other end of the spectrum, the .357 magnum and .44 magnum have much more power than is needed for home defense. These guns have a substantial recoil and are simply too much to handle for someone who's inexperienced with powerful handguns. It's true that virtually anyone can go to a firing range with a magnum and handle it fine. But when it comes to defensive shooting in your home, you're going to be under extreme stress. Under those conditions you'll have to be very experienced with such a gun to use it safely and effectively.

Another disadvantage of these weapons is their extreme penetrating power. A magnum can actually fire a bullet into the engine of a car. Such a bullet can go right through your wall, across the street into your neighbor's home, and still have enough power left to kill someone. When you fire one of these guns inside your home, you don't know where the bullet will stop. Even if you were to hit an assailant square in the chest, the bullet may still go right on through him and out through an exterior wall. For self-defense at home, the use of a .357 or .44 magnum constitutes overkill.

Fig. 6-1. H&R .38 revolver

This brings us to the .38. This is the handgun that is most often used by police departments, and about 99 percent of the experts recommend this one for self-defense at home (Figure 6-1). You may also consider a .38 special. The special is designed to fire cartridges with a slightly larger powder charge, so it has more stopping power than a standard .38. Thirty-eight special ammunition has more recoil than a standard .38 round, but it is not nearly as powerful as a magnum cartridge.

Smith & Wesson used to make a .38 special with an unusual safety feature for a revolver. Along the back of the grip is an extra piece of metal. When you hold the gun in a normal grasp, your palm presses this piece of metal into the grip, releasing a safety that will then allow the trigger to be pulled. The gun cannot be fired unless this metal plate is pressed in.

This means that it is much more difficult to accidentally fire the gun. It also means that a child with hands too small to grip the gun properly would have a hard time firing it. Of course, this doesn't mean that a child *couldn't* fire it; it just means that it would be more difficult for him to do so. Unfortunately, this model was discontinued several years ago, and used ones now bring high prices when they can be found.

When selecting a revolver, keep in mind that although guns of a given caliber are usually available in several different sizes, you should not buy the smallest model you can find just because it seems handier. Many police revolvers are of the smaller, lightweight variety because of a need to conceal them beneath clothing. Since you don't have that requirement, you should stay away from the smaller models. A heavier handgun is likely to be more stable and therefore more accurate—up to a point. If your arms quiver while you're trying to hold a huge gun up in the air, you won't be able to hit much with it.

Another consideration is barrel length. The longer the barrel, the more accurate the gun will be. If your home is dark, or there's no time to carefully look through the sights, a longer barrel will definitely enable you to aim the gun more accurately. A little peashooter with a two-inch barrel won't be nearly as accurate as a target model with a six-inch barrel, and a rifle or shotgun will be even more accurate, especially in near darkness.

Many police revolvers have shorter barrels, but again, this is primarily for concealment purposes. A four- to six-inch barrel is probably the best choice for home use.

Since some guns are attempted counterfeits of the quality brands such as Colt or Smith & Wesson, you should be careful when buying a used gun from someone you don't know. Take a good look at the name stamped into the metal. It will sometimes be spelled just slightly different; perhaps Smyth & Wesson rather than Smith & Wesson.

Be especially leery of cheaper guns, cheap foreign models in particular. Not only is their accuracy often less dependable, they also can be dangerous. Firearms must be designed to continually withstand a tremendous amount of stress. Each time a gun is fired, a powerful explosion takes place inside it, and every once in a while a gun will literally blow up in someone's hands. Such accidents are virtually unheard-of with quality brands that have been properly cared for.

The better made guns may have safety designs or advantages that you're not even aware of. An excellent feature that is built into many high quality guns is an internal guard that prevents the gun from discharging if it is dropped. If you drop a gun without this mechanism so that it lands on the hammer, the force of the blow may knock the firing pin against the cartridge hard enough to fire it. Even though a gun may have this guard, you should still be very careful about dropping it or throwing it around. Accidents can still occur.

If your gun doesn't have this safety feature, it isn't a bad idea to keep an empty chamber beneath the hammer. This will prevent the firing pin from being forced against a live cartridge if the gun is dropped. But as soon as the trigger is pulled or the hammer is cocked, the empty chamber will be rotated out of the way, and a live cartridge moved into firing position. You have to give up one shot in order to gain this extra margin of safety, but it may be well worth it.

Fig. 6-2. H&R top-breaking .38

Most revolvers made today either break at the top, allowing the entire barrel and cylinder assembly to swing down together (Figure 6-2), or the cylinder swings out sideways. There is no significant advantage or disadvantage to either design unless you are considering a cheap brand. A defective top-breaking model can blow open and severely injure the shooter.

Caution should also be exercised with an older gun, even though it may have been in your family for years. Before using it you should have

it checked and approved by a gunsmith. Many of these guns were not
designed to handle the more powerful gunpowder that is used in modern
ammunition. As a result, if you use such a gun, you may be dangerously
overstressing it without knowing it.

Single Action vs. Double Action

Revolvers are either of single action or double action design. The
double action design has advantages and safety features that make it by
far the most desirable for home protection. A single action model
requires the shooter to first cock back the hammer before the trigger will
fire the gun, but with a double action revolver there's no need to first
cock the hammer; you simply pull the trigger. As the trigger is pulled it
rotates the cylinder to bring a new cartridge into firing position, moves
the hammer back, and then lets the hammer fall forward, firing the
bullet. Or, you can still cock the hammer on a double action revolver and
fire it as if it were a single action model.

A double action revolver can be fired more rapidly than a single action
model unless one fans the latter in the style of a wild west gunslinger. But
for anyone other than an expert trick shooter, fanning a gun isn't
practical for self-defense.

A standard double action revolver has no mechanical safety that is
moved on or off. The safety in this sort of gun resides in the fact that the
trigger must be pulled back firmly (the amount of pressure varies from
gun to gun) in order to fire it. If, however, the hammer has been cocked
back for single action firing, it's a different story. A slight pressure on the
trigger or just a good bump can cause the gun to fire. That's why a
revolver hammer should never be cocked unless you're preparing to fire
the weapon.

Automatics

Quality is even more important in an automatic than in a revolver.
There are many more moving parts and much more that can go wrong.
The cheaper makes are much more apt to jam or malfunction, or simply
break.

The most common sizes are the .25, .32, .38, 9mm, and .45. As with
revolvers, the smaller caliber automatics shouldn't be relied upon for
self-defense. The .38, 9mm, and .45 all have adequate power to stop an
assailant.

The term "automatic" as applied to these handguns is actually a misnomer. A true automatic weapon will continue to fire as long as the trigger is depressed (a machine gun is an automatic). The "automatic" handguns discussed here are actually semiautomatics. That is, a new cartridge is automatically introduced into the firing chamber after each shot, but the trigger must be pulled each time a shot is to be fired.

Automatics have a slide that is slammed back when a bullet is fired. As the slide moves back, it cocks the gun and the empty shell is ejected. A new cartridge then moves up into the firing chamber from a clip inserted into the hand grip.

This may sound as if there's a lot going on, and there is; it happens so fast that all you can see is a blur as an empty shell pops out of the gun. An automatic can literally be fired just as fast as you can pull the trigger.

Probably the best known automatic is the .45 (Figures 6-3, 6-4). Sometimes said to be the safest handgun in the world, this is the standard sidearm used by the U.S. military since early in the century. And whether or not it really is the *safest* handgun, it does have many excellent safety features.

Fig. 6-3. Colt .45 automatic

For example, the hammer on a .45 has half cock and full cock positions, but the gun can be fired only from the full cock position. If the hammer were to slip out of your grasp as you were pulling it back, it would fall back only to the half cock position, so the gun would not accidentally discharge. In order to fire the gun, it must be firmly grasped in your hand so that your palm presses a grip lock into the back of the hand grip. The trigger can't be pulled unless this lock has been depressed.

Still other internal locks keep the gun from firing unless the slide is locked all the way forward, and there is a standard thumb-operated on-off safety that locks the trigger in place. Although the .45 can be fired with the clip removed, some automatics have an additional lock that will prevent this. Depending on your point of view or situation, it may or may not be an advantage to have a gun that will fire with the clip removed (Figure 6-4).

The .45 has a somewhat exaggerated reputation for being inaccurate. It has been said that you could kill an elephant with a .45, but you would have to hit him first. Actually, the gun can be fired with good results, but it takes some practice. In the hands of someone who has spent a little

Fig. 6-4. .45 automatic with the clip removed and the slide locked back

time with it, the .45 has more than enough accuracy for the distances encountered inside a home.

Cartridges for the larger caliber handguns, revolvers as well as automatics, can be somewhat expensive. This means that practice sessions with such pistols can cost more than a little. For example, twenty-five jacketed hollow point bullets for a .45 automatic sell for about $8.95.

A conversion kit is available for the .45 that will enable you to fire .22 cartridges when practicing—a significant savings in the cost of ammunition. But with the price of the kit at $200, you'll have to practice a lot for the device to pay for itself. More over, .22 cartridges don't cause nearly as much kick as do .45s, so if you want meaningful practice you'll want to fire the larger ammunition.

Revolvers vs. Automatics

For the inexperienced shooter a revolver is probably the wiser choice. It is simpler to care for, it is much simpler to operate, and it usually is less expensive. If you decide to buy a cheap gun, which is not recommended, an inexpensive revolver is likely to be a much better choice than a cheap automatic.

One frequently cited drawback of automatics is the ammunition they must use. There has to be a layer or jacket of hard metal over the soft lead bullet, or it may be scratched and deformed as it goes through the feed mechanism of an automatic. The result often can be a jammed gun. A jacketed bullet is undesirable for personal defense at home, too, because even if it hits a wall or an assailant, it may retain its basic shape and perhaps keep on going. The soft lead bullets fired by revolvers are more likely to flatten out when they hit something, so they are less likely to keep going or to ricochet.

This disadvantage of the automatic and its ammunition can be avoided, however, by using jacketed hollow point bullets. These aren't deformed by the feed mechanism of the automatic, and they are specifically designed to flatten out when they hit something. This flattening will not only reduce the ricochet, but will cause the bullet to do more damage when it hits.

If a cartridge fails to fire after you pull the trigger (a misfire), a person with a revolver simply pulls the trigger again, and a new cartridge is rotated into position. With an automatic, though, the shooter must stop and pull the slide back in order to eject the defective round and get another one into the firing chamber. Be aware, however, that a misfire should be handled in such a manner only if you are involved in a true defensive firing situation. If a misfire occurs when you're practicing with the gun, you should continue to point it at the target for about thirty seconds before doing anything else. The bullet may still fire after a slight delay.

As it turns out, this advantage of the revolver—quickly getting another cartridge into position after a misfire—may turn into a disadvantage. Even if you've rotated another round into position, the offending cartridge will still be in the gun—you could be holding a time bomb. If that cartridge eventually fires, the gun can blow up and take your hand with it. Although it takes a couple of seconds longer to work the slide on an automatic to get a new round into position, you'll be rid of the misfire.

Actually though, the average person who shoots only occasionally and who uses good ammunition probably will never even see a misfire. The chances of a misfire occurring just when you have to fire at an attacker are almost nil, so all things considered, this advantage of the revolver over the automatic is very slight indeed.

More common than a misfire in an automatic is the problem of jamming. A cartridge may fail to move all the way into the firing chamber, or it may not be ejected completely, so that the gun jams and can't be fired. This requires the shooter to pull the slide back and sometimes even shake the gun upside down in order to remove the offending round. The chances of a jam can be minimized if the proper ammunition is used, but even that may not avoid the problem completely. This is a principal reason for not buying a cheap automatic; as a general rule, an inexpensive brand is much more likely to jam than is a quality make.

An automatic can be fired more rapidly than a revolver, though this too is a very minor difference. After a little practice anyone should be able to fire a revolver quite rapidly, but then firing a gun as fast as possible is not advisable for anyone other than an expert. When firing in such a manner, the average person is unlikely to hit his target unless it's at point-blank range.

Many of the larger automatics hold one to four more bullets than a typical revolver, and when another clip is loaded and available, an automatic can be reloaded much quicker than a revolver. It's doubtful, however, that you'll be involved in a protracted firefight in your own home. After the first few shots have been fired, someone is likely to have been hit, or the assailant will probably beat a hasty retreat. On the other hand, if you were to fire several quick shots at an assailant without hitting him or chasing him off, those extra few rounds might prove to be very valuable.

A safety problem inherent in automatics is that after each shot is fired the gun is cocked and ready to fire again with only a slight touch of the trigger. The danger is that in a stressful situation it will be all too easy to fire an automatic again without meaning to. A revolver requires you to either cock the hammer back or deliberately pull the trigger again.

Another problem with an automatic is that the spring in a fully loaded clip can eventually weaken, causing the gun to jam on the last few cartridges. This doesn't mean that the spring of a fully loaded clip will necessarily fail. I stored a full clip for seven years without once touching it, and it still works fine. One way to avoid this problem is to load the clip with one or two fewer cartridges than it is designed to hold. This will keep the spring from being constantly under maximum tension.

Still another spring problem may result with an automatic if a cartridge is kept in the firing chamber. Many automatics are cocked whenever a round is in firing position; that may weaken the firing springs after a period of time. If the springs weaken enough, the gun wouldn't fire when the trigger is pulled.

An automatic with an exterior hammer doesn't present this problem, since you can lower the hammer once a cartridge has been introduced into the firing chamber. If you don't keep a round in the chamber, you'll have to work the slide mechanism before the gun can be fired. This will take only a couple of seconds if you are familiar with the pistol, but it will make some noise.

This noise can be advantageous or not, depending on whom you ask. Many people feel that it is desirable, because it tells an intruder that someone is waiting for him somewhere in that dark house with a gun. Unless he's completely irrational, some say, he isn't going to come after you. On the other hand, if he doesn't believe that you have a gun, he may indeed come after you. Most people would rather have a criminal make a hasty retreat than have to shoot it out with him.

Many of the larger automatics have a built-in safety feature that can be a lifesaver if a child gains access to the weapon. As previously noted, it takes a fair amount of strength to pull the slide back and introduce the first cartridge into the firing chamber of one of these pistols. The .45 has this characteristic, though the spring tension will tend to lessen a little with use.

An average-size woman can manage to pull the slide back, but it takes a little practice and considerable effort. There is therefore little possibility that a small child could get the slide back and introduce a bullet into the firing chamber. This feature makes these automatics safer than revolvers when they're kept in a home with small children.

An automatic is also easier to conceal than a revolver, since it's flatter. But that's of little value to a person who's concerned with defending himself or herself at home.

In summary, the best reason for choosing an automatic over a revolver is the fact that some of them may be safer around children. But if you've no children to worry about, the few advantages of the automatic are relatively insignificant, leaving the revolver as the better choice.

Used Guns

You should be very careful when buying a used gun. You may get a gun that's as good as new for much less money, or you may find yourself with a stolen gun or one that will malfunction when you need it most.

If you do buy a used gun, it is important to get it from a reliable gun shop where a gunsmith has examined it. A gunsmith can tell what condition a firearm is in, but the average person can't. Buying a gun from a stranger could mean trouble even if it functions properly. If the gun has ever been used in a crime, the police may feel they have good reason to ask if you have an alibi for the time of the shooting in which the gun was used.

Ammunition

The array of ammunition available for handguns often seems to be endless. And as it turns out, there are as many opinions as to which is the best cartridge as there are cartridges. One may be a little larger, but another has a higher velocity; while a third type may have a small frontal area, it has an extra charge of powder.

What we are really concerned with when it comes to self-defense is a bullet's stopping power or knock down capability—its impact energy. There are three basic factors that determine the impact energy of a bullet: its weight, its speed, and its shape.

The following table gives a comparison of several of the most common cartridges. A bullet's weight is stated in grains (gr.) and its velocity in feet per second (fps).

Cartridge	Bullet Weight	Muzzle Velocity	Impact Energy (at muzzle)
.22 short	29 gr.	1,095 fps	77 ft. lbs.
.22 long rifle	40 gr.	1,255 fps	140 ft. lbs.
.38	145 gr.	685 fps	150 ft. lbs.
.38 special	158 gr.	855 fps	260 ft. lbs.
.357 magnum	158 gr.	1,450 fps	690 ft. lbs.
.45 automatic	230 gr.	810 fps	335 ft. lbs.

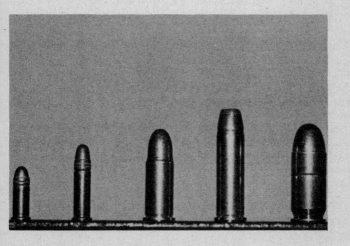

Fig. 6-5. Left to right: .22, .22 long rifle, .38, .38 special hollow point, .45

Since a bullet's velocity decreases as it travels away from the gun, its impact energy will be less as the distance to the target increases. For this reason, velocity and impact energy are sometimes computed at various distances from the gun's muzzle. But the distances usually involved in self-defense in the home are so short that these deceleration effects can be ignored. For our purposes the muzzle velocities given in the table provide an adequate basis for comparison.

The table provides some interesting information. First of all, take a look at the .22 long rifle. This cartridge contains a larger charge of powder than the standard .22 short cartridge and can be fired from many .22 pistols. The .22 long rifle has a very high muzzle velocity, but it has a very small bullet. This is what can make a .22 bullet so dangerous. It fires with a tremendous velocity, but it has little frontal area to slow it down. The result is that a .22 can still have enough velocity to kill someone more than a mile away.

Smaller caliber ammunition is therefore your worst choice for self-defense in the home. The bullet doesn't have much impact energy, so you'll have to hit an assailant in a vital spot in order to have a good chance of stopping him, but yet it is capable of killing innocent people far away.

Take a look now at the .38 special and .357 magnum cartridges. These both fire the same weight bullet, 158 grain, but the .357 has more than 2½ times the stopping power of the .38 special. This is due to the tremendous velocity that is generated as a result of the magnum's extra charge of powder.

Impact energy, or the knock down capability of a bullet is very important in a self-defense situation. If a person weighing 100 pounds hits you on the arm, it might move you a little, it might not, depending on your weight. But if a 300-pound pro football player hits you on the arm, the force probably will knock you down.

This is what a bullet with more stopping power will do for you. If you hit an assailant in the arm with a bullet that has considerable impact energy, you stand a good chance of knocking him down and stunning him, even if you haven't struck a vital area. If you do knock down an assailant, he's less likely to be able to return your fire or to attack you. You can then fire another shot, if necessary, or keep the assailant covered if he surrenders.

On the other hand, if you hit the intruder in the same spot with a low caliber bullet such as the .22, it will draw blood, but it may not keep him from shooting or stabbing you. As stated before, there's been many instances of criminals being shot with low caliber bullets in supposedly vital areas only to live long enough to kill the defender.

A bullet with more impact energy will therefore provide you with more security, not only because it has more power, but also because your aim doesn't have to be nearly as accurate. When using more powerful ammunition, it isn't as critical that you hit an assailant in a vital spot.

Hollow Points

What has been discussed thus far is a bullet's impact energy. But two bullets with exactly the same impact energy may cause different amounts of damage if they are of different design or material.

The soft lead bullets used in revolvers flatten out somewhat when they strike something, so they usually do more damage than a jacketed bullet of the same weight, velocity, and initial shape. This spreading out also means that the bullet is less likely to pass through an assailant and continue on to strike someone else. This is not to say that a regular lead bullet will not do that, but it is less likely to do so than a jacketed bullet.

The bullet that is least likely to ricochet or to go through an assailant or a wall is the hollow point. The hollow point is basically a standard shaped bullet with a hole drilled into its nose (Figure 6-6). When a hollow point strikes something, it flattens out into a jagged piece of metal with a greatly increased frontal area.

Hollow point bullets have occasionally been outlawed, even for police and military use, because they have often been considered inhumane. But quite a few police departments have begun to use such bullets again, since there is less possibility of rocochets that will strike innocent

Fig. 6-6. .45 automatic hollow nose (left) and standard cartridge

bystanders. If you use such bullets, you'll have a better chance of stopping your attacker and less chance of killing a member of your own family or a neighbor. You can decide for yourself if that sounds inhumane or not, but before you buy them or put them into your pistol, determine first if they are legal in your state and community.

Plastic Bullets

These are low-powered cartridges with a plastic rather than lead bullet. While they are occasionally used for short range target practice, they should not be used for self-defense. Though they have relatively little power, these bullets can still be deadly, so they should be treated with the same respect you give to any bullet.

Wadcutters

Wadcutters are specifically designed for target shooting. They have very sharp shoulders, so they will cut a nice round hole in a paper target. As with plastic bullets, these should not be relied upon for self-defense, but they are still potentially deadly and caution should be exercised.

7.

Firing the Handgun

If you don't already know what you're doing, don't read a book on shooting and then try to teach yourself. You certainly wouldn't read a book on flying and then jump into an airplane all by yourself. A book on the subject of flying would definitely be very helpful, but only in conjunction with the proper instruction.

That's how this section should be used. Read it before you go for instruction, then review it after you've been with an instructor. This overview may touch on any points that your instructor doesn't cover.

To find an instructor, ask at your local firing range. If you don't have a range, or if they know of no one, check with your police department or the shop where you bought your gun. You may also ask the National Rifle Association in Washington, D.C. They keep lists of approved instructors and should be able to supply you with the names and addresses of competent people near you. An instructor approved by this organization will have received training that strongly emphasizes safety. If you just happen to meet someone on the firing range who is willing to show you how to shoot, you may or may not have met someone who really knows what he is doing.

Target shooting emphasizes many different areas; body stance, grip, trigger pull, breathing, aiming, and more. People who are interested in a handgun purely for defense at home may consider this sort of shooting to be a waste of their time. It isn't. Before you seriously consider defensive shooting, you should be very familiar with your gun and how it shoots. And the best way to do this is through basic target shooting.

Someone who wakes up in the middle of the night and fires at a figure in the dark probably will not have the time or the inclination to stop to consider if his grip is just right, if he is breathing properly, and if he is using the correct sighting technique. These points that are so vital to accurate shooting will be done properly under such circumstances only if they are second nature.

If you have practiced the basics enough, you'll be much more likely to automatically do things correctly when you have to, thus greatly increasing your chances of stopping an assailant. You must learn the fundamentals, no matter what the activity, before proceeding to more advanced tasks, and learning to fire a gun is certainly no exception.

But, the argument goes, if you're facing an intruder in a dark house—a very definite possibility—you won't be able to see your gun sights. So what good will all that target shooting do you then? Well, it will do you a great deal of good. If you can't see the sights, you will have to rely to a great extent on feeling that you are aiming correctly—a feel developed in target practice.

All of these considerations, such as grip, breathing, and aiming, are significant in that a mistake in any one area can affect your accuracy considerably. The best way, and often the only way, to determine how various factors are affecting your accuracy is to shoot at a target. If you go out into a field and shoot at a can, you usually can't tell where the bullet goes when you miss. On the other hand, when shooting at formal targets, unless you miss the entire thing, you can see exactly where your shot went. If it didn't go where you meant it to, you can figure out why it didn't and what you must do to correct the problem. After a while, you'll know as soon as you fire the gun what, if anything, you did incorrectly and where the bullet actually went.

This ability to be instantly aware of where you're shooting and why is especially important in defensive shooting. If your first shot misses your assailant, only feel may be able to tell you in which direction and how far. Then you can correct your next shot for better results.

Safety

Most people are aware that you should always treat a gun as if it were loaded. That warning is a very familiar one. But wait a minute. Stop. Don't just lightly read over this and go on. Think about it. You must be consciously aware of the danger involved with a gun, and you must consciously treat a firearm as if it were loaded. Respect for the danger the weapon poses cannot be a mere afterthought. Many people are killed each year by guns that were "not loaded."

This means that you should never point a gun at anyone unless you are prepared to shoot to kill—even a gun that is obviously unloaded. And you must never believe anyone else when you are told that a gun is unloaded. If your instructor hands you an unloaded gun, you should still check it for yourself. Don't worry about annoying him; a good instructor will appreciate your conscientiousness.

When checking a revolver to see if it is loaded, you should actually swing the cylinder out for close inspection. An automatic should have the clip removed and the slide pulled back, so you can examine the barrel. Don't look down the business end! Your fingernail, inserted into the firing chamber, should reflect light coming down the barrel pointed toward the sun.

It's not a good idea to leave your gun where others may have access to it, but if you must, be sure to unload it, even if the other people are experienced gunmen. Then when you return, even if you believe no one else can have even touched it, check to see if it is still unloaded. A gun is always loaded until you have personally checked it, and even then you must treat it as if it were still loaded—don't point it at anyone.

A handgun is much easier to accidentally point at someone than is a rifle or shotgun, because of its size. Just a flick of your wrist can point a handgun ninety degrees away from where it was aimed. Likewise, if you just turn slightly to look at something, you may unknowingly point the weapon at someone.

When transporting a revolver, the cylinder should be unloaded and swung out; an automatic should have the clip removed and the slide locked back. Don't load the weapon until you are ready to begin shooting, and whether the gun is loaded or not, keep your finger out of the trigger guard until you are ready to fire. Safety rules may vary slightly from firing range to firing range, so make sure that you know what you should or should not be doing before preparing to fire.

Before you fire a single shot, no matter where you are, you must know where the bullets will stop. A bullet that strikes a hard object such as a rock or bottle can ricochet in an entirely unexpected direction. Bullets can even ricochet off water, so be very careful when shooting into a river or a lake. You may inadvertantly kill someone whom you can't even see.

Simply loading a gun can also be dangerous. It is all too easy to point the weapon in several different directions during the process, so you should make sure that your gun can't accidentally discharge. Let the hammer down and engage the safety if possible. And before you load any kind of gun—revolver, automatic, rifle, or shotgun—open it so you can check the barrel for obstructions. A cleaning rag left in the barrel of a gun could cause it to blow up in your face.

Before you begin target shooting, or any kind of shooting for that matter, invest in a couple of inexpensive pieces of safety equipment. First, you need a good pair of safety glasses. If you already wear glasses, make sure that they contain safety glass. A ricochet or a piece of debris kicked up by a bullet can put out an eye in an instant.

The second thing to protect is your hearing. Use earplugs or earcovers that are specifically designed to block out loud noise. Some materials may seem to block out part of the noise, but much of the damage may still be occurring. You may believe that a little shooting won't harm your hearing, but you pay a price every time you are exposed to loud noises without proper protection. Guns are no exception.

Once you've finished firing a revolver, if you've a cocked hammer, you should lower it. Otherwise, the pistol remains in a dangerous state of readiness. This requires a careful technique if the hammer is to be lowered onto a live round. If the hammer slips away from you or you lower it too hard, the gun could fire.

As a result, you should first make sure that the gun is pointing in a safe direction. Then, holding the gun in your firing hand, get a good grip on the hammer with the thumb and forefinger of your free hand. It's a good idea to position your forefinger in front of the hammer, so that if it does snap forward unexpectedly, your finger will catch it.

Once you have a firm grip on the hammer, you can pull the trigger and then gently lower the hammer as described above. Practice this technique with an unloaded gun before you try it with live cartridges.

It is possible, with some pistols, to do all of this with one hand by placing the thumb of your firing hand on the hammer. But if the hammer has a very strong spring or if you are a little sweaty, you run the chance of it slipping out of your grasp.

When you've finished firing an automatic, you should engage the safety and remove the clip. Then you can pull the slide back to remove any cartridge that may still be in the firing chamber. Finally, you can lower the hammer if it has one. When lowering the hammer of an automatic onto a live round, you have even more reason to be careful. If the gun were to discharge, the slide can easily break a finger or two as it snaps back, and this can cause you to drop the gun or accidentally fire it one more time.

Grip

A handgun should be gripped very tightly. Not so tightly that your arm and hand shake, but you should have a firm hold on the gun. There are two reasons for the tight grip. First, it gives you better control of the pistol and therefore more accuracy, especially if the gun has much recoil. The gun is more likely to move around in your hand if you hold it loosely. Second, it's much safer to hold the gun tightly, since there's less chance that it will jump out of your hand.

Since hands and guns both come in different shapes and sizes, not everyone holds a gun exactly the same way. Even the experts don't always follow the same procedures. For example, one instructor may say that the thumb should be placed a little higher on the gun when firing an automatic, but then you see a super marksman with his thumb held low. So, grip the gun in a position that feels good to you, and check with your instructor to make sure that he doesn't see anything wrong with it. If he does, you may find that the grip he recommends is uncomfortable at first but feels fine after a little practice.

If you aren't able to hold your gun comfortably, the pistol grip may be too large or too small. A gunsmith can usually take care of this for you. If you have small hands, you may have trouble reaching the trigger of a larger gun, even if you hold it properly and the grip is the correct size. This can affect both accuracy and safety. If a gunsmith isn't able to help, you probably should trade in your gun for one that suits you.

Some people recommend different grips for target and combat shooting, but ignore that advice if your main concern is self-defense. Settle on one grip and stick with it.

Without meaning to contradict the last statement, there are two basic grips that you should learn. These are the one-handed and two-handed grips. For anyone other than an expert marksman, the two-handed grip provides significantly more support, more stability, and therefore more accuracy. This is especially true for a woman who is shooting a heavy pistol. The one-handed grip is used mainly for target shooting; it's less useful for defensive shooting, but familiarize yourself with it, too. In an emergency you may find yourself in a position that allows you to shoot with only one hand.

Both one- and two-handed grips have several variations. Again, do what seems to suit you best, with agreement from your instructor.

In order to use a two-handed grip, first hold the gun in a normal one-handed grip, as illustrated. Your supporting hand can then be used in one of three basic ways. One method is to grasp the wrist of your firing hand to add support to your arm (Figure 7-1). This technique is not usually recommended, however, because your wrist and the gun itself are not nearly as stable as with the other two methods.

Fig. 7-1. Grasping wrist of firing hand

Probably the most common way to use the supporting hand is to wrap all four fingers around the three fingers of the firing hand that are already on the grip (Figure 7-2). Your supporting forefinger should be just under the trigger guard. If desired, the supporting thumb can then be placed above the firing thumb, pulling down on it. By pulling the firing thumb downward, you will be tightening the grip of your firing hand without having to squeeze the gun any harder. This technique of pulling down the firing thumb may not work for you on all guns, however. Depending on how your hand fits your pistol, you may find that you are pulling your thumb down out of position rather than tightening your grip.

Fig. 7-2. Supporting hand wrapped around firing hand

The third way to use your supporting hand is to form a cup and place the butt of the gun into that palm (Figure 7-3). The fingers of the

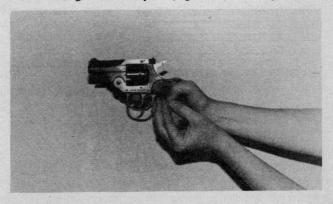

Fig. 7-3. Supporting hand cupping the pistol butt

supporting hand are then wrapped up over the fingers of the firing hand on the front of the grip.

Although these are the three most common two-handed grips, they are certainly not the only ones. Depending on your hands and the gun itself, you may find a variation of one of these grips more suitable for you.

A common error when using a two-handed grip is relaxing the firing hand grasp. This mistake is easy to make, since you get the feeling that you have a more secure grip on the gun because you're using two hands. You must also keep the pressure of your grip constant. If you vary your hand pressure while you're aiming and pulling the trigger, the gun will move and affect your accuracy.

Stance

Your stance and orientation toward the target will differ depending on whether you use a one-handed or two-handed grip. When firing with your right hand alone, stand facing the target with your body turned about sixty degrees to the left; sixty degrees to the right when firing left-handed. Your free hand can then be placed in your pocket, behind your back, on your hip, or wherever you feel most comfortable.

Whether shooting with one or two hands, your weight should be distributed equally on each foot—don't lean one way or the other. Your feet should be spread apart about twelve to eighteen inches, approximately shoulder width, or half your stride. The reason you don't want your feet close together is because your balance won't be as good. The recoil from the gun will affect you less if your feet are spread, enhancing your accuracy and ability to fire rapidly.

When using the two-handed grip, stand squarely facing the target without turning your body either way. Some people lean back a little to counteract the weight of the gun, but don't overdo it. This is something that your body will probably do automatically without you even having to think about it. Again, do what's comfortable for you, with approval from your instructor.

Breathing

Proper breath control is one of several techniques that are important, whether firing at a target or an assailant. Although they may not seem important if you've not fired before, these factors all add up and seriously affect your accuracy. Although you may not realize it, if you breathe while aiming, the gun will move.

One of the more common ways to control your breathing is to inhale while extending the gun and preparing to sight on the target. As the gun is being lowered onto the target, let out a little of that breath and then hold it. With a little practice this will become second nature; you won't even be aware of it.

Eyes

Contrary to popular belief, you should shoot with both eyes open; don't close one and squint with the other. This is important in defensive shooting, especially so if your assailant is moving, and if it's dark. Using both eyes under such circumstances will allow you to find your target much more quickly and accurately.

There has also been widespread confusion and misinformation about where the shooter should focus his eyes. When you hold a gun out in front of you, you can focus either on the sights or on the target but not on both at the same time. You'll be able to see both at the same time, but they won't both be clear—one will be blurred. When target shooting, focus your eyes on the gunsights. It's important for the front and rear sights to be lined up correctly, but you can't do this very well if you are focused on the target.

When you focus on the target, it's easy to let the alignment of the sights drift. The gun will shoot wherever the sights are lined up—possibly missing the target entirely. On the other hand, if you focus on the sights, it will be almost impossible for the gun to be aimed completely off the target without you noticing it.

Aiming

Proper aiming involves many different techniques. One aspect that is undebatable, however, is how the front and rear sights should be lined up with one another (Figure 7-4).

As the diagram shows, the front sight should be placed in the middle of the groove in the rear sight, and the tops of the two sights should be level. When you want to aim a little higher, the entire gun should be raised slightly, so that the sights remain in this same relative position. If you just raise the muzzle, the front sight will then be above the rear one.

Opinions vary as to where you should place the sights on a bull's-eye.

Fig. 7-4. Correct sight alignment. The front sight blade should appear
centered in and level with the rear sight aperture.

Some people place them slightly below the bull's-eye, so that a sliver of
white is showing. Others place the sights right on top of the bull's-eye, so
that no white is seen. Still others place the sights right in the middle of the
bull's-eye.

This last method may seem to be the most logical, but it's not necessarily so. If you're using dark sights, it's often difficult to discern minor
inaccuracies in your aim when the sights are centered on a dark bull's-
eye. But, if the bull's-eye seems to rest atop or slightly above the sights,
small movements will show up much more readily.

But for a novice shooter, seeing these slight movements is not always
desirable. A beginner is likely to overcompensate if he sees the sights
move a little. As he stops and starts his trigger pull and tries to move the
sights a hair this way or that, he often causes more problems than he
solves. A large deviation from the target should certainly be corrected,
but slight deviations often amount to little compared to the shooter's
attempts to correct them.

The proper aiming technique is the one that works best for you. But
for practical purposes the slight difference in accuracy that each of these
methods will produce won't be of much concern unless you're shooting
in a target match. Knowledge of these techniques is useful in order to
learn if you're making any other mistakes, but remember that criminals
don't stand still and wear shirts with bull's-eyes painted on them.

When you look at a target, no matter how far away it is, you are looking in a straight line. A bullet, however, doesn't follow a straight line. It follows a curved path due to the effects of gravity and air resistance. At long distances the trajectory of the bullet may rise above your line of sight and then drop back down to hit the target. If you practice long distance shooting, this should certainly be considered, but for the distances encountered inside a home, this effect is insignificant. Likewise, you can ignore the effects of wind and problems encountered when shooting up or down a hill. For our purposes we can assume that a gun shoots in a perfectly straight line.

When you first begin shooting at targets, don't be surprised if you can't hold the gun perfectly steady on the bull's-eye. Not even the experts can do this, though they are much better at it than a beginner. The only way to hold a gun's sights exactly on one spot is to clamp it in a vise, and the human body, however trained and strengthened, is not going to function as perfectly as a vise.

As you attempt to hold your gun steady on a target, it will move around, but this area of movement will get smaller and smaller with practice. Many people make the mistake of trying to jerk the trigger as the gun passes through the bull's-eye, but that jerk is likely to throw the shot off considerably.

A more successful technique is to hold your aim in the smallest area possible and slowly *squeeze* off the shot. This should enable you to hit somewhere within your area of movement. More experienced shooters are able to increase their trigger pressure only when the sights are centered exactly on the bull's-eye, but this is very difficult for a novice to do without adversely affecting his accuracy.

After the gun fires, you should concentrate on returning your aim to the center of the target as quickly as possible. This will prepare you for rapid firing which may be needed against an assailant. If you're in the habit of letting the gun drop after each shot, you may develop a tendency to lower your arm slightly just as the gun fires.

Trigger Pull

It may seem as if there is only one way to pull a trigger, but this is one of the areas where an inexperienced shooter is most likely to foul up. Everyone has a tendency to jerk the trigger when a gun is on target. This is undesirable, because such a jerk is enough to make you miss not only the bull's-eye but the entire target.

The proper method of pulling a trigger is to squeeze it. This means a steady pressure, not a rough jerk. An additional problem associated with jerking a trigger is flinching. If you know exactly when the gun will go off, you'll have an involuntary urge to flinch. This flinch can also cause you to miss the entire target. But when you squeeze a trigger, you aren't exactly sure when the gun is going to fire, so the tendency to flinch is lessened significantly.

You've already learned that your grip shouldn't change as you pull the trigger. Squeezing rather than jerking will also help to alleviate that problem.

An area of some debate is what part of your forefinger should be placed on the trigger. Some people say you should use the tip, some say the first joint, and others recommend the second joint. Actually, this will largely be determined by the size of your hand and how it fits your gun. The important thing is to concentrate on pulling the trigger straight back. Applying pressure to one side or the other will move the gun slightly in that direction.

Most people can fire more accurately single action than double, since the single action trigger pull requires you to move the trigger less than the double action pull.

If you suddenly find yourself in a defensive firing situation, you probably won't have time to fire single action, but if you do have time to do so, your accuracy probably will be improved. Since you may have to fire either single or double action during an emergency, practice both. In general, you'll find that if you can fire double action accurately you will also be able to fire single action accurately. However, since the reverse doesn't necessarily hold true, your emphasis when practicing should be on double action firing.

Some people have the trigger pull on their guns lightened, since they feel that this improves their accuracy. Many of these people end up with what are called hair triggers. These are very dangerous and should not be used, especially in a gun that is to be kept at home for self-defense. This doesn't mean that you shouldn't have your trigger pull lightened if it is so heavy that you have trouble with it, but just don't overdo the connection.

Many experts recommend a procedure called dry snapping to perfect your grip, aim, and trigger pull. This is simply aiming and pulling the trigger without live ammunition. Since the gun isn't going to fire, it will be easier to practice your trigger pull without jerking or flinching. Dry snapping with no cartridge in the gun can be bad for the firing pin, however, so you should load the gun with empty shells. After a while the firing pin will wear down the shells, so you should replace them fairly often. And even though you are using empties, don't point the gun at anyone.

Quick Drawing

There is one word that effectively covers this subject—don't. Quick drawing is a good way to shoot yourself in the leg, as many people learn to their sorrow every year. In fact, this practice is considered so dangerous that it is rarely seen in shooting matches or allowed on a firing range. It is especially dangerous to carry in a holster a cocked gun with no safety; it can be accidentally discharged very easily.

Very few people have any need to wear a gun in a holster at home anyway. If you've properly prepared your doors, windows, and locks, anyone trying to break in is more than likely to make enough noise to alert you in time to get to your gun, wherever it is.

If you do decide, however, to practice drawing from a holster, do so with an empty gun. The main thing to concentrate on is that you don't begin to apply pressure to the trigger until the gun has cleared the holster and is almost lined up on the target.

8.

Shotguns

Overall, the most effective weapon for home defense is a twelve gauge sawed-off shotgun. That notion often triggers a negative reaction from people who don't fully understand it, since a sawed-off shotgun tends to conjure up images of mobsters and bank robbers.

Federal gun laws permit you to have a shotgun with a barrel as short as eighteen inches and an overall gun length as short as twenty-six inches. The average standard shotgun barrel is approximately twenty-eight inches long; police models usually have a barrel of about nineteen or twenty inches.

There are two good reasons for shortening the barrel of a shotgun. First, it makes the weapon a little lighter, more maneuverable, and therefore more practical for indoor use. A full length barrel can be rather awkward to use when you're peering around corners inside a house.

The second reason for shortening the barrel is that the shot will spread out. This effect is the main advantage of a shotgun. Instead of firing a single bullet as a rifle or a handgun does, each shotgun shell contains a number of lead balls which spread out into a wide pattern (Figure 8-1). As a result, your aim doesn't have to be nearly as accurate in order to hit your target. You needn't carefully aim a shotgun; you simply point it.

Fig. 8-1. Number eight shot and 00 buckshot

When you're confronted by a moving assailant in a dark house, this is an extremely valuable advantage.

The force generated by a shotgun is phenomenal. At close range the blast can lift a large man completely off the ground and throw him several feet through the air. A shotgun has the added advantage of being a strong psychological deterrent. The sight of a shotgun is more likely than any other weapon to stop a criminal in his tracks.

People who aren't familiar with shotguns often shy away from them because of their reputation for being big, loud, and having a powerful kick. Actually, this reputation is largely overstated. There are very few people who cannot easily and safely handle a shotgun after just a little instruction and practice. In fact, one of the shotgun's main advantages is its ease of operation.

Shotgun Sizes

The size and the competent firepower of a shotgun is stated in terms of its gauge. The smaller the gauge the larger the gun. The standard shotguns, in decreasing size, are the 10, 12, 16, 20, and 28 gauge, and the

.410 (pronounced four ten). "Four ten" refers to the inside diameter of this shotgun's barrel, rather than its gauge, which would be about 67.

The term gauge refers to the weight of a lead ball that would just fit into the barrel. The lead ball that would fit into a 10 gauge barrel would weigh 1/10 pound, one that would fit into a 12 gauge would weigh 1/12 pound, and so on.

Although several sizes are available, it is fairly simple to determine which shotgun you should use. The 10 gauge is much more powerful than is practical for home protection, or even for most hunting needs. It is basically a high-powered long range gun designed for hunting geese. The 28 gauge and the .410, on the other hand, are designed primarily for shooting small animals; they are inadequate for protection against an assailant.

This leaves the 12, 16, and 20 gauges. I recommend the 12 because of its extra power. If you're uncomfortable with a 12 gauge, however, try the 16 and then the 20 gauge. These two shotguns still have plenty of stopping power.

Several things can be done to reduce the kick or recoil of a shotgun if that's a problem. First, try out a heavier gun; lighter models transfer more of the recoil to the shooter. It also will help if a thick rubber recoil pad is mounted on the butt of the stock. This will cushion the shock considerably.

Proper handling and use of a shotgun will also lessen the recoil effects. The gun should be held tightly against your shoulder, so the gun will merely *push* you instead of slamming back against you.

Choke and Spread Effects

The term "choke" refers to the narrowing of the barrel that is designed into almost all modern shotguns. Notable exceptions are police and riot control weapons. A gun with no choke at all is called a cylinder bore or full bore. A choked barrel is narrower toward the muzzle, so shortening it a few inches will remove all of the choke.

The purpose of the choke is to minimize the spread of the shot, thus increasing the effective range of the gun. For purposes of self-defense, however, this extra range is meaningless, and it is desirable to have the shot spread out as far as possible. The more the shot spreads out the less need there is for pinpoint accuracy.

Even with a gun with full choke (the maximum amount of choke) the shot will spread somewhat, but it doesn't do so nearly as much as when fired from a cylinder bore weapon. Neither design spreads much in the first few feet; out to four or five feet the shot is spread about 1 to 1½ inches. As a result, aiming at short distances is more important, though little skill is required.

At seven to eight feet the difference in spread begins to show with the choked pattern being a little less than two inches, while the full bore would cover almost three inches. At a distance of ten feet the comparison is three inches to four or five inches.

It is past this point that the difference in spread becomes truly significant. At thirty feet the pattern is nine inches choked, versus nineteen inches with a cylinder bore. Consequently, as the distance to the target increases, requiring more accuracy and skill in aiming a rifle or a handgun, the increasing spread of the shotgun pellets makes such accuracy and skill far less important.

Shortening the Shotgun

As already stated, you can legally shorten the barrel of your shotgun to 18 inches—without having to get permission or fill out any sort of paperwork. But this eighteen-inch figure is very important. If your barrel is 17.9 inches long, you are in possession of an illegal firearm, and that carries very stiff federal penalties. It is therefore a good idea to stay on the safe side by shortening the barrel to no less than 18½ inches.

How you measure this length is also very important. With the gun closed and unloaded, a rod is inserted into the end of the barrel as far as it will go. A mark of less than eighteen inches on this rod had better not be showing.

Basically, the shortening of a shotgun barrel is very simple; all it takes is a hacksaw. But in practice there is a little more to it than this. If you botch the job badly enough, it will not only affect the way the gun shoots, it also can be dangerous. Unless you really know what you're doing, you should have a gunsmith shorten the barrel for you. He should be able to do the job so that the gun will still shoot a proper pattern and will not pull to one side or the other when fired. The price for this is very low, usually between fifteen and twenty-five dollars, depending on the gunsmith.

Another thing a gunsmith can do for you is put the front sight back on the gun, if it had one. If you ever have to use your gun for self-defense, you probably won't use the sight at all, but it certainly won't hurt to have it, either.

You might also consider shortening the stock of your shotgun. As you hold the gun in position to fire it from the hip, the stock should extend back to your elbow. Since you'll clamp the stock between your elbow and your side when firing from this position, any part of the stock that extends back past your elbow is just excess weight that may make the gun a little more cumbersome. But if the stock is shortened too much, you may suffer a loss of control, since you won't be able to use your elbow to brace it against your side.

If you do decide to shorten the stock, don't forget about the twenty-six-inch overall limit. It doesn't matter how long the barrel is if the total length of the gun is less than twenty-six inches, and shortening the stock very much could get you down into that area. A rubber recoil pad usually should not be included when figuring the twenty-six-inch restriction. Even though the pad may be screwed on securely, the authorities may not consider it to be a permanent, nonremovable part of the gun.

You should also be aware that a greatly shortened stock can compromise both your safety and comfort. When firing from the hip, you can easily get a modified stock out in front of you far enough for it to be jammed back into your midsection.

Choosing a Shotgun

If you get together three people who know something about shotguns and ask them which make and model should be used for self-defense at home, you probably will get four different answers. There are, however, a few features that you don't need and therefore needn't pay for in a gun that's to be used only at home. Fancy engraving is one such. This can greatly increase the attractiveness and the price of a gun without adding anything to its effectiveness.

Many shotguns have a ventilated rib running along the top of the barrel. This radiates the heat that builds up when the gun is fired frequently in a short period of time. This is a nice option to have when using a gun outdoors, but you're not going to be firing it that many times in your home. Nor do you need a high quality gun designed for skeet or trap shooting. Those guns are designed to withstand much more use than one that is to be used for hunting or self-defense.

If you want a gun that can be used for hunting, too, check into the models that are available with interchangeable barrels. This will increase the price somewhat, but it may be cheaper than buying two guns.

Single Shot Shotguns

The cheapest and simplest shotgun is the single shot break action. This type has a barrel that "breaks open" and hinges down. A single shell can then be inserted into the gun. This model is not generally recommended for self-defense, because you must reload after each shot—not a very desirable situation when facing an assailant in the middle of the night.

Bolt Action Shotguns

Next up the price scale is the bolt action shotgun. These guns usually hold several shells, but the shooter must operate a bolt with his firing hand after each shot in order to introduce the next shell. As a result, the gun can't be fired as rapidly as some other models that cost just a little more.

Automatic Shotguns

At the upper end of the price range are the automatic shotguns. These are actually semiautomatic weapons, in that the trigger must be pulled in order to fire each individual shot, but as with an automatic pistol, a new shell is automatically fed into the firing chamber after each shot.

Although an automatic shotgun may seem very desirable, it suffers many of the same drawbacks that are inherent in automatic handguns. There are quite a few moving parts, which means that more things can go wrong, and after each shot the gun is ready to be fired again with only a slight touch of the trigger. With your adrenalin flowing, it would be very easy to accidentally fire this type of gun without meaning to.

Actually, the main advantage of the automatic shotgun—speed in firing several shells—isn't much greater than the double barrel or pump shotguns, which will be discussed next. These two models can be fired almost as fast as the automatic, but they are much simpler, more dependable, and cheaper. The pump and double barrel are the two designs that are most often recommended by experts as the shotgun you should have for self-defense at home.

Pump Shotguns

Most pump shotguns can hold five or six shells, but a brand-new shotgun usually has a wooden block in the magazine that keeps it from holding more than three shells at a time. This plug is inserted at the factory, so that the gun will comply with federal laws governing the hunting of ducks and geese. These laws prohibit you from using a gun that will hold more than three shells at a time, but there is nothing illegal about removing the plug unless you are hunting those birds. Indeed, there is no reason not to remove the plug if the gun is to be used for home defense, since you'll then be able to load more shells.

The pump shotgun has several advantages. It is simple to operate; it has few moving parts, so there's little chance of a malfunction; and the pump design allows the gun to be fired very rapidly. In fact, with just a little practice, the average person can fire this gun almost as fast as he can an automatic.

As you hold the gun in a normal grip, right hand at the trigger and left hand supporting the barrel, your left hand is gripping the slide mechanism. You simply pull the slide straight back to the stop and then shove it back forward in order to introduce a shell and cock the gun. As the slide is pulled back, any shell that is already in the firing chamber is ejected. When the slide is pushed forward again, a new shell is moved into position from the magazine.

This movement can be accomplished very smoothly, easily, and quickly without having to remove the gun from its firing position at your shoulder or hip. Be careful, however, not to pull the trigger while operating the slide.

The safety on this type of gun usually consists of a short rod that runs through the trigger guard and is pushed from side to side to lock or unlock the trigger. When the red side of the rod is exposed, it means that the safety is not engaged, and the trigger can be pulled. Other models may have a safety on top of the gun that is pushed on and off with the thumb.

Pump shotguns incorporate another safety device called the slide lock. This automatically locks the slide in place when the gun is cocked. The release for the slide is usually located near the trigger guard, but you may have a model that doesn't have a release button. Instead, the slide may simply be moved forward a fraction of an inch in order to unlock it.

The slide lock can provide an extra measure of safety if it is utilized correctly. Before you put any shells into the gun, engage the safety and operate the slide mechanism once. This will cock the gun and engage the slide lock. Then load the gun by slipping the shells into the loading port just forward of the trigger.

This is the safest way to store the gun in your home. There is no shell in the firing chamber, so if the gun is dropped or if a child releases the safety and pulls the trigger, nothing will happen. Furthermore, a child will have to unlock the slide and operate it before a shell moves into firing position.

If you wake up in the middle of the night and hear an intruder, simply push the slide release, pump the slide, and click the safety off. You can do it even quicker than you can say it or read it. With most guns you can pump the slide with your left hand and push the safety off with your right forefinger, all at the same time. Your finger is then in position to slide right back onto the trigger. As soon as you fire, the slide is automatically unlocked, and you can pump the gun without having to hit the slide release again. Some pump shotguns operate slightly differently, but these procedures work for most of them.

Another advantage of the pump shotgun is the distinctive sound that the slide makes when it is pumped back and forth. Suppose an intruder has broken into your home. It's dark and he believes that no one is home, or perhaps he knows that you *are* home, and that's his reason for being there. Suddenly, from the dark bedroom the sound of a shotgun being pumped sounds through the quiet house. Only the most stupid or most dedicated intruder isn't going to get out of there as fast as he can.

Even though he may be armed, if he is at all rational, he'll be disinclined to come stalking after you in that dark house when he knows that there will be a shotgun aimed at him. Of course, there are a few criminals who won't stop at that point. These are the ones who don't know what the sound is and who don't have enough sense to realize that it may be a gun—a truly irrational psycho, or a drug addict who is so spaced out that he doesn't know what is going on.

Although it's highly unlikely that you'll ever have to fire more shots at an intruder than a pump shotgun holds, still another advantage of the pump is that you can reload simply by slipping more shells into the magazine. You don't have to stop to swing the barrel down or remove a clip.

As with handguns, a disadvantage of keeping a shotgun always cocked is that the springs inside the gun may weaken after a long period of time. Some guns are more prone to this than others, so ask the dealer about it when you buy. A clerk in a large department store isn't likely to know that much about the merchandise, so if you want to get expert advice, go to a store that is primarily in the business of selling and repairing guns. You will then be dealing with people who know the guns they handle inside and out.

If you have children to worry about, you probably will be much better off leaving the gun cocked with no shell in the firing chamber, so that the slide lock will provide added protection. As long as you check your gun regularly, or better yet go out and fire it, you should be able to discover any long term deterioration before it becomes a significant problem.

But if there are no children to be concerned about, you may want to bypass the slide lock, so that the gun will be in a more advanced state of readiness. Simply load the magazine, unlock the slide if it's locked, and pull it back about an inch. Now if you have to grab the gun in the middle of the night, rather than first having to unlock the slide, you simply pump it. Again, in the same movement, you can push the safety off and then slide your finger right back onto the trigger. Or, you can have the gun even more ready for use by loading it, pumping it once, and then engaging the safety. Then all you'll have to do in order to fire is click off the safety.

Another consideration when leaving a gun loaded and inactive for a long period of time is the spring in the magazine. This too can weaken, creating problems when the last of the shells are being injected into the firing chamber. The simplest way to avoid this problem is to load the magazine with one shell fewer than it will hold, sparing the spring maximum stress. But if you examine and fire the gun regularly, you'll be able to spot any problems of this sort as soon as they occur.

Double Barrel Shotguns

An often cited advantage of the double barrel shotgun is that the sight of it is even more of a deterrent to an assailant than is a single barrel. Actually, though, it's unlikely that an intruder who stops for a double barrel shotgun will attack in the face of only a single barrel. The psychological advantages of a double over a single are probably more significant when confronting a crowd, not just one or two intruders in your home.

Most doubles are like having two guns welded together, in that you have two of just about everything except the stock. For this reason a double will cost you more than a comparable single barrel gun. Most doubles have the barrels side by side, others have one barrel on top of the other—"over-under" as it is called. For self-defense, it makes no difference which model you choose.

Normally there are two triggers on a double barrel shotgun, one in front of the other. Some guns, however, have only one trigger. On some models you can select which barrel the single trigger will fire first, but on most guns the firing order is fixed. For self-defense it makes no difference which model you use.

With double triggers it is possible to fire both barrels at the same time, but that's not recommended. In the first place, you'll gain little by doing so, and in the second the recoil will be so great that you may end up flat on your back.

The disadvantage of a double barrel is that you get only two shots before you have to reload. Of course you can get off those two shots very quickly indeed. It's been said that if you can't do away with an intruder with two shots from a shotgun, you may as well not try. On the other hand, if you do fire once and miss, or if you hit him with some of the shot but don't disable your assailant, you'll then have only one shot left—not a very desirable situation, especially if the intruder is armed.

The main advantage of the double over the pump is its simplicity of operation. This is truly an advantage for someone who is very inexperienced and nervous with shotguns. The barrels break open and hinge down, so that any used shells can be pulled out and new ones inserted. This also enables you to look right through the barrels and positively tell at a glance if the gun is empty or not.

When the barrels are snapped shut again, the gun may or may not be ready to fire, depending on the model. There are two basic designs—those with external hammers and those without them. Although they are rarely seen on guns made today, external hammers can provide an extra margin of safety. Once the shells have been loaded and the barrels have been snapped shut, the hammers must still be manually cocked before the gun can be fired.

Some people feel that external hammers are dangerous, because you may catch one on something, clothing for example, and pull it back to the cocked position without realizing it. But when a gun is to be kept at home under the bed and used only in an emergency, that shouldn't be a significant concern.

The hammerless models are automatically cocked when you open and close the barrels. Most of these models also have a safety that is automatically engaged when the gun is closed and cocked, so you must move the safety off before you can fire. But not all models have this automatic safety feature. On those guns that don't, the shooter must remember to engage the safety himself.

A significant drawback of a double barrel shotgun is that it can be rather dangerous to keep it loaded if other people may have access to it. When a hammerless model is loaded, the only thing that prevents it from discharging if someone touches the trigger or drops it is the safety. And rare as that happens, safeties have been known to fail. Models with external hammers aren't much safer when loaded, since it's quite simple for even a child to cock back the hammer.

If you live alone with no one else around who can ever touch the gun, you can safely keep a double barrel loaded and ready. But if that's not the case in your home, you'll have to consider keeping your double unloaded.

It doesn't take long to load a double barrel. You simply hit the barrel release, the barrel swings down, and you insert two shells. This is easy to do, but if you have to fumble around in the dark for shells while you're half scared to death, it can take much longer than you'd like. This is therefore a big advantage of the pump over the double—it is much safer to leave the pump loaded.

Conclusion

The bottom line is that a 12 gauge pump is the best shotgun for most folks for self-defense at home. If the 12 gauge is too powerful, try a 16 and then a 20 gauge.

If you want a very simple gun and are unable to comfortably use a pump, use a double barrel. But remember, if others may have access to it, especially children, you'll be wise to keep a double barrel unloaded.

Firing the Shotgun

When using a shotgun for self-defense, there's no need for meticulous aiming through the sights. Instead, whether shooting from the shoulder or the hip, just point the barrel at the center of your target and fire. This is another advantage of a shotgun over a handgun, since you may not be able to see the sights if you're firing at an assailant in the middle of the night.

In order to fire right-handed from the shoulder, stand with your body turned about forty-five degrees to the right of the target and the butt of the gun held firmly against your right shoulder. Keeping the gun tight against your shoulder will lessen the recoil effects. Have your feet spread comfortably, about twelve to eighteen inches. You need not follow some strictly prescribed set of angles and measurements, but you'll want to get into a stance that will be comfortable and will keep you from being thrown off balance when the gun is fired.

As you aim, or rather point, from the shoulder, it's important to get your head over toward the gun far enough to look out along the top of the barrel, instead of looking down on it or over at it. This usually will require your cheek to rest against the stock. Once you're in position, you can change your aim from side to side by simply twisting your body back and forth. The gun will follow.

When firing a shotgun from the hip, your grip will basically be the same as if you were shooting from the shoulder; your stance and the angle of your body in relation to the target should be about the same as well. Clamp the stock between your elbow and your side with the gun about level with and parallel to your firing forearm. Be careful, though, that you don't get the butt of the gun out in front of you, or it may slam back into your midsection when you fire. As when firing from the shoulder, if you have to turn to one side or the other to follow a target, you should swivel from the waist rather than attempt to move only the gun.

Some people are hesitant to fire a shotgun from the hip position because they're uncertain about the recoil effects, but most people actually find it to be easier to cope with the recoil if they fire the gun from this position. However, unless you're a real expert, you'll be able to fire more accurately from the shoulder than from the hip. That's why you should plan to use the gun in that manner unless you're so rushed that you don't have time to bring it all the way up to your shoulder.

When firing a double barrel shotgun, the question of which trigger to pull first often comes up. One theory is that the front trigger should be pulled first, so your finger can then slip right back to the rear trigger and be ready to fire again. But for an inexperienced shooter, or even an experienced one under stress, it would be very easy for the trigger finger to slip back to that rear trigger and fire the gun again without meaning to. This could be dangerous, not to mention the fact that you would then be standing there with an empty gun. If the rear trigger is pulled first, it will only take a fraction of a second longer to move your finger up to the front trigger than vice versa, and there will be far less chance of inadvertently firing the gun again.

Shotgun Ammunition

A shotgun shell differs from a handgun or rifle cartridge in that it contains a number of small, or sometimes not so small, lead pellets or balls called shot. In order to insure that all of the pellets get a good uniform push as the gunpowder explodes, a wad of material, appropriately called the wad, is packed between the shot and the powder (Figure 8-2).

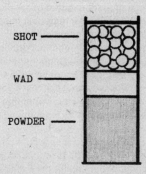

SHOT

WAD

POWDER

Fig. 8-2. Cutaway diagram of a shotgun shell

The owner of a shotgun has a wide range of shells from which to choose, the primary difference being in the size and number of pellets each contains. A shell loaded with the largest size shot will contain only a few pellets; one loaded with small shot will contain hundreds or even thousands of pellets. Sizes range from number twelve shot (about like finely ground pepper) to 000 (pronounced triple ought) buckshot (Figure 8-3). Buckshot, as the name implies, is a shell containing shot large enough for hunting deer.

A standard 12 gauge 00 buckshot shell contains nine lead balls, each

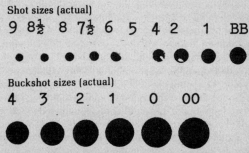

Shot sizes (actual)

9   8½   8   7½   6   5   4   2   1   BB

Buckshot sizes (actual)

4   3   2   1   0   00

Fig. 8-3.

about the size of the bullet fired by a .32 handgun. If you fire five of these shells from a 12 gauge pump or automatic shotgun as fast as possible, you'd be firing a total of forty-five lead projectiles, any one of which alone can stop an assailant. At close range very few submachine guns can do as much damage in the same amount of time.

When choosing a shotgun shell for home defense, your concerns are twofold. You need a shell with enough power to stop an assailant, but a shotgun blast that tears through a wall may kill someone on the other side. One thing to bear in mind, though, is that if you use a shell that is so weak that it won't penetrate an interior wall of thin plaster or sheetrock, it probably can't be relied upon to stop an intruder at greater than point-blank range.

As the size of the shot increases, the effective range also increases; 00 buckshot will travel more than 700 yards, with a lethal range of about 100 feet. For this reason 00 buckshot is the shell most often used by law enforcement officials. The police need a shell that will give them plenty of range, since much of their work is outside, but someone concerned with home security doesn't have to worry about that sort of distance. As a result, while 00 buckshot may be the best shell for police work, it might not be the most desirable thing to use inside your home.

On the other end of the spectrum, number twelve shot will stop an assailant but only at very close range. These small particles will travel about 100 yards, but they won't be effective at anywhere near that distance. You'll want to use a shell that will enable you to stop an assailant with one shot from any spot inside your home, and number twelve shot isn't likely to give you that dependability.

Where, then, between number twelve shot and 00 buckshot, is the happy medium? Unfortunately, there is no simple clear-cut answer; it really comes down to a matter of opinion, with the general concensus being somewhere between number four buckshot and number eight shot for use inside an average apartment or home. Number eight shot has about 500 pellets, number four buckshot about 27.

Take a look around your home. If there's nowhere that you can stand and be more than about twelve feet from another person (a fairly small home), then a number eight shell is all you need. But if you may have to fire down a hallway and into another room, you need a shell with larger pellets. If in doubt, you probably are better off using a shell with pellets that are a little too large. One important advantage of a shotgun shell is that it doesn't have the dangerous range that a bullet does. But no matter what size shell you decide to use, be sure to refer to the section of this book on floor diagrams and planning.

There is one other shotgun shell—the rifled slug—that can do even more damage than 00 or 000 buckshot, but it isn't practical for home defense. A slug is a large bulletlike ball that is twice as large as the bullet fired by a .38. Police SWAT teams use these to blow their way through locked doors and such. Slugs will easily penetrate several walls, so they can be very dangerous inside a home. With a slug you'll also loose the shotgun's advantage of firing a load of shot that spreads out into a wide pattern.

You can even get tear gas shells for a shotgun, but you don't need tear gas for home defense. It might be great for controlling a mob, but if you fire one of them inside your home, the gas probably will affect you as much as it does the intruder.

Whichever shell you choose, make sure that you use the proper gauge shell in the proper gun. Doing otherwise, even though it may seem to fit, can be very dangerous.

Since each shotgun has its own personality, especially if it has been modified, it's a good idea to examine the spread of its pellets by firing at large sheets of paper at various ranges. You may also find that the spread will vary according to the shell you use. When practicing or test firing, be sure to observe the same safety precautions that you should when firing bullets. Although the lethal range of most shotgun shells is fairly short, a pellet hitting someone in the throat or the eye at even a long distance can do a great deal of damage. There is also the danger of clumping. If several of the pellets clump together as they leave the barrel, their range will be greatly increased, so you may harm someone who is well beyond the normal danger range.

As with handguns, when transporting a shotgun to a firing range, it should be unloaded. Have the barrel broken open or the action open, whichever is applicable, and keep your fingers outside the trigger guard until you are ready to fire.

Rifles

A rifle is not recommended for home defense. If you want to shoot something far away, it's the only weapon to use, but you shouldn't depend on one for protection at home. A handgun has the advantage of being lightweight and compact, so that you can pull it out, aim, and fire quickly. Shotguns have the advantage of requiring less skill and accuracy. But a rifle has neither of these attributes.

Since rifles are usually high-powered weapons made for long distance shooting, you have a much better chance of sending a bullet through a wall and killing an innocent third party. But, as with a handgun, you are firing only one bullet at a time and must therefore be able to shoot accurately with little time to aim in poor light conditions.

Even small, relatively low-powered rifles such as the .22 can be deadly up to a mile away. But as with any small caliber weapon, if you don't hit your assailant in a vital spot, you probably won't disable him. And in the case of a large, enraged assailant, even a hit in a normally vital spot may not stop him immediately.

If you live out in the country with very little traffic around your home, and if you have no neighbors for at least two miles, then you may be able to safely use a rifle for self-defense. But only if you are very skilled with it and know exactly what you are doing; and even then you'd still be much better off with a shotgun.

9.

Defensive Shooting at Home

Defensive shooting, used by the police and the military, differs significantly from simple target shooting. The two-handed grip is strongly emphasized along with the use of cover or barricades, both for concealment and additional support of the weapon. For those times when little or no cover is available, various shooting positions have been developed that will provide stability when firing as well as enabling the shooter to present a smaller target to an assailant.

This sort of firing also requires a liberal amount of common sense. If an intruder is carrying a gun, don't you step out into the open and order him to drop it. That's an excellent way to get shot.

Aiming

If you've enough time to take careful aim at an assailant, then by all means do it. But defensive firing assumes that you probably won't have that time. Or, even if you do have time, when firing in dim light, you may not be able to see your sights well enough to use them.

When firing defensively, the shooter simply points the gun at the target and fires quickly without ever looking through the sights. With a shotgun this type of firing is very simple and relatively accurate. When you point a shotgun at a target, the barrel sticks out far enough to enable your peripheral vision to pick it up, and you can see fairly well where it is aimed, even though you aren't looking directly at the gun.

When using a handgun it's important to use this same technique. The gun should be held well out in front of you at eye level, so that it will be well within your field of vision when you're looking at the target. You'll find that you are aiming your arms as well as the gun. Once you're familiar with your weapon, you should be able to assume the proper grip and arm position and have a fairly accurate idea of where the gun is aimed, even when you're in almost total darkness.

When you're practicing this sort of quick firing it's important that you not attempt to aim the gun by use of the sights. Concentrate on pointing the gun and getting the shot off quickly. If you have to depend on the sights, your firing will be considerably slower, and that can be fatal in a defensive firing situation.

What you're seeking is the proper feel of your arms, your grip, and the gun. With enough practice you should learn exactly how it feels when you're properly aiming the gun where you are looking.

Shoot a handgun from the hip, cowboy style, only when it is vital to get a shot off as quickly as possible. Firing from the hip will not be nearly as accurate as bringing the gun up with both hands to eye level, but it will get the first shot off a little faster. You're in a tradeoff—speed for accuracy. After considerable practice you can become fairly proficient in shooting from the hip, but for the average person who shoots only occasionally, the standard two-handed firing position is much more accurate.

When you do shoot from the hip, it is important to get the gun out in front of you far enough for you to see it with your peripheral vision. The technique of getting it out there as quickly as possible is best described as a punching sort of motion. Try to punch the gun straight out at the target as if you were punching with your fist.

When pulling the trigger remember that a wild jerk can easily throw your aim off enough to cause you to miss the entire target. The best way to perfect your trigger control is through slower practice on a target.

A good way to practice your aiming at home is to quickly point the gun at various targets, and then, holding the gun perfectly still, look through the sights to see how well you are lined up. Before using either of these methods, however, you should be certain that the gun is unloaded. But even then, never practice by aiming at another person.

An excellent way to improve your ability to fire a shotgun quickly and accurately is to spend some time on a skeet range. You must fire quickly at a small target that is suddenly hurled into view and then zooms rapidly out of range. Instructors are usually available at these ranges; just a little time at such a place should be very beneficial.

A good way to improve your handgun accuracy with a moving target is to shoot at balloons. Considerable caution must be exercised when doing this, though, since you may be firing over a wide area, perhaps wildly at times. Make sure that the entire area of fire is clear and that you know exactly where your bullets will stop. Don't just shoot toward a stand of trees, since someone may be within your range but out of sight.

Most combat shooting instructors recommend that you fire two shots at a time, and it's a good idea to practice in this manner, squeezing off two shots very close together. This technique makes sense, especially if your assailant is armed. Although your first shot may hit him and knock him down, he may be only slightly wounded. That's no time to stop and wait to see what the intruder is going to do next.

As soon as your assailant hits the ground, he is likely to begin firing back at you if he can. While he is off balance and falling, you are in an excellent position to make sure that he doesn't fire again. The same reasoning applies, perhaps even more so, if your first shot misses him completely. If that is the case, you'll want to have a second shot on its way to the target quickly.

Barricades

Barricade shooting makes use of a barrier for support of the firing arm and the gun as well as protection from your assailant's fire. A good barricade also will allow you to hide from an assailant who's stalking you, and, possibly even enable you to fire the first shot.

Homes are full of vertical barricades, doorways being the most common. When you are peering to your right around the edge of a wall or doorway, you can shoot right-handed and still remain fairly well concealed. The amount of cover you have—cover means protection—depends upon the materials that make up the wall, and its thickness. If you're on the right side of such a barricade leaning over to your left, you must shoot left-handed in order to remain concealed.

When in position to fire right-handed, place your left hand flat against the wall or doorway with your fingers pointing up. Your thumb should be extended out to the right, past the edge of the barricade. Your thumb now forms a V into which the wrist of your firing hand will fit (Figure 9-1). When using a shotgun simply rest the weapon in this V about where your supporting hand would normally be gripping the gun (Figure 9-2).

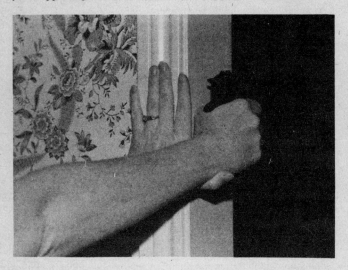

Fig. 9-1. Support the wrist of your firing arm on the outstretched thumb of the braced, other hand.

The gun itself should not touch the wall or barricade. Instead, your supporting hand should be between the gun and the barrier. If you allow a gun to rest directly on a solid object, the recoil may cause it to jump, affecting your accuracy and your ability to quickly get away a second shot.

The way you position your feet in this firing position is very important. When firing with your right hand, your left foot will be placed forward, just inside the edge of the barricade, so that it's not exposed. Your right foot is then swung back behind you, concealing your right leg and hips (Figure 9-3).

Fig. 9-2. Support the shotgun on the outstretched thumb of the braced, non-firing hand.

Fig. 9-3. Proper firing position behind a wall.

Once you're in the proper position, you may feel somewhat awkward. That's normal. Try to be balanced on your feet as much as possible. Don't lean over so far that your supporting hand has to hold you up.

A common error when using this position is failing to swing your foot far enough back behind the body. This leaves the rear leg and hip exposed. Properly done, when shooting right-handed this position leaves only the thumb of your left hand, your right arm and shoulder, and the right side of your face and head exposed as a target (Figure 9-4). If you practice this position while looking into a large mirror, you will immediately be able to determine if you're doing it correctly.

When using any sort of barricade or support, it is very important that the muzzle of the gun be clear of all obstructions. If the bullet were to strike something just a short distance from the gun, the effect would be similar to that of a small bomb; debris would probably fly back and hit you in the face.

Fig. 9-4. When you're properly positioned, you expose very little of yourself to your assailant's view.

Perhaps the best barricade in your home is your bed. This is where you're most likely to be if someone breaks in during the night, so it will certainly be readily available. The best way to utilize your bed is to sit on the floor on the side away from your assailant. The ideal position will depend somewhat on your height and that of the bed, but most people find that they should either sit cross-legged or kneel. Don't stick your legs up under the bed, though, since this may hamper your ability to move quickly if you have to.

Now rest your arms, or your supporting elbow if holding a shotgun, on the top of the bed. Whenever you use any position lower than a standing position, you may aim too low without realizing it, so pay special attention to the elevation of your gun.

Depending again on your height and the height of the bed, you may have to prop up your arms on a pillow or two to give the gun exactly the right elevation. You won't have time to arrange pillows if the assailant is almost upon you as you grab your gun, but if you have time to wait for him, put yourself into perfect firing position.

Check your home for possible barricades; couches, dressers, tables, and other things normally found around the house can provide excellent concealment along with good support for your weapon. But don't fool yourself into thinking that you are automatically safe if you duck behind something such as your couch. As already noted, most of the weapons available today will shoot right through a door or a wall. But then, whatever protection they offer is far better than nothing at all and certainly should be utilized when available.

Night Firing

It may be very dark when your assailant breaks in—so dark that you may have trouble even seeing him. You hold the advantage in your own home, in that you know your way around in the dark. Even though an intruder may have been in your home before—a delivery person for example—he isn't going to know his way around it as well as you do.

For this reason darkness is a weapon to be used against an intruder. You will be on the defensive with time on your side, so you can simply wait in the dark, forcing the intruder to come to you. If the entire house happens to be in darkness, you may be able to mark your assailant's progress by the noise he makes. He is likely to find your home to be an obstacle course. For your part you should remain perfectly still. Other than noise, the main thing that will give you away in the dark is movement. A static object is much more difficult to see.

Under some circumstances you may have to venture through your home looking for an intruder, but those situations are rare. If you feel that a child in another room is in danger, you may be forced to take the offensive, but simply wondering if someone has broken in is no reason to go exploring.

If you decide to go after an armed intruder who is quietly waiting for you somewhere in your home, the odds will be on his side. It won't matter how well you know your own home. Any slight noise you make along with your movements will enable the intruder to spot you long before you find him. The probability of your being killed in such a circumstance is high.

However, if you hear one of your children being attacked, that's a different story. In that case you'll know exactly where the intruder is. It's no longer a case of the criminal quietly waiting for you. On the other hand it could be a trick or a trap to draw you out, so you'll still have to be very cautious; don't just rush right in without thinking.

If you do have to go through your home looking for an intruder, the safety rules that normally should be followed when carrying a gun no longer apply. The weapon should be carried loaded with the safety off, ready to fire with a pull of the trigger. As you move through the house, don't hold the gun up or down as you would under normal circumstances. Keep it pointed out in front of you ready to fire instantly if the assailant suddenly attacks. Be careful, though, that you don't stick the gun way out ahead of you when you round a corner. If you do that, the intruder may see you before you can see him.

Be very cautious about turning on lights, including a flashlight. You'll not only tell the intruder exactly where you were, but your eyes will no longer be adjusted to the dark. Going after a criminal with a flashlight is especially risky, since your light provides him with an excellent target. Remember, the dark is your ally when you're in your own home; use it to your full advantage.

Figures 9-5, 9-6, and 9-7 show quite well how important it is that you use your lighting properly. Let's suppose that lights are on in other parts of your home, but your bedroom is dark. Figure 9-5 shows the target that an intruder would present as he enters your bedroom. Figure 9-6 shows what the assailant would see, and 9-7 shows what is actually waiting for him.

Fig. 9-5. The target an intruder presents when entering a bedroom

Fig. 9-6. What the assailant would see

Fig. 9-7. What is waiting for the assailant

You may find yourself in a situation that requires you to reload your gun in the dark. Most guns are fairly easy to load in darkness, but it does require a little practice to be able to do it quickly and quietly. Practice loading with your eyes closed until you can do it smoothly and comfortably by feel alone.

Crouch Position

In this position the shooter stands with his weight equally distributed on both feet, facing the target, but he is crouched down so that he creates a smaller target for his assailant. This position has been described as standing like a monkey, since the knees are bent quite a bit, and one leans forward slightly.

The crouch position is most suitable when you must fire quickly without time to prepare for your attacker—when you've no time to seek cover. The position is one that feels natural, since it is instinctive to crouch somewhat when attacked.

Sitting Position

To assume this position simply sit down with your feet flat on the floor, your heels about twelve inches in front of you, and your legs close together. When possible, sit with your back against a firm support such as a wall. You can then either rest your arms on top of your knees, or you can squeeze them between your legs in order to provide even more stability.

One problem, however, is that when your arms are placed down between your knees, the gun will not be aimed upward; it will be approximately level. As a result, this squeezing technique isn't very useful if you're sitting on the floor and firing at short range—exactly what you'll do in your home. For short range firing you probably will have to slouch down, bend your elbows, and raise your forearms slightly in order to get the gun high enough.

When firing a shotgun from the sitting position, spread your feet and legs far enough to create props for your elbows. You'll find that the elevation of the gun is not such a problem when firing a shotgun from this position.

Prone Position

Since this position is most advantageous when no cover is available, you probably won't have to use it inside your home; the average house or apartment is full of doorways and furniture. If the assailant is far away, this position presents him with a small target, and the floor makes an excellent support for your arms.

This position is all right for handguns, but it isn't very practical when firing a shotgun at short range. The problem with the shotgun at short range is that it takes quite an effort to get the barrel high enough to hit your assailant anywhere above the knees. In fact, if you try this, you probably will find that in order to aim the shotgun high enough, you're no longer holding the gun properly. This is certain to affect your aim quite a bit, and the recoil is likely to bruise your shoulder or possibly even break your collarbone.

In order to use a handgun in this position, you lie flat on your stomach with your head held up, facing straight ahead. Your arms are out-stretched in front of you in a two-handed grip, and the supporting hand may have to be placed under the gun, palm up, so that the butt doesn't touch the ground.

As with a shotgun, you probably will find that in an average size room a handgun will be aimed too low, so you'll have to raise the weapon. The best way to do this is to bend your arms at the elbows; keep your upper arms firmly on the ground, and raise your forearms and the gun.

Kneeling Position

Unlike the prone position, the kneeling position easily can be used at short range with either a handgun or a shotgun. Due to the added stability that this position gives the shooting hand, it is especially advantageous when shooting at more distant targets.

To assume this position, drop to your right knee if you are shooting right-handed. Your left foot is flat on the floor, so that the left knee is pointing toward the target. Now plant your left elbow on your raised knee and use your left hand to brace the gun.

This position usually works best if you use the supporting hand as a cup for the butt of the pistol. You will probably need to sit back on the heel of your right foot; that will enhance stability and will allow you a level or slightly elevated aim.

When kneeling to fire a shotgun you've several options. You can place your left elbow on your left knee (shooting right-handed) and hold the gun in a normal grip; you can straighten up and hold the gun normally without using your knee for a brace; or you can fire from the hip.

Be very careful, though, when kneeling on one knee and firing from the hip. If you're sitting on one heel and holding a shortened shotgun back a little farther than normal, that is, with your trigger hand back at your side rather than out in front of you just a bit, you may accidentally blow off your knee.

10.

Confronting the Intruder

Once you hear an intruder breaking into your home, or realize that one has already broken in, it probably is too late to figure out exactly what you should do. In order to react properly in that limited amount of time, you'll have had to thoroughly think things out beforehand. The actions you take will depend largely on where the intruder is, where any children are, and how your home is laid out. Everyone faces a different set of circumstances.

There are two very basic and important points to bear in mind when making your contingency plans. First, you should strive to avoid any confrontation with an intruder. If you're just waiting for the chance to blow away a criminal, you have the wrong attitude. That's a good way to get killed.

Second, dismiss any thoughts you may have about capturing this threat to society. That's a job for the police. The sole purpose of your arming yourself is to protect yourself and your family. In order to do that you must make everything work to your advantage. Use your head; a gun is to be used only as a last resort, if all else fails. Again, if you have any other attitude, you are reducing the chances that you and your family will come through the episode unharmed.

Floorplans

When you've no children to worry about, things are very simple. No matter what the layout of your home is, you can simply lock the bedroom door if someone breaks in. In fact, you can sleep with it locked. But if you have children to consider, it's a very different story.

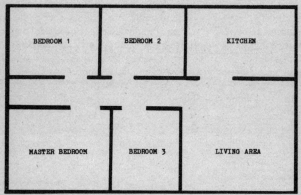

Fig. 10-1. Common four bedroom floorplan

Figure 10-1 shows a fairly common four bedroom design with all of the bedrooms located at one end of the house. In this case it probably will be a good idea to set up a child's room as the security room. Then rather than having to carry a sleepy child back across the hall to your bedroom, you can just duck into his room and lock the door. Don't forget that besides a strong door with secure locks, the child's room should have an emergency exit and a telephone.

If your plan is to run across the hall to the child's room and lock yourself in, don't forget to take your gun with you when you go. Although you may safely make your way into the security room, you may need your gun if the intruder attempts to break into that room. If you don't take your gun you face the danger that he may find your weapon and threaten to fire through the door unless you open it. He can make this same threat if he has his own gun with him, but you can respond by firing back if you've armed yourself.

Another option is to close the hall door and lock it, securing the entire end of the house. This should work unless the intruder has broken in through one of the bedrooms instead of the living or kitchen area.

When an intruder enters your home through an occupied bedroom, you have a serious problem no matter how your home is laid out. You'll have to decide whether to wait for the criminal or confront him. You'll certainly be in a poor position to do any shooting if the intruder is near one of your children. It probably will be wiser in that situation to wait quietly and listen. If the assailant attacks one of your children, you'll probably hear something, and then you have little choice but to go after him. But if he leaves that room to search other parts of your home, you'll be in a much better position to defend yourself. The criminal may even move on into the living area, giving you the opportunity to get into your security room. Since time is critical in such a situation, you can see how advantageous it will be to have set up a child's room as a security room.

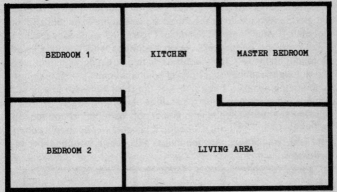

Fig. 10-2. A typical split bedroom arrangement

Figure 10-2 shows a typical split bedroom arrangement with the master bedroom separated from the others. With this sort of layout, you'll have problems no matter where an intruder breaks in. He'll almost always be between you and your children. That also means that you'll have to be very careful about shooting at someone in the central area of the home, since even if you're positive that someone has broken in, one of the children may wander into that area in response to the noise. Neither do you want a shot at the intruder to pierce a wall behind him and strike one of your children.

The smaller your home is the fewer options you have to consider or worry about. If you hear someone breaking into your two bedroom apartment, you just haven't got much room in which to maneuver. But the smaller the home, the easier it is to hear an intruder as he attempts to break in, so you should be able to react quickly.

Another thing to consider is the position of your bed. When you suddenly wake and realize that an intruder has broken in, your fastest defensive move is to roll off the bed on the side opposite the bedroom door. You'll then be in an excellent defensive firing position.

But take a look at Figure 10-1 again. You'll find that if a gun is fired from any position in the master bedroom toward the door (presumably where an assailant would enter), any stray bullet will go into one of the other bedrooms. If there are people in those rooms, you'll not be able to safely fire your gun from your own bedroom. As you can see, this is the sort of strategy that must be thought out beforehand.

In the situation described you'd have to step out into the hall, or better yet, use the vertical barrier shooting position and fire down the hall at the intruder. If your floorplan resembles Figure 10-2 you'll have much the same problem, unless you're using a shotgun with very small shot. Buckshot or virtually any bullet is likely to go right through a couple of interior walls and may strike one of your children.

Referring again to Figure 10-1, if the third bedroom is a usually unoccupied guest room, then the position of your bed largely determines whether you can safely fire your gun or not. With the bed positioned as in Figure 10-3, if you roll off beside it in order to fire at an incoming assailant, you can see that the bullets will still go into the other two bedrooms.

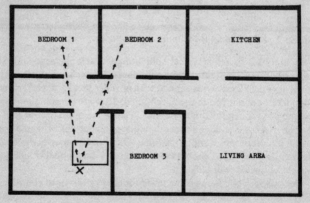

Fig. 10-3. Position of shielding bed restricts safe field of fire.

But if you position the bed as in Figure 10-4, you can roll off the bed and hold your fire until the intruder steps into your room. Then any stray bullets will go into the empty third bedroom.

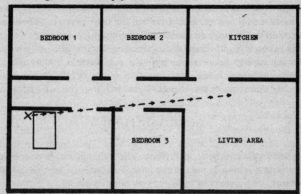

Fig. 10-4. Position of shielding bed enhances safe field of fire.

Figure 10-5 illustrates a bed position that will not only allow your shots to go into the other two bedrooms, it offers you no protection at all from an intruder entering your room. In fact, you won't even be able to use the bed as a brace for your gun. This probably is the worst way to position your bed.

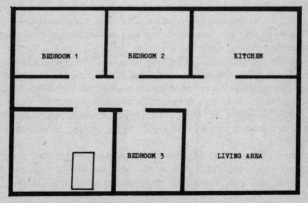

Fig. 10-5. Positioning the bed this way offers you no protection.

These few examples should help guide you when you examine the layout of your own home. Obviously, it would take several volumes to present all possible floorplans and strategies.

Figure out if you'll be able to safely fire at an intruder from your own bedroom, and if repositioning your bed will help. If you can't fire safely from there, you'll probably be better off trying to get into the hall or into a child's room. Establishing a security room is a fine idea, but you may not have time to get everyone into it if you wake to find an intruder already inside your home. You should, therefore, be fully prepared for a situation that requires you to defend yourself from your own bedroom.

Returning Home

What if you walk in on an intruder who's already inside your home? Surprising a criminal could prove fatal. You may not be able to get to your gun, or worse, your assailant may have found it.

The best advice is, don't walk in on such a person. Be aware of anything that doesn't look quite right whenever you return home. If you notice that someone has damaged your door, or if you find a window open that shouldn't be, stop. Don't go in and look around, go somewhere else and call the police. The intruder may still be inside, or if he has left, you may disturb things that can help the police in their investigation.

Make it a habit to knock loudly or ring your doorbell before opening the door. This may allow an intruder to beat a hasty retreat, thus saving you from a dangerous confrontation. Of course, some criminals won't leave when they hear you returning, so you should remain alert and aware even after you are "safely" inside.

Another obvious tip-off of the presence of an intruder is the chain lock being engaged when you try to open your door. This is a technique often used by burglars to warn them that someone has returned. As soon as the intruder hears the door bang against the chain, he probably will attempt to escape through a rear or side exit. Don't run around the house to try another entrance. You may run right into the criminal as he's trying to get away.

One way to keep an intruder from finding your gun and using it against you is to unload it every time you leave. For most people, however, that's an impractical solution, few of us have the time or inclination to load and unload a gun several times a day.

Setting Your Priorities

When an intruder breaks into your home, there are several things that you can or should do. You may have enough time to do each of them, or you may not have enough time to do any of them. Your own situation will dictate what you should plan to do first and last. The following general sequence for the various moves and options is certainly not meant to be an ironclad declaration of what steps you must take and the order in which you should take them.

If you've prepared your home properly, you should be able to hear an intruder as he breaks in. If you're alone, immediately lock yourself into your security room. When there are children to worry about, first get your gun. Then, if you're sure that you've enough time, quickly turn off any lights around you and activate the alarm system and outside lights. Then get the family into the security room if you can safely do so.

Once you're inside the security room, call the police and activate your alarm system and exterior lights if you haven't already done so. If there's an exit in that room, consider getting out and going to a neighbor's. However, the lights and any alarm system may have frightened off the intruder; you don't want to run into him somewhere outside. You may want to get out if you can still hear him moving around inside, but you are in a very secure position sitting in a locked room with your gun. The only way the intruder can get to you is to break through the door, and it will be simple for you to use a bed or a chair as a brace and wait with your gun aimed at the door.

This sequence of events can, of course, be varied if the situation dictates, but there's reasoning behind such a structuring of your actions. Recently, a lady who lives alone in her house had just gone to bed for the evening when her doorbell rang. Since she didn't feel like talking with anyone, she simply ignored it. A few minutes later she heard someone breaking in through her back door. She quickly called a neighbor who immediately came over to investigate. As the neighbor walked around the house, the intruder apparently heard him and ran off.

This reaction is typical of many criminals. When they think that they've been discovered, they flee. In this case the intruder didn't think anyone was at home, since there was no answer at the door. As soon as you activate an alarm or exterior lights, an intruder will know that he's been discovered, and there's a good chance that he'll be scared off right away. If an intruder doesn't run off when he realizes that he's been heard, you can be sure that he is dangerous and is probably not there simply for burglary.

Getting your gun should be one of your first actions, because you may encounter the assailant as you try to round up your children, and then it will be too late to get your weapon. Of course, this assumes that your gun is readily available, and that all you have to do is grab it. If it's stored unloaded in the back of the closet somewhere, you may be better off forgetting it, since it may take you so long to get to it and ready it for firing.

Calling the police is the last thing to do, not because it isn't important, but because they probably won't be able to help you immediately. The steps other than calling the police warrant your quick action.

If you can control the lights in other parts of your home from your bedroom or security room, it may be a good idea to turn them on. You should not, however, turn on the lights in your part of the house, since that will make it easier for the intruder to find you. Remember, in your own home you have the advantage in the dark.

If you're unable to get into a room with a door that you can lock, just wait in the dark with your gun pointed at the door, and force the assailant to come to you. As already shown, lights from other parts of your home will silhouette the intruder as he comes into the darkened room looking for you; your eyes will still be adjusted to the dark, his will not. And remember to remain still, since motion can give you away, even in the dark.

An added advantage of passively waiting for an intruder is that he may quietly give up and leave. If you aggressively seek him out and confront him, you may provoke an attack that neither one of you really wants.

Once you've made it into a locked room, stay there. Though a security room should have both a telephone and an exit, you may find yourself in a room that has neither. If so, stay put. Don't get curious after a few minutes and open the door to peek out. The intruder may be waiting for you. Stay there all night until you're sure that it's daylight and people are moving about outside. At that point you can cautiously open the door and then get out of the house as quickly as possible. Don't stay inside and look around, because the intruder may still be there.

If you do end up face to face with an intruder and point your gun at him, you are certainly under no obligation to shoot him—as long as he doesn't attack you. But you should be aware that the simple act of pointing a weapon at such a person, rather than subduing him, may very well have the opposite effect and trigger a violent attack. As a result, if you ever do point your gun at an intruder, you must be ready, willing, and able to use it.

You should not infer from this that you should never aim your gun at an intruder. Actually, a criminal may be even more inclined to attack you if you don't have a gun.

If your attacker has a gun, and if you are in a situation that legally entitles you to fire, you should shoot first rather than just pointing your gun and waiting to see what he does. Forget all that stuff you've seen TV heroes do. They always let the bad guy fire the first shot before they do anything. In real life that's almost certain to get you killed.

But use some common sense in such a situation. If a criminal has a gun pointed directly at you at short range, it probably isn't a good idea to try to grab for yours. Such a move can get you shot when the intruder has the drop on you.

Firing a warning shot at an intruder is rarely a good idea. You not only run the risk of the bullet hitting innocent children or neighbors, but the shot, rather than causing the intruder to freeze, may panic him into an attack. When your opponent has a gun, it's particularly dangerous to fire a warning shot, since he may well respond by shooting you.

Some police literature for laymen cautions against pulling a gun on a burglar, because burglary is a nonviolent crime. But if someone breaks into your home, how do you know if he is there only for burglary? If you don't get your gun, you may not know until it's too late that you're facing a violent person. Remember that you should not seek a confrontation with an intruder even if you do have a gun.

You should certainly avoid getting between an intruder and his escape route. If you do, even though you may be armed and he is not, he may suddenly attack you in a desperate bid for freedom. The criminal is not necessarily going to react rationally. If you stand to one side of his escape route, he may still make a wild break for it, but at least you won't be in his way. He won't have been forced to make his way out "over your dead body."

When the Criminal Is Outside

If you hear suspicious noises outside your home, don't go out and look around, even if you have a gun with you. The odds are on your side as long as you are safely inside and the intruder is still outside. If you think that you've heard a prowler, turn on all of your outside lights, activate your alarm system if you have one, turn off your inside lights, get your gun, retreat to the security room, and call the police. By turning off the lights inside your home and turning them on outside, you'll be able to see out, but the prowler won't be able to see in.

If you aren't sure if you've actually heard a prowler, you can still go through the same steps, but instead of turning on the alarm system and letting it blare the entire time you're waiting for the police, you may choose to activate it for just a few moments. This will let anyone out there know that he's been discovered.

If a criminal is actually in the process of breaking in when you spot him, you'll have to react a little differently. For example, if you find someone breaking in through your door with the chain lock still in place, you can try to close and lock it again. Of course, if the criminal has broken the lock or destroyed the jamb, you may not be able to relock it. In that case you should immediately get your gun, go to the security room, activate your outside lights and alarm system, and call the police.

If you see a criminal breaking in through a window and you then point a gun at him, you could be the one who gets shot. When you're standing inside a lighted room at night, an intruder outside can see you as well or better than you can see him. He may also be in a position to duck down and fire through the window, offering you a very small target; you may be standing right in the middle of the room with no cover at all.

And remember, in many states it is illegal to fire at an intruder until he has actually endangered your life. The simple act of coming through your window may not be considered an act of violence against you.

Caught Without Your Gun

What if you suddenly wake up in the middle of the night and realize that someone is in your bedroom? Making a wild grab for your gun in such a situation can be very dangerous. You'll have to decide if you can get to it and fire it before the assailant can get to you. But if the intruder is armed, any sudden move on your part may be fatal. If an intruder is actually in the same room with you, you probably won't have enough time to get your weapon unless it's under your pillow.

Your best course of action is to pretend to be asleep. Do your best to avoid a confrontation with the intruder; provoking him could elicit a violent reaction. If he's not yet harmed you, perhaps he doesn't intend to do so. If he leaves the room for a moment, you can then quietly grab your gun and roll off on the other side of the bed. Some police pamphlets recommend that you loosen the covers, so that you can move quickly if you have to, but it may be hard to do this without making enough noise for the intruder to realize that you aren't asleep.

If you are unexpectedly confronted by an intruder when it's obvious that you aren't asleep, remain as calm as you can and do exactly as he says. Make no sudden moves and say nothing to antagonize him. Don't raise your voice, and make sure that any others involved, children included, follow your lead. Let the criminal make the first move. He may not be inclined to commit any violent acts unless he's provoked. If you scream you may force him to attack you to shut you up—permanently.

Don't try to be a hero for the sake of a few material goods; they aren't worth your life or the lives of others in your home. If a criminal wants to take something, by all means let him and be thankful that he wants nothing more. The newspapers occasionally report about someone who, under such circumstances, attacks a criminal with bare hands or some impromptu weapon such as a lamp. But many of these people end up dead. When your life or the lives of your family are actually in danger, then do whatever you can to defend yourself, but this does not apply to the protection of material goods.

Without being obvious about it, while you are calmly doing as the intruder tells you, note things such as his hair color, eye color, scars, clothing, height, weight, build, and the like. But again, don't make it obvious, or he may decide that it isn't wise to leave a witness behind.

As does any dangerous situation, this one requires common sense and good judgment. If your assailant is a stumbling drunk who is unarmed and can barely stand up, you may be able to run out of the house.

What If He Gives Up?

So you've confronted an intruder and he gives up without a fight. Now what? First of all, forget the stuff you see on TV about frisking the guy or trying to tie him up. Don't get close to him. Stay at least eight feet away, and make sure that no one else gets anywhere near him or between the two of you.

The assailant you face may appear docile and seem to have meekly surrendered, but what do you think is going through his mind? He is trapped, he is scared, and he is desperately trying to think of some way to get away. If he 'hinks he can make a sudden move and get your gun, he probably will do so. Even if he looks like a scared kid, he may be fully capable of killing you, so you mustn't drop your guard for a second.

Have you called the police yet? If you have, all you have to do is wait, but if you haven't, this is your next concern. You can't just stand there forever. It's simple enough when there is a phone right there in the room, but if the phone is in the next room or down the hall, you have a problem. You certainly can't wander off and leave the criminal alone, or he may grab a makeshift weapon and attack you. If other people are with you, you can have them make the call, but if you're alone you'll have to order your prisoner to walk very slowly in front of you with his hands on top of his head or behind his neck until you can reach the phone.

The best thing to do when trying to keep someone covered for a while is to have him face away from you, so that he can't see what you're doing. Better yet, have him lie down on his stomach with his hands clasped behind his neck. This sort of position is advantageous to you, because the intruder can't directly attack you. His first movements will have to be devoted to getting himself back into position to lunge at you. As long as you remain a safe distance from him, you'll have adequate warning of any such attempt.

If the intruder begins to slowly move toward you, you order him to stop or else. But if you appear to be scared and helpless with a shaking gun hand, he may decide that you won't shoot. If you ask him to please stop in a frightened, subdued voice, you may only enforce his opinion. Even though you certainly will be frightened at such a time, you should not speak in a hesitant, timid voice. Rather, you should speak loudly, throw in plenty of four-letter words, and try to sound both angry and dangerous.

For example, you might shout, "Stop right where you are, you g---d--- bastard, or I'll blow your f---ing ass off!!!"

There is a good chance that this sort of approach will stop an assailant right in his tracks. This will clearly convey the message that you won't hesitate to fire. Of course, this method shouldn't be used if you're not in control of the situation. If you're facing an intruder without your gun, such actions could trigger an attack. Or, if you have an intruder covered and he is passively standing there with his hands up, you might not want to goad him with such a line. Moreover, in some jurisdictions, your threat of deadly force against an intruder who is not threatening you is itself a criminal act.

When keeping an intruder covered, keep your gun in the best firing position. This means keeping your handgun out in front of you in a two-handed grip or keeping a shotgun at your shoulder. This may get a little tiring after a while, so if the criminal is facing away from you or is on the floor, you probably can afford to relax slightly and lower your shotgun to your hip.

After It's Over

What if the intruder gets away? One of the most important things to do right away is to call the police and report the crime. Many people don't bother to report a crime, because they believe that the police can't do anything after it's all over. Well, maybe they can and maybe they can't, but they certainly can't do anything if you don't report it.

One danger in not reporting a crime is that it can encourage criminals to strike other people in your neighborhood or even hit you again. If the residents of a neighborhood never report incidents to the police, the word gets around and criminals will be attracted to that area.

An additional reason for reporting a crime is that victims are sometimes entitled to government compensation. This can amount to a considerable sum of money—thousands of dollars in some states—but you must report the crime to be qualified. The laws vary from state to state, so if you're ever the victim of a crime, check with your state officials to see if you are eligible.

If you can report how an assailant gets away, it may help the police. Don't chase him down the street, but if you can, try to look out a window and see where he goes. Try to give the police a good description of the assailant, what he took, and what he touched. While you're waiting for the police, make sure that you don't touch anything that the intruder touched or left behind.

If the criminal didn't get away cleanly, that is, if you shot him or just shot at him, call the police and a lawyer. Don't make any sort of statement to the police until you've talked to your lawyer. You may think that you know all of the legal implications, but perhaps you don't. You should politely but firmly tell the police that you are exercising your right to speak to an attorney. If it is in your best interests to make a statement, your attorney will advise you to do so.

Something else to consider if you have killed or wounded a criminal is that he may have family and friends who are mad at you for shooting good 'ole Uncle Butch who was always bringing them used televisions and jewelry. They may not care that he was attacking you in your own home. Under such circumstances it may not be a bad idea if you move in with friends or relatives for a while.

For the same reason you should try to keep your name, address, and picture out of the news reports. This is often rather difficult, however, since the newspeople aren't worried about 'ole Uncle Butch's friends coming to get them—that's your problem.

11.

The Law of Self-Defense: State by State

The laws that are presented and discussed in this chapter pertain only to self-defense as it applies to a person faced with a criminal intruder in his or her home. It cannot be assumed that these laws apply equally to acts of self-defense outside one's home or to acts of self-defense in the home against someone other than a criminal intruder. In fact, once one departs from the specific situation that this book addresses, the laws pertaining to self-defense are often radically different.

Clearly the laws of self-defense vary considerably from state to state, but they may vary within a given state as well. Politics, personalities, and public opinion often influence police enforcement, a district attorney's decision to prosecute, and a judge's rulings.

The author of this book is not an attorney and thus cannot make any guarantees as to the accuracy or authenticity of the legal information presented for each state. The attorney listed as the source for a given state is solely and completely responsible for the accuracy of the material that he or she has presented for that state. But, accurate as that information may be, it has already been noted that the law may be treated differently in different areas. You should check with an attorney in your area to find if there are any local rules or regulations that may apply to you. You should also find out exactly how your local laws are enforced.

Another consideration is that laws are occasionally changed, added, or deleted. It is therefore a good idea to check back with your adviser from time to time to see if there have been any changes that may affect you.

You'll be much better off if you do not attempt to push the law to the nth degree. Due to the fact that a law may be upheld differently in different areas, you could be in serious trouble if you're right on the edge. It is therefore much better to be well within the law than in that sometimes gray area.

For example, if the law in your state says that you can legally shoot someone who is jiggling your window after dark (an exaggeration), you should not automatically do so. It would be much better to give a warning, wait until the person actually begins to break in, etc. The point is, if you do not have to, you should not necessarily use deadly force the instant the law says that you may.

Another reason for avoiding the use of deadly force whenever possible is the possibility of retaliation against you by the criminal or his survivors. If you wound a criminal so that he is crippled for life, he may feel that he actually has a right to revenge himself at some point.

In your reading of the individual state entries, please be sure to read the entire entry. Do not take any phrase, sentence, or paragraph out of context. Remember, too, to note the difference between "use of force" and "use of deadly force."

Trespassers

One is generally not allowed to use deadly force against a simple trespasser. Obviously, you cannot shoot someone just for walking across your lawn, even if you have "no trespassing" signs posted. And in many states, even if a criminal has broken into your home, he is still considered to be a simple trespasser as long as he has not committed or threatened to commit any other criminal acts.

If a criminal manages to talk his way into your home, he may not even be considered a trespasser, since he is there with your permission. If you subsequently become suspicious and ask him to leave, he usually would be considered a trespasser at that point. But still, unless he endangers your life, most states do not permit you to use deadly force in an attempt to expel him.

Armed Booby Traps

Do not set one of these unless you want to go to prison. There are numerous cases of desperate, frustrated burglary victims who set booby traps on their doors or windows. Invariably, these hapless people either end up in jail themselves or find themselves fighting a damage lawsuit brought by a criminal, or both.

Proving Right to Use Deadly Force

If you shoot someone who breaks into your home, you may find yourself in court trying to prove that you were actually entitled to use such force. If the criminal is there to testify, you can be sure that he will have a good story prepared that will make it seem as if you were the aggressor and that he meant you no harm at all.

When it is obvious that the person was actually breaking in (broken locks, windows, etc.) it will be much easier to prove your case. If you shoot a criminal while he is preparing to break into your home, he can claim that he was just a Peeping Tom or a trespasser. And if you are unable to prove that you were clearly within the law when you acted, you will have a much more difficult time defending yourself against a civil suit brought by the criminal or his survivors.

Provoking the Attack

If you have provoked your attacker, however slightly, you may no longer be entitled to use deadly force to defend yourself. For example, suppose you have had an argument with someone outside your home, and you retreat inside but continue to shout insults at him. If the person then attempts to enter your home and attack you, you would be on shaky legal ground if you use deadly force against him. In fact, some states specifically say that you cannot use deadly force against an assailant in your home if you have attempted to draw him into such an attack.

Using Deadly Force in Defense of Another

In order to determine whether you are entitled to use deadly force against an assailant who is attacking a third party, you must place yourself in the third party's shoes. If you would be entitled to use deadly force were you in that person's shoes, then you usually can use such force in order to assist that person. Thus, if an intruder were to attack your spouse with a knife, you would be entitled to use deadly force (assuming your wife was not at fault or the provoker), even though you might not be in danger at all at that point.

Threatening the Use of Deadly Force

In general, you cannot threaten someone with the use of deadly force unless you are in a situation that legally entitles you to use deadly force. Suppose you spot a trespasser in your back yard who looks very suspicious. If you attempt to scare that person away by pointing a gun at him, you probably would be acting illegally, since you could not legally shoot someone for simply standing in your yard. The trespasser, however, might be entitled to use deadly force against you, since he might reasonably believe that his life was in danger.

Furthermore, in many states if a third party sees you pointing your gun at an innocent person, the third party would be legally entitled to come to that person's aid by using deadly force against you. The trespasser could also call the police and possibly have you arrested for threatening him. The point to be remembered is, don't go around pointing guns at people. You should never point a gun at anyone unless you are in a situation that legally entitles and may require you to use it.

Danger Has Ceased

When a person is in a situation that legally entitles him to use deadly force, but the danger he is confronted with ceases, he usually is not entitled to continue the use of deadly force against his attacker. Suppose a criminal breaks into your home and attacks you with a knife. If you shoot him in the leg so that he falls down and ceases his attack, he would no longer be presenting a life-threatening danger. Thus you usually would not be entitled to continue your counterattack on that person.

In the same vein, if the assailant backs away and starts to leave as soon as he sees your gun, you usually would not be entitled to use deadly force. Some courts have held, however, that if you were attacked by a person with a gun, even though that person may stop his attack and retreat, you could consider him to be an imminent danger if he is still in position to turn and fire at you. Therefore, when facing an assailant who is armed with a gun, not a knife, in some jurisdictions you may be entitled to use deadly force as he backs away from you.

Of course, you can carry this only so far. If you have a long range hunting rifle and the fleeing assailant has a short range shotgun, you would not be legally entitled to shoot him from a distance of half a mile.

Danger As It Would Appear to a Reasonable Person

You cannot legally use deadly force against an intruder unless he has attempted to "force an entry in a manner sufficient to lead a reasonably prudent person to believe that he intends to commit a felony or to inflict some serious personal injury upon the occupants of the house."[1] The danger that entitles you to defend yourself with deadly force must be of such nature that any reasonable person in your position would feel as you do.

Suppose a very large, ominous-looking man comes to your door and asks to use your telephone. You may have good reason to be wary of the man, but if you shoot him, you probably will end up in prison. The man has done nothing to indicate that he meant you any harm at all. All you had to do was tell him that he could not come in. Even though you may have truly believed that he was dangerous, a reasonable person under those circumstances should not have acted in that manner. In order for a person to constitute a real danger to you, there normally must be some threat or act or combination of the two that demonstrates that a serious danger does indeed exist. If your perception of the situation had been altered by the fact that you were intoxicated, you once again would not have been reacting as a reasonably prudent person.

Anyone faced with a situation which truly seems to threaten his life usually is entitled to use deadly force even if there was in fact no danger. Suppose a stranger—a practical joker—attempts to scare you by pointing a loaded gun at you when you open your front door. Although there is no real danger, any reasonable person in that situation would believe that there was, and therefore the use of deadly force probably would be found to be justified.

A case in California involved a couple of drunken soldiers who came to a woman's home and began loudly banging on the door demanding to be let in. The woman responded by throwing acid in their faces. As a result, she was arrested and later convicted of assault. In this case the two soldiers had shown no intention to break into the home, even though they were causing a disturbance and frightening the woman.[2]

Warning Before Using Deadly Force

In many jurisdictions you are required to give warning before using deadly force. This does not mean that you are automatically entitled to use deadly force as long as you have first given a warning. Rather the opposite is true. You must first be in a situation that entitles you to use deadly force.

When the laws of the state require you to give such a warning, you are not expected to do so if it would endanger your life. For example, if an intruder slashes at you with a knife, there obviously will be no time for a warning before you defend yourself. If you take time to give a warning under those circumstances you probably will be considerably increasing the danger to yourself.

Source of Danger

You don't necessarily have to be threatened with a gun or a knife in order to reasonably feel that your life is in danger. If your assailant is much larger than you and is wielding a club, he'll be able to cause serious bodily harm or even kill you. Likewise, a large gang of juvenile delinquents, although they may be individually smaller than you, in some circumstances may also cause you to reasonably believe that your life is in danger.

Killing in Defense of Property

Most states do not allow the use of deadly force to protect property. Suppose you discover an intruder who is stealing your TV set. In most states you would not be entitled to use deadly force to stop him. But if the criminal pulls a knife and attacks you, you would be entitled to use such force.

The point to be noted here, though, is that you would still not be entitled to use deadly force to protect your property. You would be entitled to use such force only in order to protect your life.

Excessive Force

There are many situations that allow you to use force, but not excessive force. Thus, even though your state laws may not allow the use of deadly force to protect property, you are usually permitted to use a certain amount of force to keep a criminal from walking away with your belongings.

The general rule is to use like force with like force. For example, if a small unarmed burglar attempts to resist you by pushing you down, you generally are not allowed to retaliate by shooting him.

Right to Use Deadly Force in Defense of Habitat

In most states the old phrase "a man's home is his castle" simply does not apply when it comes to the right to use deadly force. If you catch a criminal breaking into your home, you usually are not entitled to shoot him to prevent him from breaking and entering. You are entitled to use force to stop someone from unlawfully entering your home, but in most states that force must not be excessive. Someone who shoots an unarmed kid is going to have a hard time proving that his life was in danger when he did so. On the other hand, an eighty-year-old grandmother who shoots a 250-pound escaped convict will have a much better case.

If a criminal points a gun at you while he's breaking into your home, you'd be justified in defending yourself with deadly force. But in most states you'd not be entitled to use that force because the criminal was breaking in; rather it would be based on the fact that your life was actually in danger.

Any rights you may have to defend yourself against an unwanted intruder do not apply when that person has a legal right to be in your home. A policeman with a search warrant is a good example.

Imminent and Immediate Danger

Before you can use deadly force, the danger that you face must be imminent and immediate. Suppose an intruder is leaving your home peacefully, so you have no legal right to shoot him. But then he pauses and declares that he will return in an hour and kill you. Although you know that he is absolutely serious, you cannot legally use deadly force against him at that point. In this case the danger to you, though it may be real, is not imminent and immediate.

The reasoning behind these two words is that a person should call the authorities if the danger is not imminent and immediate, rather than take the law into his own hands. A person is not required to wait so long for an attack to occur, however, that he endangers his own life. If an intruder begins to pull a gun out of his pocket, you don't have to wait until he points it at you or actually fires a shot before you can reasonably consider the danger to be imminent and immediate.

Likewise, if an assailant has a knife, you'd not be expected to wait until he actually got within striking distance, as long as other facts led you to anticipate an attack. But if the intruder sits down on your front porch and begins to sharpen his knife in preparation for an attack, he would not be presenting an imminent and immediate danger.

Alabama Law of Self-Defense

Source: Gerry E. Adams, Attorney at Law
         1275 Centerpoint Road
         Birmingham, AL 35215
         (205) 836-4586

Mr. Adams currently practices law in Birmingham, where he is a member of the law firm of Massey, Adams, Veitch & Crenshaw P. C. The firm has a general practice of law with emphasis in the area of criminal law.

In the state of Alabama a person has the legal right to use deadly physical force to prevent certain criminal actions. First, we should focus our attention on the current law as it is set forth in the Alabama Criminal Code Title 13A. The sections relevant to our discussion will be found in Title 13A-3-20 through 13A-3-26.

All laymen should of course realize that this brief synopsis cannot be applied rigidly to all fact situations because there nearly always is an exception to any given rule. To explain thoroughly would require a complete legal education.

Generally, a person is justified in using deadly physical force in a variety of situations. The key word in our discussion of the law is the word "reasonable." One can use deadly physical force if one reasonably believes that the other person is about to use unlawful deadly physical force (i.e., murder); or the other person is about to use physical force to commit a kidnapping, burglary, rape, robbery, sodomy, or assault in the first or second degree; or the other person is about to use physical force against an occupant of a dwelling while attempting or committing a burglary of such dwelling. So if we interpret the code literally, as it is stated, then a person has the right to use deadly physical force even if someone has not actually broken into the dwelling. But again the key word is whether a "reasonable" man would believe someone was "about" to commit a burglary.

One cannot justify the use of deadly physical force if he can retreat or avoid the use of deadly physical force with complete safety. However, under the present Alabama Criminal Code, there is no duty to retreat if you are in your place of business or in your dwelling and were not the original aggressor. If deadly physical force is used, Alabama law is clear that the one who claims self-defense must be completely free of fault in provoking the altercation. Alabama law does not require the imminent danger of death or grave bodily harm to actually exist to establish the grounds of justifiable homicide. It is sufficient if you actually believe, and have reasonable ground to believe, that you are in imminent danger. You can never use deadly physical force for the prevention of trespass upon property alone. One can use deadly force in defense of the dwelling, but not of the property by itself.

Alabama has no requirement that you must warn someone before using deadly physical force. You could threaten to use such force only when you would be justified in using it.

The law is silent as to what right someone has to the use of deadly physical force if the assailant were leaving after committing the act of rape or burglary. If the assailant was walking out the door or was already walking away in the yard then there would be no threat of imminent grave bodily harm or death. If the assailant had committed a rape and was still present in close proximity, then the danger of imminent grave bodily harm or death is still present, and the use of deadly physical force would then be justifiable.

Anytime deadly force is employed, such as the use of a firearm, extreme care should be exercised. If you should use such deadly force and in the process should kill or wound an innocent third party bystander, the fact that you were justified in using this deadly force on your assailant has no bearing as to the third party. Not only would you be liable for criminal prosecution as to the third party, but, in addition, civil remedies for money damages could be instigated in conjunction with the criminal charges. An example of this situation would be where someone justifiably used deadly physical force such as a firearm, but fired a hail of bullets in a reckless or negligent manner.

The burglary of your dwelling entitles you to use deadly physical force against the criminal intruder while he is inside your home. You do not have to be protecting any one particular person, but just protecting a victim in the course of a burglary.

The Alabama law defines Deadly Physical Force as follows: "Force which, under the circumstances in which it is used, is readily capable of causing death or serious physical injury." It goes on to define serious physical injury as that which would cause disfigurement or protracted loss or impairment of any bodily organ. So under our law if you were justified in using deadly physical force and shot to wound your assailant and it should result in permanently maiming your assailant, then you would probably be justified in your actions.

Alaska Law of Self-Defense

Source: Gary W. Brown
         Attorney at Law
         4220 B St., Suite 200
         P.O. Box 10-4299
         Anchorage, AK 99510
         (907) 561-2232

Mr. Bowen received his B.S. degree from the U.S. Military Academy at West Point and attended the Southwestern University School of Law at Los Angeles, graduating in 1978. After graduating he served as an attorney with the Judge Advocate General's Corps, U.S. Army. He now practices law in Anchorage with the the firm of Lamb and Bowen.

The Alaska State Legislature recently enacted a revised criminal code which became effective January 1, 1980. Because the revised code is so new, very few cases have reached the Alaska Supreme Court interpreting its provisions. Therefore in interpreting the new code previous State Court decisions may be of doubtful validity.

Before any intelligent analysis of the use of deadly force in Alaska can be made, the terms must be defined. AS 11.81.900(b) (12) states: "Deadly force means force which the person uses with the intent of causing, or uses under circumstances which he knows create a substantial risk of causing, death or serious physical injury; deadly force includes intentionally discharging a firearm in the direction of another person or in the direction in which another person is believed to be." Nondeadly force is described as any force other than deadly force.

Pursuant to AS 11.81.355(a) (2), you may not use deadly force to stop someone from simply breaking into your home. Breaking into an occupied dwelling may be criminal, but it is not such a criminal activity as would warrant the use of deadly force. However, the breaking and entering of the dwelling place is one element of the crime of burglary in the first degree (AS 11.46.300). If a person enters a dwelling or unlawfully remains in a dwelling with the intent to commit a crime therein he commits the crime of burglary. It is not always possible to tell whether the individual doing the breaking in is intent upon committing a crime therein.

For example, every year several airplanes crash within the state; trappers become lost and disoriented; hikers and campers are unexpectedly caught in foul weather conditions. In those cases a person might come upon a remote dwelling and the breaking in may simply be for the purpose of self-preservation, since the winter temperatures may plunge to sixty below zero. If someone were breaking into a dwelling simply for the purpose of avoiding exposure, the owner would not be justified in using deadly force to expel the entrant.

It appears from the Statute that some other act would be necessary to justify the use of deadly force, although that additional act need not necessarily be the target offense. Moreover, AS 11.81.350(c)(2) states: "A person in possession or control of any premises, or an express or implied agent of that person, may use deadly force upon another person when and to the extent he reasonably thinks is necessary to terminate what he reasonably believes to be a burglary in any degree occurring in the occupied dwelling or building."

Ultimately, if an owner/occupier of a dwelling is to use deadly force against one breaking into the dwelling, he must reasonably believe that that breaking in is for the purpose of committing a crime within the dwelling and not for some innocent or otherwise lawful purpose. A technical trespass on the real property of another is not such conduct as to justify deadly force. AS 11.81.350(b) further provides that a person may use deadly force upon another when and to the extent he reasonably believes it necessary to terminate what he reasonably believes to be the commission or attempted commission of arson upon a dwelling or occupied building.

While the commentary from the *1978 Senate Journal* indicates that in some circumstances a warning is required before using deadly force, there is nothing in the new statute which requires one to give a warning prior to using deadly force in his home. Also, AS 11.81.335(b)(1) specifically states that a person need not retreat inside his home before using deadly force, provided the owner is not the initial aggressor and the use of deadly force is otherwise justified.

The new code allows a person to come to the aid of any third person when the rescuer reasonably believes that the third person would be justified in using force to defend himself. The intervener may use that degree of force which he reasonably believes the third person would be justified in using in his own defense.

Further commentary from the *1978 Senate Journal* suggests that where deadly force is not appropriate, a threat of deadly force may be. However, care should be used with threatening deadly force, especially when such threat is accompanied by a display of a dangerous weapon. AS 11.41.210(a)(2) provides that a person commits the crime of assault in the second degree if he intentionally places another person in fear of imminent serious physical injury by means of a dangerous instrument. Consequently, a threat to use deadly force in one's own home may be justified, when the threat of the use of deadly force outside one's home, absent extraordinary circumstances, may constitute the commission of a Class B felony!

One should be very careful about using deadly force in an attempt to stop a criminal who is attempting to escape from a dwelling after committing a crime. It appears that the use of deadly force could be used to make an arrest or terminate an escape for rape, assault and similar crimes against a person. But the use of deadly force would not be justified to arrest or stop the escape of a burglar unless the target crime within the dwelling house was an act involving force against an occupant.

The use of a gun at home for self-defense is not unlawful in the state of Alaska. One who keeps a gun for self-defense, however, must realize that the scope of the right to use deadly force is limited in Alaska by the foregoing statutes. The reasonableness of a homeowner's actions may ultimately be judged by a jury of his peers. While this offers little guidance at a time when split second decisions must be made, the homeowner who retains a weapon for self-defense should use the weapon only with a great degree of care and only if he is skilled in its use. If a homeowner exceeds the force reasonably necessary to prevent criminal conduct he may be liable for civil damage even if the State decides not to prosecute. Consequently, if he were to wound or kill an innocent bystander or even a trespasser, he could be liable for substantial damages. A homeowner would likely have sufficient assets to satisfy any judgment for damages in a civil suit.

The discharge of a firearm causing injury on another is likely to be considered an intentional act which would prevent and preclude discharge of the judgment debt in a bankruptcy proceeding! It would therefore behoove any homeowner who maintains a weapon for self-defense to be thoroughly familiar with the characteristics of his weapon, skilled in its use, and use it only as a last resort to prevent undue intrusion upon himself, his family, or third persons whom he reasonably believes he has the right, duty, and obligation to protect.

Arizona Law of Self-Defense

Source: Martin P. Rosenzweig
                 Attorney at Law
                 P.O. Box 4174
                 Scottsdale, AZ 85261

Mr. Rosenzweig currently practices law in Scottsdale, Arizona, where he is a partner in the law firm of Bruno & Rosenzweig. The firm has a general practice of law with emphasis in the areas of criminal law, personal injury, and real estate.

In the state of Arizona, the general rule is that the use of deadly physical force to prevent certain criminal actions is justified under special circumstances. The precise sections relevant to this area of the law are found in the Arizona Revised Statutes, Sections 13-404 through 13-411.

The language in the Arizona Statutes implicitly sets out a distinction between the use of physical force and deadly force by requiring a "reasonable" belief that deadly force be "immediately necessary" to prevent an arson, burglary, kidnapping, manslaughter, child molestation, armed robbery, aggravated assault, or murder. No warning before using such force would be necessary. With respect to a homeowner defending himself against an intruder, the mere unlawful entry into his own home would not seemingly justify the use of deadly force, but rather physical force only. The distinction hinges in part on the stage to which the crime has progressed and whether or not in fact someone's life is being threatened.

Once, however, a justification to use deadly force is established, as where the "intent" to perform the crime is manifested coupled with the exhibition of a gun which indicates the "immediate necessity" of deadly force, there is no duty to retreat before acting. In other words, as the elements of the crime are established to a point where a reasonable or objective person would feel his life was endangered during the commission of a crime, deadly force could be used.

If a crime does in fact progress to this stage, there is no duty on behalf of an individual to retreat before using deadly force. This, however, is not meant to be carte blanche authority for the use of such force when seemingly justified. Deadly physical force as defined in the Arizona Statutes means "force which is used with the purpose of causing death or serious physical injury or in the manner of its use or intended use is capable of creating a substantial risk of causing death or serious physical injury." If the individual using this force did so in a reckless or negligent manner so that an innocent bystander or third party was injured or killed, liability both criminally and civilly could ensue. Furthermore, if the altercation was provoked by or the situation wrongly ascertained by that same individual, criminal prosecution or civil litigation could likewise be instituted.

The use of deadly force to prevent an escape is permitted in Arizona if the intruder is using or has the apparent capacity to use deadly force, is an escaping or fleeing felon, or is a felon who is resisting arrest with physical force. Again, the "reasonableness" standard is important here, for as long as there is a "reasonable belief" that one of these factors is present, as where the pointed gun is visible (apparent capacity to use deadly force) or the unlawful exit of a house is seen (reasonable belief that an intruder has committed a felony). The irony here is that there seems to be greater latitude to use deadly force in order to stop an escape than to prevent the crime itself.

The rationale in such instances is the defense of the public at large or third persons. A person is justified in using deadly physical force against another to protect a third person if it is reasonable to believe that such force is immediately necessary to protect that third person against deadly force. Thus, even, if an arson, burglary, kidnap, child molestation, aggravated assault, armed robbery, manslaughter or murder of a homeowner or upon his premises is not likely, the use of deadly force can be justified.

As far as protecting personal property inside one's home is concerned, Arizona law allows only nondeadly force that is reasonably necessary to be used. However, it must be noted that any situation giving rise to a defense of property in one's residence could easily escalate into self-defense, defense of a third person, or the prevention of an escape. The use of deadly force would then, as discussed previously, be justified and, therefore, permitted.

Finally, in Arizona the law expressly permits one to threaten the use of deadly force in order to protect a third person or himself against the use or attempted use of merely unlawful physical force (it need not be or appear to be deadly physical force), to protect one's personal property inside a residence, to prevent a crime, or to prevent an escape. In other words, there are very few restrictions or limitations upon an individual for a threat of deadly force, as long as it remains just that—a threat.

Arkansas Law of Self-Defense

Source: Don Bassett
         Attorney at Law
         9110 Chicot Road
         Little Rock, AR 72209
         (501) 562-6495

Mr. Bassett is currently engaged in the general practice of law in Little Rock,
Arkansas, as a sole practitioner. He is a member of the American and Arkansas
Bar Associations and is licensed in Federal as well as State Courts.

In the state of Arkansas, a person's right to use deadly physical force is set
forth in Arkansas Statutes Annotated Section 41-501 et. seq; and gives a person
the right to legally use deadly physical force in certain instances.

The summary of the law of the state of Arkansas cannot, and is not intended
to cover all possible fact situations, but merely expresses the general law in the
state.

Generally a person is justified in using deadly physical force in defense of a
person if he *reasonably* believes that the other person is "committing or about to
commit a felony" involving force or violence or if he reasonably believes the
other is using or is about to use unlawful deadly force. What this means in
layman's terms is if a person reasonably believes that another is or is about to
commit some act of violence to the person of another, e.g. murder, rape, arson,
burglary, etc., he is justified in using deadly physical force to protect himself or
another person.

Further, a statute passed in 1981 guarantees the right of an individual to
protect himself, the lives of others in his home, and property in his home against
"harm, injury, or loss by persons unlawfully entering or attempting to enter or
intrude" in his home and states that such right is a fundamental right to be
promoted as public policy. The statute further creates a legal presumption that
the force used to accomplish the protection of the aforesaid was exercised in a
lawful and necessary manner and places the burden of producing clear and
convincing evidence on those pressing for a contrary finding. In the statute, the
courts of this state are ordered to comply strictly with the legislative mandates
set forth therein.

Yet another 1981 statute relieves anyone using deadly physical force in the
protection of himself, the lives of others in his home, and property in his home
from civil liability. That is to say the survivors of a person killed while intruding
or attempting to intrude unlawfully into a home cannot subsequently sue the
residents for wrongful death, etc.

Under current law in Arkansas, a person is not required to retreat prior to
using deadly physical force if in his dwelling and if he was not the aggressor in

the violence. In the event the original aggressor is retreating or escaping one cannot use deadly force to prevent his escape unless such force is used by, or at the direction of, a law enforcement officer. The key in determining whether the use of deadly force against an intruder who is withdrawing is whether the person using such force was in reasonable belief that he was in danger which was immediate urging and pressing.

Although not specifically required under current Arkansas law, the writer would strongly recommend the use of a warning (if there is time) prior to the use of deadly force. This is so because the persistence of the intruder after the warning is given would reinforce the reasonableness of the conclusion that the intruder was about to use violence or physical force. Again, it is not required and failure to give warning will not override the presumption, provided for by the statute, that the use of force was exercised in a lawful manner.

Mere threats made by a person outside the home, e.g., standing in the yard, are not justification for the use of deadly physical force. There must be the reasonable belief that the other person is about to commit some felonious violent act.

Anyone who uses a firearm, even when justified under Arkansas law, should do so with extreme care since there could be a criminal and civil liability in the event that a third party such as a visitor in the home should be injured or killed. Arkansas law only protects an individual from criminal and civil liability as to an intruder, not third parties.

A common misconception which many Arkansas citizens have is "If you shoot someone breaking into your house, you had better drag them in." This is simply not true and you are entitled to protect your residence and the inhabitants therein so long as there is the *reasonable* belief as set out above.

lifornia Law of Self-Defense

Williams
.orney at Law
300 17th St., Suite F
Bakersfield, CA 93301

In the state of California, the killing of another person in self-defense is justifiable and not unlawful:

1. When the person who does the killing has reasonable ground to believe and does believe that there is imminent danger that the other person will kill him or cause him great bodily injury, and

2. A reasonable person under the same circumstances would believe that it was necessary to kill the other person to prevent death or great bodily injury to himself.

In order to justify killing another person in self-defense, actual danger or great bodily injury is not necessary. On the other hand, a bare fear of death or great bodily harm is not sufficient.

In order to justify a killing it must be established:

1. The circumstances must be sufficient to excite the fears of a reasonable person that there was imminent danger of death or great bodily injury, and

2. The party killing must have acted under the influence of such fears alone and under the belief that such killing was necessary to save himself from death or great bodily injury (CALJIC 5.12).

An assault with the fists does not justify the person being assaulted in using a deadly weapon in self-defense unless that person believes and a reasonable person in the same or similar circumstances would believe that the assault is likely to inflict great bodily injury upon him (CALJIC 5.31).

Furthermore, the use of deadly force is justifiable when it is used by a person who is resisting an attempt to commit a forcible and atrocious crime. CALJIC 5.16 defines a forcible and atrocious crime as any felony, the character and manner of the commission of which threatens, or is reasonably believed by the defendant to threaten, life or great bodily injury so as to cause in him a reasonable fear of death or great bodily injury. Murder, mayhem, rape, and robbery are forcible and atrocious crimes.

A person may defend his home or habitation against anyone who manifestly intends or endeavors in a violent or riotous manner, to enter that home or habitation and who appears to intend violence to any person in that home. The amount of force which the person may use in resisting such trespass is limited by what would appear to a reasonable person, in the same or similar circumstances, necessary to resist the violent or unlawful entry. He is not bound to retreat even though a retreat might safely be made. He may resist force with force, increasing it in proportion to the intruder's persistence and violence if the circumstances which are apparent to the homeowner are such as would excite similar fears and a similar belief in a reasonable person (CALJIC 5.42).

The lawful occupant of real property has the right to request a trespasser to leave the premises. If the trespasser does not do so within a reasonable time, such occupant may use force to eject the trespasser.

The amount of force which may be used to eject the trespasser is limited by what would appear to a reasonable person, under the existing circumstances, to be necessary (CALJIC 5.40).

Actual danger is not necessary to justify self-defense. If one is confronted by the appearance of danger which arouses in his mind, as a reasonable person, an honest conviction and fear that he is about to suffer bodily injury, and if a reasonable man in a like situation, seeing and knowing the same facts, would be justified in believing himself in like danger, and if the person so confronted acts in self-defense upon such appearances and from such fear and honest convictions, his right of self-defense is the same whether such danger is real or merely apparent (CALJIC 5.51).

An example would be the case of a homeowner who shoots an intruder who points an authentic-looking toy gun at him. Although there may have been no actual danger, it would be reasonable under such circumstances to believe that there was an actual danger.

It has been stated that a belief that leads one to the use of deadly force must be reasonable. If a person were to resort to the use of deadly force based on an unreasonable belief, but no malice aforethought was involved, that person would not be guilty of murder, but he could be charged with manslaughter.

A person who is threatened with an attack that justifies the exercise of the right of self-defense, need not retreat. In the exercise of his right of self-defense he may stand his ground and defend himself by the use of all force and means which would appear to be necessary to a reasonable person in a similar situation and with similar knowledge; and he may pursue his assailant until he has secured himself from danger if that course likewise appears reasonably necessary. This law applies even though the assailed person might more easily have gained safety by flight or by withdrawing from the scene (CALJIC 5.50).

A person may also use deadly force to defend another person. However, the person to be defended must be in a situation that would legally entitle him or her to use deadly force.

The right of self-defense exists only as long as the real or apparent threatened danger continues to exist. When such danger ceases to appear to exist, the right to use force in self-defense ends (CALJIC 5.52).

Thus, if an intruder were to break into a woman's home and rape her, the woman would not have the right to shoot the rapist as he walked out of her home, since there would probably be no more danger at that point.

The right of self-defense ceases to exist when there is no longer any apparent danger of further violence on the part of an assailant. Thus where a person is attacked under circumstances which justify his exercise of the right of self-defense, and thereafter he uses such force upon his attacker as to render the attacker incapable of inflicting further injuries, the law of self-defense then ceases to work in favor of the person attacked (CALJIC 5.53).

This summation of the law of self-defense has been presented primarily from the standpoint of one who is attacked by criminal in his or her home. A claim of self-defense may not be justified in the case of a person who was the original aggressor in an incident, unless that person in good faith endeavored to decline further combat and fairly and clearly informed his adversary of his desire for peace and that he has abandoned the contest. Furthermore, a person will not be allowed a claim of self-defense when he has entered into a quarrel with another party with the intent of creating a real or apparent necessity of exercising self-defense.

Colorado Law of Self-Defense

Source: Amy S. Isaminger
         Attorney at Law
         610 Preston State Bank Building
         8111 Preston Road
         Dallas, TX 75225
         (214) 369-7035

Ms. Isaminger currently practices law in Dallas, Texas, and Pueblo, Colorado. She is a sole practitioner with a general practice of law in Texas and associates with the firm of J. E. Losavio, Jr., in Colorado.

Colorado has several statutes dealing with self-defense, choice of evils, and the use of physical force. These defenses are all limited in that they may only be used in very specific situations. To inform the reader properly about the state of the law of self-defense in Colorado one must look first to the statutes which define when a person may use force to defend himself, others, or property. Then one must look at the case-by-case interpretation of those laws by the courts.

The relevant Colorado laws governing self-defense are found at Colorado Revised Statutes Section 18-1-701 through 18-1-710.

Physical Force in Defense of a Person

By statute, a person may use physical force upon another person to defend himself or a third person from what he reasonably believes to be the use or imminent use of unlawful physical force by that other person. One may use the degree of force he believes necessary to defend himself.

One may use deadly force only if nothing short of it will do *and* one of the following exists:

(1) If one truly believes he or a third person is in imminent danger of being killed or receiving great bodily harm; or,

(2) If the other person is using or appears to be using physical force against the occupant of a house or business establishment while committing a burglary; or,

(3) If the other person is committing or appears to be committing kidnapping, robbery, sexual assault, or assault.

Now, self-defense is a natural right and is based on the natural law of self-preservation. It is not limited in Colorado to where an assailant intends to commit a felony. It may also be used in defense of another, such as a family member or friend. A person may jump in and assist another, as long as he is not the initial aggressor. And, the right to assist applies with peculiar force where a relationship exists, such as father, son, brother, spouse.

One can act on appearances in defending himself. When a person believes he is in danger of being killed or of receiving great bodily injury, he may act on such appearances and defend himself, even to the point of killing another, even though it may turn out the appearances were false or he may have been mistaken about the real danger. The standard is that a "reasonable and prudent person" would have done the same..

Another requirement is that the threat be imminent and immediate. It must be a present danger, such that it puts a person in sudden fear for his life. It cannot be a threat made one day, a long-standing grudge wherein you decide to seek a person out and harm him before he harms you.

One cannot use physical force against another if (1) he provokes the use of force by another, (2) he is the aggressor, unless it is justified to protect another person, or (3) the force is a product of combat by agreement not authorized by law.

There is no requirement in Colorado that a person "retreat to the wall." Also, there is no requirement that a person escape the peril if possible. A person also does not have to shout out a warning or forewarn the other person that he is going to use force to protect himself.

Physical Force in Defense of Premises

One may use reasonable force to prevent a trespass on any house, building, realty or other premises a person controls or possesses. Deadly force may only be used as stated above in defense of a person or oneself, or, if it is necessary, to prevent an attempt by a trespassor to commit first degree arson. One cannot use deadly physical force in defense of property alone.

There is no law in Colorado governing the use of physical force by a private citizen in making an arrest or preventing an escape. If a criminal is leaving a home after committing a crime, the threat of injury or death is over; therefore, deadly force would not be necessary.

The use of deadly force should always be a last resort. If you use deadly force against another and accidentally injure an innocent party, you may suffer criminal and civil penalties. Also, many persons mistakenly harm themselves or family members when in the course of attempting to protect themselves from either real or false dangers. Suffice it to say, one should proceed with great caution whenever the physical well being of any person is at stake.

Connecticut Law of Self-Defense

Source: John R. Gulash, Jr.
         Attorney at Law
         1 Lafayette Circle
         P.O. Box 9118
         Bridgeport, CT 06601

The following information is taken from Title 53a of the Connecticut penal code:

"Sec. 53a-19. Use of physical force in defense of person. (a) Except as provided in subsections (b) and (c) a person is justified in using reasonable physical force upon another person to defend himself or a third person from what he reasonably believes to be the use or imminent use of physical force, and he may use such degree of force which he reasonably believes to be necessary for such purpose; except that deadly physical force may not be used unless the actor reasonably believes that such other person is (1) using or about to use deadly physical force, or (2) inflicting or about to inflict great bodily harm.

"(b) Notwithstanding the provisions of subsection (a), a person is not justified in using deadly physical force upon another person if he knows that he can avoid the necessity of using such force with complete safety (1) by retreating, except that the actor shall not be required to retreat if he is in his dwelling . . . or place of work and was not the original aggressor . . . , or (2) by surrendering possession of property to a person asserting a claim of right thereto, or (3) by complying with a demand that he abstain from performing an act which he is not obliged to perform.

"(c) Notwithstanding the provisions of subsection (a), a person is not justified in using physical force when (1) with intent to cause physical injury or death to another person, he provokes the use of physical force by such other person, or (2) he is the initial aggressor, except that his use of physical force upon another person under such circumstances is justifiable if he withdraws from the encounter and effectively communicates to such other person his intent to do so, but such other person notwithstanding continues or threatens the use of physical force, or (3) the physical force involved was the product of a combat by agreement not specifically authorized by law.

"Sec. 53a-20. Use of physical force in defense of premises. A person in possession or control of premises, or a person who is licensed or privileged to be in or upon such premises, is justified in using reasonable physical force upon another person when and to the extent that he reasonably believes it is necessary to prevent or terminate the commission or attempted commission of a criminal trespass by such other person in or upon such premises; but he may use deadly physical force under such circumstances only (1) in defense of a person as prescribed in section 53a-19, or (2) when he reasonably believes it is necessary to prevent an attempt by the trespasser to commit arson or any crime of violence,

or (3) to the extent that he reasonably believes it necessary to prevent or terminate an unlawful entry by force into his dwelling or place of work, and for the sole purpose of such prevention or termination.

"*Sec. 53a-21. Use of physical force in defense of property; larceny; criminal mischief.* A person is justified in using reasonable physical force upon another person when and to the extent that he reasonably believes it necessary to prevent an attempt by such other person to commit larceny or criminal mischief involving property, or when and to the extent he reasonably believes it necessary to regain property which he reasonably believes to have been acquired by larceny within a reasonable time prior to the use of such force; but he may use deadly physical force under such circumstances only in defense of person as prescribed in section 53a-19.

"*Sec. 53a-22. Use of physical force in making arrest or preventing escape.* (a) For purposes of this section, a reasonable belief that a person has committed an offense means a reasonable belief in facts or circumstances which if true would in law constitute an offense. If the believed facts or circumstances would not in law constitute an offense, an erroneous though not unreasonable belief that the law is otherwise does not render justifiable the use of physical force to make an arrest or to prevent an escape from custody.

"(f) A private person acting on his own account is justified in using reasonable physical force upon another person when and to the extent that he reasonably believes it is necessary to effect an arrest or to prevent the escape from custody of an arrested person whom he reasonably believes to have committed an offense and who in fact has committed such offense; but he is not justified in using deadly physical force in such circumstances, except in defense of person as prescribed in section 53a-19."

It is very important that the reader note the distinction that Connecticut law makes between the use of force and the use of deadly force. If a statute allows the use of force under certain circumstances, one should not assume that deadly force is also allowed unless deadly force is specifically mentioned.

While the statutes allow a person to use deadly force "to the extent that he reasonably believes it necessary to prevent or terminate an unlawful entry by force into his dwelling . . ." one should not read too much into this. The law does not give a resident carte blanche authority to shoot any intruder at any time. For example, suppose you discover an intruder in the act of stealing your TV set. If the criminal starts to walk off with your property, even though he may still be inside your home, you would not be entitled to use deadly force in an attempt to stop him. Deadly force would not be required to prevent or terminate his unlawful entry, since he is terminating the entry himself by leaving.

Although the law allows you to use force to prevent a criminal from stealing your property, it does not allow you to use deadly force except "in defense of person as prescribed in section 53a-19." And even though you might be entitled to use force in an attempt to arrest the criminal, you once again would not be entitled to use deadly force except "in defense of person as prescribed in section 53a-19."

Delaware Law of Self-Defense

Source: Harry M. Fisher, III
         Attorney at Law
         225 S. State St.
         Dover, DE 19901
         (302) 734-7401

Mr. Fisher is a member of both the Delaware and Florida Bars and is currently a member of the law firm of Hudson, Jones & Jaywork. The firm engages in the general practice of law in Dover and Rehoboth Beach, Delaware. Mr. Fisher's concentration is in the field of criminal law.

The use of deadly force to protect one's person and property is justified in the State of Delaware in certain limited circumstances. The statutory law concerning the use of deadly force is located in 11 Delaware Code Sections 461 through 470.

Deadly force is defined in the Delaware Code as "force which the defendant uses with the purpose of causing or which he knows to create a substantial risk of causing death or serious physical injury." Deadly force can be used against another person if one believes that such force is necessary to protect himself against death, serious physical injury, kidnapping or sexual intercourse compelled by force or threat. The use of deadly force for one's self-protection is not justifiable if the person using the force is the initial aggressor in the encounter and provoked the use of force against himself. In addition one is not justified in using deadly force if he can avoid its use by retreating safely or by surrendering possession of an item to a person asserting a claim of right thereto. However, one is not required to retreat in or from his dwelling or his place of work, unless he was the initial aggressor.

Deadly force can also be used for the protection of one's property in Delaware in certain situations. If an intruder attempts to dispossess one of his dwelling without a claim of right to do so, deadly force is justified. In addition when an intruder is attempting to commit arson, burglary, robbery or felonious theft or destruction of one's property or another's property for whose protection he acts, deadly force can be employed if the person attempting to commit the acts uses or threatens to use deadly force against you or against someone in your presence. If you believe the use of force other than deadly force against the intruder would expose you or another person in your presence to the reasonable likelihood of serious physical injury, then deadly force would be justified.

The protection of personal property alone is not sufficient to justify the use of deadly force. It must be accompanied by the threat or use of deadly force by the intruder or your belief that the use of any other force would expose you or another in your presence to serious physical injury.

Before deadly force can be employed in the protection of your property, a warning must be given to the intruder to desist from his actions unless you believe such a warning would be useless or dangerous to you or someone else in your presence. In such a case, no warning would be required.

The Delaware Code does not specifically cover the situation where a serious crime has been committed against you or in your dwelling and the criminal is escaping or attempting to escape. Therefore, the general rules concerning the use of deadly force would have to be applied to the particular fact situation.

Specifically excluded from the definition of deadly force in the Code is the threat of deadly force. Thus, deadly force may be threatened as long as the purpose is limited to creating the apprehension that deadly force will be used if necessary.

It is important to remember in Delaware a subjective standard is used to determine whether or not the use of deadly force is necessary. In other words, the actual belief of the person using the force, and not what a reasonable man would have done, governs. While the reasonable-man test is a factor to be considered, it is not necessarily the controlling factor. However, it should be noted that where one was reckless or negligent in forming such belief, the defense of justification will not be available in a prosecution requiring only a reckless or negligent state of mind. In addition, where one, although justified in using deadly force, uses it recklessly or negligently and in doing so injures or creates a risk of injury to innocent persons, he may not use the defense of justification or self-defense in any prosecution involving negligence or reckless-ness towards those innocent persons.

Although this brief synopsis has been written within the context of using self-defense or protection of property as a legal defense to a criminal prosecu-tion, it is worth noting that where a person has used any force for the protection of property and has not been convicted of any crime or offense connected with that use of force, the Delaware Code provides that such person shall not be liable for damages or otherwise civilly liable to the one against whom such force was used.

District of Columbia Law of Self-Defense

Source: Samual H. Press and Thomas M. Fortuin
         Becker & Chameides
         1819 H Street, N.W.
         Washington, DC 20006
         (202) 223-6450

Messrs. Fortuin and Press specialize in litigation. Prior to entering private practice, Mr. Fortuin was an Assistant U.S. Attorney in Manhattan and counsel with Leon Jaworski in the "Koreagate" investigation; Mr. Press served as law clerk to a U.S. District Judge. Both are residents of the District of Columbia.

On the first day of March 1980, Dieter Rechenberg, a jeweler in the Adams Morgan section of the District, killed a 17-year-old black youth who was breaking into his shop with five other youths. Rechenberg had been living in the back of the shop with his wife and young son and had been robbed there twice before. Around 2:00 A.M. on a snowy night, his wife heard noises of the break-in at the front door, and the jeweler awakened to her screams. He grabbed his shotgun and fired two buckshot cartridges at the intruders, hitting one of them in the chest. The shotgun had been properly registered with the District police. Said the jeweler: "I'm only sorry I didn't kill all of them." The slaying was deemed a justifiable homicide.

As the case of Dieter Rechenberg illustrates, you may shoot someone, stab him, or hit him over the head with a baseball bat, or use some other kind of deadly force, if he comes into your home and you believe that he intends to commit a felony or to do serious harm to you or others inside. You need not retreat from the intruder to elsewhere in the home or outside it, and you don't have to warn the intruder before using deadly force. Defense of your home under these conditions is a complete defense to both criminal prosecution and civil lawsuits for injury to the intruder, or to bystanders injured inadvertently.

To get away with it, your belief about the intruder's intentions must be reasonable under the circumstances. Among the many circumstances that can support a reasonable belief about intruders' violent or criminal intentions, are a break-in or forcible entry; night time; people sleeping or otherwise vulnerable inside the home; more than one intruder; an apparently armed intruder; threats, or menacing actions or statements by the intruder; and recent break-ins in the neighborhood. It makes no difference that your belief about the intruder's intentions turns out to be mistaken; the law requires only that your belief was actual and reasonable as you saw the situation at the time.

But what happens if you misjudge the circumstances, and you were not justified in using deadly force against an intruder? Criminal prosecution for murder, manslaughter, and assault are theoretically possible. The prosecution would have the difficult task, however, to prove beyond a reasonable doubt that the use of force was *not* justified. A civil lawsuit for battery or wrongful death of the intruder is also possible, but lawsuits like this are virtually unknown. A civil lawsuit could also be brought by a bystander who was hurt by the improper use of deadly force.

Although there are no court decisions on the subject in the District of Columbia, one also has the right under the common law to make a citizen's arrest, by using deadly force, of an escaping intruder who has committed a felony involving great bodily harm. Great caution must be exercised if you do this. It is necessary that a crime involving great injury has occurred, *and* that the intruder was the one who committed the crime. Your belief, no matter how honest and reasonable, that these facts exist is not enough; they must be true. Furthermore, you must be in hot pursuit of the escaping intruder, and reasonably believe that deadly force is necessary to apprehend him. The fleeing intruder must also be given a warning. If any one of these conditions is absent, and you kill the intruder, you could be guilty of murder. Of course, if the intruder turns to the attack, one may exercise the right of self-defense.

There are important limits on the right to use deadly force against an intruder in your home. You can do so only in the building where you are living. In the District of Columbia, your "home" probably does not include the surrounding land or out buildings such as sheds or garages. In an apartment building, your home is your apartment, and probably does not include common areas such as stairwells, corridors, and lobbies. The right to protect the home also is not a license to use deadly force against someone merely because they are in your home. You must always have a reasonable belief about the intruder's violent or criminal intentions. Thus, you have no right to shoot a pesky insurance salesman, or your mother-in-law if she gets uppity. You have no right to use deadly force against a peaceful intruder, such as a police officer or a city inspector. Neither may you provoke someone into attacking you in your home, and then use deadly force to repulse them. If you would not be justified in using deadly force, then you should not threaten to do it.

Whether you can get away with using deadly force in the District of Columbia is affected by two other important factors: the District's gun control laws, among the toughest in the country; and the discretion exercised by law enforcement personnel.

Among many other things, the District's laws and regulations concerning guns include the following: Every firearm in the District must be registered with the police. The mere possession of an unregistered firearm is not only illegal, but it also suggests an illegal purpose, which will make it more difficult to establish reasonable justification for using the weapon. Residents of the District also may not possess a pistol unless it was registered to them before February 5, 1977. There is thus a "freeze" on new handgun ownership in the District. Residents of the District also may not possess automatic weapons, sawed-off shotguns, or silencers. Doing so is a federal offense. The law requires that every firearm must be kept unloaded *and* disassembled or locked, unless kept at one's place of business. A license is required to carry a pistol outside of your home, place of business, or land. Violation of these laws is a misdemeanor, but defense of the home is a defense to the crime of illegal possession at that time, although not for possession before the actual danger arose.

In order to be convicted for improper use of deadly force to repel an intruder in the home, one must be investigated by the police, prosecuted by the U.S. Attorney, tried by a jury, and sentenced by a judge. All have some amount of discretion in how they do their jobs, and many have sympathy for District residents confronted with a housebreaker. As a practical matter, therefore, someone using deadly force to protect his home is unlikely to incur criminal penalties or civil liability even if his conduct does not quite come up to the letter of the law.

D.C. Police Chief Maurice T. Turner reflects the tolerant attitude of the police toward armed resistance to an intruder. As Chief Turner put it, "District residents ought to have the opportunity to have a handgun and to legally use it in their homes." And the chief asks, "If someone was breaking into your house, wouldn't you want a gun to protect yourself?"

Jurors sitting in the trial of someone who shot an intruder, all of whom probably have homes in the District themselves, seem receptive to the defendant's argument that he acted properly. Many judges would also be reluctant to impose stiff punishment on an otherwise law-abiding person who miscalculated in protecting his home and family. Prosecutors in the office of the U.S. Attorney presumably are aware of how a judge and jury would react in such a case, and so could be disposed not to press charges or to accept a plea to a lesser charge.

The practical realities of the justice system, however, do not affect the letter of the law that all citizens must obey in defending their homes. Although the people enforcing the laws have some discretion, each of them, from the first cop on the scene to the twelfth juror in the box, is sworn to uphold the law, and will do his duty.

This discussion of the law in the District of Columbia is of necessity brief and general. The reader is cautioned that the legal problems of any particular case should be referred to an attorney for complete and specific answers.

Florida Law of Self-Defense

Source: Stuart M. Rapee
         Attorney at Law
         12955 Biscayne Blvd., Suite 400
         North Miami, FL 33181
         (305) 895-3880

Mr. Rapee practices law in Miami, Florida, having been a member of the Bar for nineteen years. He is designated by the Florida Bar in the areas of Real Property Law, Wills, Estates, Estate Planning, and Corporation and Business Law.

Florida follows the majority of states regarding the right to use deadly physical force in defense of one's person, dwelling, and place of business. Florida differs in certain respects and these differences are outlined here. This abbreviated article cannot cover sufficient individual situations to permit the reader to blindly follow the principles outlined. It is intended solely as a guide and cannot be interpreted as legal advice.

Florida Statute 776.06 defines deadly force as that force which is likely to cause death or great bodily harm. This includes using a firearm even without the intent to kill or to inflict great bodily harm, or using a firearm against a vehicle occupied by an assailant.

Deadly force is justified when a person is resisting the commission of a felony upon him or any dwelling or place of business where he may be. The type of felony contemplated is burglary, robbery, arson, rape, other felonious assault, and murder.

An attempted felony is sifficient justification for the use of deadly force. However, the person must reasonably believe that there is an immediate danger to his life or great bodily harm. Examples include a pistol or knife being drawn against the person, when the assailant has the apparent ability to cause harm and there is a reasonably foreseeable anticipation of harm.

Florida law is silent on whether one must warn an assailant that deadly force will be used in self-defense. It is reasonable that this choice be left to the individual depending on the circumstances, since in some situations a warning may be hazardous to one's health.

Florida law is clear that when a person is assaulted in one's own home or place of business, one is not obliged to retreat. In such a situation, one may stand his ground and use such force as may appear to him, as a cautious and prudent person, to be necessary to save his life or protect himself from bodily harm or to prevent a felony from being committed upon him or his dwelling. A dwelling has been defined by the court as including the premises around the dwelling if the action is justified under the circumstances.

If a person has a means to withdraw (such as driving away from the scene of a shooting), he must do so if he is outside his home or place of business, since one must use all reasonable means in his power consistent with his own safety to avoid danger or the use of deadly force in such cases.

The use of deadly force in defense of others is more complicated, since it is justified only if a person reasonably believes that deadly force is necessary to prevent the imminent commission of a forcible felony on the other person. It is necessary, therefore, to distinguish between defending others in one's own home with deadly force from "any felony" (which is permitted), and using deadly force outside one's home in defense of others upon whom a non-forcible felony is threatened (which is not permitted). One very old case authorized treating your spouse, parents, and your children as yourself for self-defense purposes, but not your brother, sister, or other relatives.

There are no cases that discuss the use of a mere threat of deadly force when one is not entitled to use it. Under Florida law such a threat would probably be permitted, since a threat without an overt act and means to carry out the threat is not considered an assault. In practical situations, however, a threat to use deadly force is foolhardy because of the reaction it might provoke from an assailant.

After the risk of felony or bodily harm upon the homeowner of the dwelling or place of business has passed, deadly force is no longer justified, but it is a question of fact for the jury as to whether an escaping felon still presents a threat to the homeowner. If such a threat reasonably continues to exist, the use of deadly force against an escaping felon is justified. In a recent Miami case, the intruder was hiding behind a garage when discovered by the homeowner. When he attempted to escape, the owner shot and killed him. The jury acquitted the homeowner, apparently feeling that the threat to the homeowner had not yet abated.

The use of force, but not deadly force, is justified if one has reason to believe that the force is necessary to prevent or terminate simple trespass or criminal interference upon non-dwelling real estate, personal property, one's self, or another. Therefore, it is necessary to assess the degree of force that one must use.

The Court has held that if one justifiably used deadly force in a given situation, but has inadvertently injured or killed an innocent bystander, there would be no criminal responsibility. However, the criminal test is stringent, so it might still be possible for you to be held civilly responsible for damages if you had acted negligently in wounding or killing the bystander. If you were not justified in the use of deadly force, and an innocent bystander were injured or killed, you would be criminally responsible for the harm to the bystander, in the same manner as you would be if you inflicted harm on your assailant without justification.

The use of chemical Mace or similar substances is not regulated in Florida, but if the use of Mace is not justified, prosecution for assault could conceivably occur. It is probably a question of fact for the jury as to whether an assailant using Mace gives sufficient justification for the use of deadly force.

Throughout this discussion the terms reasonable, question of fact, and justification have been used. When these terms are used and one is arrested, it means that it will be up to a jury or the judge as decider of fact to determine whether reasonableness or justification exists.

It is recommended that any person having the means of inflicting deadly force, particularly with firearms, carefully plan out and understand those situations in which the use of deadly force would be justified to prevent inappropriate action when a threatening situation occurs.

Georgia Law of Self-Defense

Source: Samuel McGehee Mitchell
         Suite 209
         330 Church St.
         Decatur, GA 30030

Mr. Mitchell is engaged in the general practice of law with emphasis in the area of criminal law.

This section is written to provide a general synopsis of the current Georgia law subject to legislative revisions and future court interpretations. Georgia law makes distinctions among defense of self and third parties, defense of habitat, and defense of property.

The Official Code of Georgia Annotated (1982, Michie) §16-3-21 states: "(a) A person is justified in threatening or using force against another when and to the extent that he reasonably believes that such threat or force is necessary to defend himself or a third person against such other's imminent use of unlawful force; however, a person is justified in using force which is intended or likely to cause death or great bodily harm only if he reasonably believes that such force is necessary to prevent death or great bodily injury to himself or a third person, or to prevent the commission of a forcible felony.

A person is not justified in using force under the circumstances specified in subsection (a) of this code section if he: (1) initially provokes the use of force against himself with the intent to use such force as an excuse to inflict bodily harm upon the assailant; (2) is attempting to commit, committing, or fleeing after the commission or attempted commission of a felony; or (3) was the aggressor or was engaged in a combat by agreement, unless he withdraws from the encounter and effectively communicates to such other person his intent to do so and the other notwithstanding continues or threatens to continue the use of unlawful force."

In resisting an unlawful arrest, one is justified in using force, but only such force as is reasonably necessary to prevent the arrest; that is, force proportionate to the force being used in the unlawful detention.

Georgia courts point out that use of force in self-defense or defense of third persons is limited to situations where there is imminent danger and not where the danger has passed.

The Official Code of Georgia Annotated (1982, Michie) §16-3-23 dealing with use of force in defense of habitation states: "A person is justified in threatening or using force against another when and to the extent that he reasonably believes that such threat or force is necessary to prevent or terminate such other's unlawful entry into or attack upon a habitation;

however, he is justified in the use of force which is intended or likely to cause death or great bodily harm only if:

(1) The entry is made or attempted in a violent and tumultuous manner and he reasonably believes that the entry is attempted or made for the purpose of assaulting or offering personal violence to any person dwelling or being therein and that such force is necessary to prevent the assault or offer of personal violence; or

(2) He reasonably believes that the entry is made or attempted for the purpose of committing a felony therein and that such force is necessary to prevent the commission of the felony."

The Official Code of Georgia Annotated (1982, Michie) §16-3-24 on use of force in defense of property states: "(a) A person is justified in threatening or using force against another when and to the extent that he reasonably believes that such threat or force is necessary to prevent or terminate such other's trespass on or other tortious or criminal interference with real property other than a habitation or personal property: (1) Lawfully in his possession, or (2) Lawfully in the possession of a member of his immediate family, or (3) Belonging to a person whose property he has a legal duty to protect.

(b) The use of force which is intended or likely to cause death or great bodily harm to prevent trespass on or other tortious or criminal interference with real property other than a habitation or personal property is not justified unless the person using such force reasonably believes that it is necessary to prevent the commission of a forcible felony."

However, as Shakespeare wrote, "The better part of valor is discretion."

Hawaii Law of Self-Defense

Source: G. Stephen Elisha
         Deputy Public Defender
         200 N. Vineyard Blvd.
         Honolulu, HI 96817-3989
         (808) 548-6273

In the State of Hawaii, one may have the legal right to use deadly force for protection or to prevent certain criminal actions. The current law is set forth in the Hawaii Penal Code, Title 37. The relevant statutes may be found at Hawaii Revised Statutes §§703-304, 703-305, and 703-306.

The Use of Force in Self-Protection

Generally, the use of nondeadly force toward another person is justified when a person reasonably believes it is immediately necessary at that time for protection against the use of unlawful force by another. It is essential to note that the belief must be reasonable.

Where the circumstances are aggravated, a person may be justified in using deadly force. Deadly force is defined as that force a person uses which he or she intends to or knows will create a substantial risk of death, serious permanent disfigurement, or protracted loss or impairment of the function of any bodily member or organ. It is important to note that if a person displays a weapon with the intent to create an apprehension of the necessary use of deadly force there has been no use of deadly force.

A person is justified in using deadly force when there is a reasonable belief that it is necessary to protect against death, serious bodily injury, kidnapping, rape, or forcible sodomy.

A person is not justified in using nondeadly force to resist an arrest, even if it is unlawful. When a person intends to cause death or bodily injury and initially provokes another, he or she is not justified in using deadly force to protect against the ensuing retaliation.

In Hawaii, the duty of retreat, rather than use force, depends on the amount of force to be used. Where the force to be used is nondeadly, a person need only estimate the necessity under the circumstances as he or she reasonably believes them to be. That person has no duty to retreat and avoid the necessity of using that extreme force. However, this is only true where the retreat may be accomplished with complete safety, or where one may surrender possession of a thing to a person claiming ownership, or by complying with a demand to abstain from an action the person has no legal duty to take.

The Use of Force for the Protection of Others

In cases where force is used to protect others, a person must place him- or herself "in the other's shoes." If a person, under the circumstances, reasonably believes the person to be protected would be justified in using non-deadly force, he or she may use that force to protect another. The protector must believe the intervention is necessary for the protection of the other person. The duty to retreat is the same as under the laws of self-protection.

Use of Force for the Protection of Property

A person may use force to prevent criminal trespass, unlawful entry, or burglary in a building or on property in his or her possession or care. Force may be used to prevent theft, criminal mischief or any trespass or taking of one's own personal property or property in one's care.

The protector of property must first ask the person threatening the property to stop the interference, unless the request would be useless, it would be dangerous to make the request, or the property would be substantially damaged before the request could be effectively made.

Deadly force for the protection of property is justified where a person, without a claim of right to possession, is attempting to remove the occupier from his dwelling. In addition, deadly force may be used against a person attempting felonious property damage, burglary, robbery, or felonious theft where the intruder has used or threatened deadly force against or in the presence of the occupier. The occupier may use deadly force to prevent a crime where lesser force would expose him or her or a person present to a substantial danger of serious bodily injury.

A person may use a device to protect property if its use is reasonable under the circumstances. However, that device may not create a substantial risk of death or serious bodily injury. The device must be one commonly used for that purpose and reasonable care must be taken to warn probable intruders of its existence.

A person is not required to retreat from his or her dwelling place or place of work. The exceptions to this rule are where the occupier was the initial aggressor or where one is assaulted by a co-worker.

Idaho Law of Self-Defense

Source: Thomas J. McCabe, Esq.
         Attorney at Law
         P.O. Box 2836
         Boise, ID 83701
         (208) 336-3186

Mr. McCabe was formerly law clerk to the Honorable Ray McNichols and the Honorable Fred Taylor, United States District Judges for the District of Idaho. He is now a member of the firm of Nelson & Westberg, chartered at the above address. The firm has a general practice in most areas of civil and criminal law, especially federal and state court litigation.

In discussing the law of self-defense in Idaho, an important distinction must be made between mere self-defense and homicide committed in self-defense. With regard to nondeadly self-defense, Idaho Code §§19-201 through 19-203 provide that any person may defend himself with sufficient force to prevent the commission of an offense or injury against himself or any other person. In addition, an individual may offer the same resistance to prevent an illegal attempt by force to take or injure property in his lawful possession. A 1937 Idaho Supreme Court decision (written by a Justice who years earlier had killed a man trying to gain entry to his office to attack him) declared that any force, short of homicide, was justified in self-defense. *State* v. *Woodward,* 58 Idaho 385, 74 P.2d 92 (1937). A later case by the Supreme Court of Idaho made clear that the above sections *only* apply where there is no homicide. Where there is an actual homicide only Idaho Code §§18-4009 and 18-4010 apply. *State v. Rodriguez,* 93 Idaho 286, 460 P. 29 711 (1969).

I.C. §18-4009 says that homicide is justifiable in defense of one's habitation against one who manifestly intends or endeavors by violence or surprise to commit a felony, or one who attempts to enter another's habitation in a violent or tumultuous manner for the purpose of doing violence to any person within. Thus, no felony is necessary before homicide is justifiable in defense of your home, rather, it has to be obvious that the intruder was *intending* some felony. Arguably, any intruder in one's home in the middle of the night is intending some felonious act or he wouldn't be there. I.C. §18-4010 states that the fear of the commission of the felony has to be reasonable under the circumstances and such fear must be the sole motivating factor.

When it comes to the defense of one's dwelling, the law is silent as to whether a warning is necessary before using deadly force. However, the lack of a warning might bear on the question of the reasonableness of the homeowner's fear under the circumstances.

There is no requirement of retreat in the defense of one's habitation. The only requirement of retreat in Idaho law is where one who is the original aggressor must decline any further combat before homicide is justifiable (assuming the other party was attempting a felony or serious bodily injury). The lack of such a requirement leads me to believe retreat is not legally necessary in such a defense.

You are probably not entitled to threaten the use of deadly force if you are not entitled to use it. Such a threat might give rise to a civil suit for assault. Although such a threat does not constitute criminal assault, because there was no *attempt,* it could constitute the misdemeanor of disturbing the peace, depending upon the circumstances.

Under certain circumstances one can use deadly force to stop an intruder from escaping after he has committed a burglary, rape, assault, etc. Homicide is justifiable when necessarily committed in attempting, by lawful ways and means, to apprehend any person for any felony committed. Significant in this regard is the following situation that arose in Boise in the summer of 1981. A silver dealer was accosted by two armed robbers in his place of business. His initial resistance was subdued by a bloody pistol-whipping, after which the robbers took some silver and left through the front door. The dealer recovered, grabbed his shotgun, loaded it, and went out the back door. Seeing one of the robbers he fired the shotgun and killed him. He then fired on an innocent bystander who drove by in his pick-up truck, the silver dealer mistaking him for the other robber. The county prosecutor, after due deliberation and an analysis of Idaho law, decided not to file charges against the dealer. A legal defense fund had already been formed by the time of the prosecutor's decision, and this writer doubts that any jury in the state would have convicted.

Idaho has a statute, I.C. §19-202A, that provides as follows:

> Legal jeopardy in cases of self-defense and defense of other threatened parties.
> —No person in this state shall be placed in legal jeopardy of any kind whatsoever for protecting himself or his family by reasonable means necessary, or when coming to the aid of another whom he reasonably believes to be in imminent danger of or the victim of aggravated assault, robbery, rape, murder, or other heinous crime.

As noted previously, the location of this statute means that it does apply in the justifiable homicide situation. However, it may have had some influence on the Ada County Prosecutor when considering charges in the silver dealer case. However, the statute didn't stop the same prosecutor from bringing charges against a somewhat eccentric 73-year-old who shot and wounded a man in the older man's back yard. Interestingly enough the charge was filed for the *second* shot which missed the man as he was fleeing the yard. Apparently the wounding shot was considered justified and the second shot malicious. A jury deliberated 18 hours before acquitting the older man. His defense was that the younger man was sneaking around intending a burglary and tried to attack the older man when discovered. The second shot was allegedly fired in the air as a warning to stop.

Despite the two incidents recounted above, the law in Idaho clearly favors the homeowner who stops short of actual homicide. However, Idaho is a heavily armed state and any intruder who enters someone else's house in this state takes his life in his hands.

Illinois Law of Self-Defense

Source: Gary I. Wigoda
         Robert M. Wigoda
         Wigoda and Wigoda
         One North LaSalle St.
         Chicago, IL 60602
         (312) 263-3000

Gary I. Wigoda and Robert M. Wigoda, associated with the law firm of Wigoda and Wigoda, are currently engaged in the general practice of law in Chicago, Illinois.

The justification for the use of deadly force in self-defense, and especially in the defense of a dwelling, in the state of Illinois is quite broad. However, individuals should be acquainted with the limitations the law establishes and imposes.

The controlling law as to the justifiable use of force in Illinois is found in the Illinois Revised Statutes, Chapter 38, article 7. Deadly force is described as that force which is intended to or likely to cause death or great bodily harm. It should be noted with emphasis that force not intended to kill, but to cause great bodily harm, is considered deadly force.

As a general rule, a person is justified in the use of deadly force in all circumstances where he reasonably believes that it is necessary to protect himself or another individual from death or great bodily harm. An individual who acts in defense of a dwelling will be justified in the use of deadly force where an entry or an attempted entry is being made into the dwelling in such a manner that the person reasonably believes it is necessary to protect himself or another from an assault or offer of violence. In addition, the entry or attempted entry must be made in a manner that is violent, riotous, or tumultuous.

A person in defense of a dwelling may also use deadly force when he reasonably believes that it is necessary to prevent the commission of a felony in that dwelling. A person is not justified in using deadly force in defense of any property other than a dwelling unless he reasonably believes that such force is necessary to prevent a felony which involves the use or threat of physical force or violence against any individual. The most important aspect to this analysis is whether or not a person acts reasonably. When an individual uses deadly force, *he* must reasonably believe such force to be necessary *in the given circumstance and situation.*

Illinois law does not require a person in his home, dwelling, or any other lawful circumstance to retreat for the purpose of avoiding the use of deadly force. An individual is not justified in using deadly force in a situation which results from his provocation or initiation, unless he has exhausted every reasonable means of escape. There is no apparent need to give warning prior to the use of deadly force, however, as stated previously, an individual must always act reasonably.

An individual is not justified in using deadly force against an aggressor after the aggressor has broken off his conduct, has retreated, or is in the process of escaping. Illinois law does not intend the broad right of self-defense to be used lightly, carelessly, or for revenge.

This summary outlines general rules of justifiable use of deadly force by private individuals. The rules, requirements, and boundaries set out in this general discussion cannot be rigidly applied to all circumstances and situations as each one must be considered individually and on its own merits.

Indiana Law of Self-Defense

Source: Mary Ann Wunder
         Attorney at Law
         3997-9 Aurora
         Indianapolis, IN 46227
         (317) 783-0177

Mrs. Wunder has been a solo practitioner with a general practice of law in Indianapolis since 1979.

The pertinent provisions of the law of self-defense may be found in the Indiana Code at I.C. 35-41-3-2 and -3 with definitions at I.C. 35-41-1-2. This article is merely an introduction to the law and is not an exhaustive survey covering all situations.

A person in the State of Indiana has the right to use force, even deadly force, to stop or to prevent criminal acts which are directed against any person, the home, or the personal property rightfully in a person's possession. This right is more technically called self-defense, defense of others, and defense of property.

Self-defense is a defense to criminal charges which stem from actions that were taken to protect persons or property, and it is also a legal justification for the actions necessary. However, when a person reacts in self-defense (or uses force against another), it first must appear to him that force is necessary as a reaction, and he then may use only such force as he reasonably believes is necessary to protect himself, another person, or his property.

Deadly force is justified in defending your home from a criminal attack whether it be unwelcome entry or an injury to the home—arson, for example. The use of deadly force outside your home to protect yourself, another person, or your other property is justified only when there is a probability that some serious harm will come to you or another person or there is a probability that a criminal act directed toward you or another person will result in injury—rape or battery, for example. A general purse-snatching does not justify the use of deadly force.

Self-defense is not a justification for your actions in all situations. If you commit a crime and in so doing injure someone who reacts against you—even if that person threatens or injures you—you do not have a defense to that injury. If you entice or provoke another to act in such a way that you believe it is necessary to use force against him, you do not have a defense for any injuries to the other. If you are the aggressor in a fight, you cannot use self-defense as a justification unless you first withdraw and communicate your withdrawal to the other person.

A creditor attempting to repossess your property is not justified in injuring you if you object to his repossession. Similarly, you as a creditor cannot justify an injury you inflict on your debtor if he objects to your repossession.

Property you are justified in protecting includes your home and furnishings, your pets and livestock, property belonging to others which you rightfully have in your possession, and property in your home which belongs to members of your family or boarders.

You do not have to retreat from the threat of an attack. However, when you stand and fight, you must first believe that your fight is necessary to ward off or prevent the attack, and your fight must not be more forcible than the force necessary to ward off or prevent the attack. For example, a torch against a match is probably too much force with which to react.

You may capture an attacker or prevent his flight if you are certain that he is a felon or if you merely have probable cause to so believe. The amount of force you are justified in using is that which is reasonably necessary to restrain him. Deadly force is justified only if you believe that a threat of serious injury to yourself or another person is continuing.

Whenever the danger ceases your right to react with force also ceases. For example, let us assume that you fire a warning shot at someone who is breaking into your home. You then see the intruder running away from your home and fire a second shot. While the first shot may be justified, it is very doubtful that the second would be since the danger had passed when you fired it. However, if the criminal were to turn in his flight and shoot at you, the danger would still exist, so you likely would be justified in firing back at him.

In general, you must remember that you are justified in using force to protect property only when you reasonably believe that force will be necessary to protect it, and, furthermore, you may use only such force as you believe is necessary under the circumstances. Deadly force is only justified when protecting your home or when a serious injury or death is likely to occur.

Deadly force is a force which creates a substantial risk of serious injury to a person. That serious injury includes a substantial risk of death; unconsciousness; extreme pain; impairment of function or loss of function of fingers, toes, or organs; and permanent disfigurement.

Iowa Law of Self-Defense

Source: Neil A. Barrick
         Attorney at Law
         850 Insurance Exchange Bldg.
         Des Moines, IA 50309
         (515) 244-3200

Mr. Barrick, currently a member of the Robert E. Conley Law Firm, has a general practice of law in Des Moines, Iowa.

All readers should be cautioned that an extensive review of case law in Iowa and elsewhere would be necessary to fully understand and apply the law of self-defense and/or the use of reasonable force. This synopsis is not intended to fully address every possible situation.

In the State of Iowa, a private citizen has a legal right to use reasonable force, including deadly force, to resist or prevent certain crimes. Reasonable force, including deadly force, and use of the same are defined in the 1981 Code of Iowa, Sections 704.1—704.7. Reasonable force is defined as:

> force which a reasonable person, in like circumstances, would judge necessary to prevent an injury or loss, and no more, except that the use of deadly force against another is reasonable only to resist a like force or threat.

Deadly force is that force which is used for the purpose of causing serious injury or death or which creates a strong possibility that serious injury or death will result. For example, the discharge of a firearm in the direction of a person when his/her presence is known is specifically held to be a use of deadly force.

As a rule, a person is justified in the use of reasonable force to prevent or terminate criminal interference with his/her possession or other right in property, as long as he/she believes, as a reasonable person, that he/she is in imminent danger of the loss of property and that the use of force is necessary to prevent the loss. The force used must be "reasonable," however, and not disproportionate to the threat posed to the individual. An actual breaking and entering of one's premises or actual commission of some other crime need not occur before reasonable force is employed. The key, again, is whether a "reasonable" person would believe a crime was about to be committed and whether said person would reasonably determine that some degree of force was necessary to prevent the same.

Generally, a person who is confronted with the use of unlawful force against him/herself is required to avoid the confrontation by seeking and using an alternative course of action. If, however, the person is in his/her own home or place of business or employment, or on property he/she is lawfully occupying, retreat is not required before use of reasonable and/or deadly force. Nor is retreat required if an alternative course of action is available, if the alternative entails a risk to one's life or safety or the life or safety of a third person.

It is not necessary that there be actual danger before reasonable force is employed. In fact, the danger may not exist at all. The danger perceived is to be viewed from the standpoint of the person against whom the force or threat is directed and is also judged in light of the "reasonable man" standard.

Iowa has no written requirement that a warning be given before the use of deadly force. Again, it must be shown that the use of such force is reasonable under the circumstances present.

Use of deadly force can be threatened as long as it is in defense of person or property and not for the commission of an illegal act. Threatened use of deadly force, when not for purposes of defense, is considered a criminal assault.

According to Section 804.9 and 804.10 of the Code of Iowa, deadly force can be used by a private citizen after a crime has been committed in an attempt to stop the perpetrator of the crime. The person attempting to stop or arrest said perpetrator can use the force he/she reasonably believes necessary to make the arrest as long as there is reason to believe that a crime was committed in the person's presence.

One cannot justify the use of deadly force unless he/she is completely free of fault in provoking the incident giving rise to the use of such force. If, however, the provocator withdraws from his act, and this is clearly indicated, and the victim continues the physical contact or uses a force disproportionate to the initial attack or danger, then the provocator may be justified in using deadly force in protection of himself.

If an innocent bystander is injured as a result of your use of deadly force, you may be subject to criminal as well as civil prosecution as your actions relate to said innocent party. As a result, any time deadly force is employed, extreme care and caution has to be the rule. Deadly force should, in this writer's opinion, be used only as a last resort.

Kansas Law of Self-Defense

Source: Robert W. Strohmeyer
         Attorney at Law
         1932 North 77th
         Kansas City, KS 66112
         (913) 299-1718

Mr. Strohmeyer graduated from the Washburn University of Topeka School of Law and was admitted to the Kansas Bar in 1979. He is now actively involved in the general practice of law in Kansas City.

Under Kansas law, K.S.A. 21-3212, "A person is justified in the use of force against another when and to the extent that it appears to him and he reasonably believes that such conduct is necessary to prevent or *terminate* such other's unlawful entry into or attack upon his dwelling." The case law in Kansas is clear that deadly force may be used under the proper circumstances; what we are really talking about here is "reasonable" force under the circumstances.

As an example, if someone broke a hole in your window and then attempted to enter, while armed, deadly force could be used to repel that attack. Further, if you came home and found an armed intruder in your home, you could use deadly force to terminate the entry. Contrarily, however, if someone stands in your front yard and throws rocks at your house, you do not have the right to use deadly force to get the person to stop throwing rocks.

It is important to stress that a person defending his dwelling may use any force that it appears to him and he reasonably believes is necessary. This is important if one is charged with a criminal act in defending his dwelling, because the final judge of what is a reasonable belief under the circumstances is a jury of twelve persons. Hopefully, one would not have to get as far as a jury trial to prove that he was justified in his use of force.

A defender in his own home is not required to issue a warning before using force to prevent someone from unlawfully entering his dwelling. Nor does the defender have to retreat before using force in his own home when he is not the provoker or aggressor. The law in Kansas recognizes a person's right to stand his ground in his own home when faced with an unlawful intruder.

A person is also allowed to use force to protect others in his home from attack by an unlawful intruder. K.S.A. 21-3211 states: "A person is justified in the use of force against an aggressor when and to the extent it appears to him and he reasonably believes that such conduct is necessary to defend himself *or another* against such aggressor's imminent use of unlawful force."

Questions often arise concerning a victim's right to use force against a criminal as he is attempting to escape from the scene of the crime. If a criminal were leaving the dwelling, there might not be any further danger to the victim, so the use of deadly force would not be allowed for reasons of self-defense. Force may be used, however, to make a citizen's arrest. The provisions of K.S.A. 21-3216 are as follows:

"(1) A private person who makes, or assists another private person in making a lawful arrest is justified in the use of any force which he would be justified in using if he were summoned or directed by a law enforcement officer to make such arrest, except that he is justified in the use of force likely to cause death or great bodily harm only when he reasonably believes that such force is necessary to prevent death or great bodily harm to himself or another.

"(2) A private person who is summoned or directed by a law enforcement officer to assist in making an arrest which is unlawful is justified in the use of any force which he would be justified in using if the arrest were lawful."

Anyone who uses deadly force against another person should be extremely cautious and use it only when absolutely necessary. Any force used outside the bounds of these statutes would open the person using such force to possible criminal and civil liability. Furthermore, if you were to injure an innocent third party while legally, but recklessly, using deadly force against an intruder, you could be liable for both civil and criminal penalties in regards to the third party.

Kentucky Law of Self-Defense

Source: Michael B. Hayes
Attorney at Law
City of Louisville
727 West Main St.
Louisville, KY 40202
(502) 587-3524

The law of self-defense in Kentucky is known as "Justification" and is found in Kentucky Revised Statute (KRS) Chapter 503. The defense of "justification" actually means the justifiable or legal use of force. KRS 503.020 states that justification is a defense for any prosecution of an offense.

It should, however, be pointed out to laymen that there are many exceptions to this rule. It is also at times difficult to determine exactly what qualifies as a justification defense without the help of one thoroughly trained in the law.

Before we discuss the defense of justification, two important terms are defined in KRS 503.010:

I. "Deadly Physical Force" means force which is used with the purpose of causing death or serious physical injury or which the defendant knows to create a substantial risk of causing death or serious physical injury.

II. "Physical Force" means force used upon or directed toward the body of another person and includes confinement.

These definitions should be kept in mind as our discussion progresses.

A. Self-Defense

Generally, physical force is lawful to protect oneself when the user believes it necessary for self-defense against unlawful force. Deadly force can only be used in self-defense when the user believes it necessary to protect himself against: 1. death; 2. serious physical injuries; 3. kidnapping; or 4. sexual intercourse compelled by force or threat. There is also no law that the user of deadly force, who is confronted with death or serious injury, be required to retreat. He may kill in self-defense so long as he believes that use of such deadly force is necessary. This belief, however, may not be wanton or reckless. If the user of deadly force was wanton or reckless in his belief that such force was necessary, then he has lost his defense of justification.

Physical force, and therefore, deadly force may not be used to protect oneself against unlawful force by anyone even when believed necessary when: 1. resisting an arrest, believed to be unlawful, and made by a police officer (this does not apply if more force is used than reasonably necessary to effect the arrest); 2. The user provokes another into an assault for the purpose of using the assault as an excuse to kill or seriously injure that person; 3. The user is the initial aggressor and has not withdrawn and communicated his withdrawal to the person assaulted.

B. Protection of Another

KRS 503.070 outlines the right of one to defend another. In many ways, protection of another is identical to self-defense. An individual who defends another has the same rights and limitations he would have if he were defending himself. If mere physical force is used, the defendant is justified in protecting a person if that person could use such force *under the circumstances as they appear to the defendant.*

Deadly force can only be used to protect against death, serious physical injury, kidnapping, and forcible sexual offenses. One further limitation on the use of deadly force is that the defendant will be judged in the light *of what the circumstances actually are* and not as they appear to the defendant. This is to say that the protected party may be entitled to use deadly force before the defendant can use such force on his behalf.

Current Kentucky law abolishes the need of a special relationship to the defendant, such as a spouse, child, parent, brother, or sister, before the defendant is entitled to defend another. Also keep in mind that if a defendant uses deadly force to protect another he is to be judged by the actual circumstances; if he used non-deadly force he is to be judged by the apparent circumstances.

C. Protection of Property

KRS 503.080 outlines Kentucky Law as it concerns protection of property. The use of physical force is justified to prevent what the defendant believes to be an unlawful destruction of, or entry upon, real property or an unlawful taking or destruction of tangible, moveable property.

Deadly force can be used only in three situations. The first allows the defendant to use deadly force to prevent another from disposing him of his dwelling. If disposition occurs under a claim of right, such as a deed of title, then deadly force is not justified, rather the rightful claimant must have the dispute settled by the court. The second situation allows deadly force against a burglar who is using or about to use physical force against an occupant of a dwelling. This protection is slightly more liberal than under self-defense in that under this situation the defendant need not believe that he or others are in danger of death or serious physical injury. The "apparent" peril to an individual of a burglary into his dwelling justifies the use of deadly force. The third situation justifies the use of deadly force to prevent arson of a dwelling or other building.

Louisiana Law of Self-Defense

Source: Michael R. Connelly
          Attorney at Law
          604 St. Ferdinand St.
          Baton Rouge, LA 70802
          (504) 344-4369

Mr. Connelly is a partner in the law firm of Rogers and Connelly which is engaged in the general practice of law in Baton Rouge. Mr. Connelly has an expertise in constitutional law with particular emphasis on the Bill of Rights.

As in most other states, Louisiana allows the use of deadly force to protect a person from death or great bodily harm. However, unlike most other jurisdictions, Louisiana has recently liberalized its law to allow the use of deadly force where death or great bodily harm are not necessarily imminent.

The basic laws are provided in Louisiana Revised Statutes 14:20 through 14:22. La. R.S. 14:20 provides that:

1. A homicide is justifiable when committed in self-defense by a person who reasonably believes he is in imminent danger of death or great bodily harm and kills to defend himself and

2. when committed by a person in order to prevent a "violent or forcible felony" involving danger of death or great bodily harm. This second section also provides that the person using the force must reasonably believe that "such an offense is about to be committed and that such action is necessary for its prevention." In addition, "the circumstances must be sufficient to excite the fear of a reasonable person that there would be serious danger to his own life or person if he attempted to prevent the felony without the killing."

La. R.S. 40:21 provides that an aggressor who initiates a conflict cannot claim the right of self-defense unless he withdraws from the conflict in good faith and "in such manner that an adversary knows or should know that he desires to withdraw and discontinue the conflict."

La. R.S. 40:22 provides that the use of deadly force is justifiable in defense of another person when "it is reasonably apparent that the person attacked could have justifiably used such means himself, and when it is reasonably believed that such intervention is necessary to protect the other person."

The most significant recent development in Louisiana came in 1976 when the Louisiana legislature amended La. R.S. 14:20 to add a third section which reads:

3. "A homicide is justifiable when committed against a person whom one reasonably believes to be likely to use any unlawful force against a person present in a dwelling or a place of business while committing or attempting to

commit a burglary of such dwelling or business. The homicide shall be justifiable even though the person does not retreat from the encounter."

That section is extemely important for two reasons. First, it substitutes the words "any unlawful force" for the normal phrases concerning the threat of death or great bodily harm. Secondly, it totally eliminates the necessity of retreat under the circumstances of invasion of a dwelling or a place of business by a thief. In the past, retreat before the use of deadly force was a general requirement of the law in Louisiana, although it was broadly interpreted by the courts. However, it is significant to note that, in cases where the courts found that retreat was impractical, it allowed pursuit of the aggressor until the nonaggressor had "secured himself from all danger."

No real interpretation of this new provision of the law has yet been made by the courts in Louisiana. However, from a practical standpoint the law is being broadly interpreted by at least some district attorneys. Two recent incidents in Baton Rouge, Louisiana, provide good examples. In one case a store owner and his son shot and killed two armed robbers attempting to hold up their place of business. In the second incident a store owner shot and killed an armed robber after he had held up the business and was running down the street to escape. No charges were filed against the store owners in either case. Of course readers should be aware that a district attorney in another area might view the matters differently.

In addition, there are other aspects of the law of self-defense in Louisiana which are unclear. For example, there is apparently no prohibition against the threat of deadly force to prevent a crime even if that deadly force cannot be used. However, deadly force cannot be used to prevent misdemeanors unless an invasion of a dwelling or place of business is involved and there is some threat of harm to the occupants.

In conclusion, the Louisiana Law of self-defense can be generally summarized as providing that deadly force can be used to prevent the infliction of death or great bodily harm to oneself or another person, to prevent the commission of a felony which involves the threat of death or great bodily harm and to prevent the use of any unlawful force against a person present in a dwelling or a place of business when a burglary is being attempted or committed. Retreat is not necessary under the latter circumstances and probably not necessary when there is virtually any invasion of a home or business. Pursuit is allowed until the threat of danger is alleviated, and where the use of deadly force is warranted. There is no requirement that a warning be given prior to its use.

Maine Law of Self-Defense

Source: Peter A. Anderson
Attorney at Law
Suite One
61 Main St.
Bangor, ME 04401
(207) 947-0303

Mr. Anderson currently practices law in Bangor, Maine, where he is a member of the law firm of Anderson, Merrill, Norton & Relyea. The firm engages in the general practice of law. Mr. Anderson is an active competitor in high-power rifle, indoor and outdoor pistol, and holds the Distinguished Pistol Shot Badge. He is a colonel in the United States Army Reserve.

This material is intended to be merely a summary and general statement of the law of the use of deadly force in Maine. Each factual situation must be carefully analyzed in the light of the precise statutory language; therefore, it must clearly be understood that this information provides merely a general guide.

The relevant provisions of Maine law are found in Title 17A M.R.S.A., §§2, 104 and 108. The Maine Criminal Code is a relatively recent enactment and therefore as yet has not been extensively interpreted by case law.

The Maine statute defines deadly force as "physical force which a person uses with the intent of causing or which he knows to create a substantial risk of causing death or serious bodily injury. Intentionally or recklessly discharging a firearm in the direction of another person or at a moving vehicle constitutes deadly force." A person in possession or control of premises, which includes but is not limited to lands, private ways, and any buildings or structures thereon, or a person who is licensed or privileged to be thereon is justified using deadly force upon another when and to the extent he reasonably believes it necessary to prevent an attempt by the other to commit arson. A person in possession or control of a dwelling place, but not "premises," or a person who is licensed or privileged to be in the dwelling place is justified in using deadly force:

1. When he reasonably believes it necessary and he reasonably believes the object of his deadly force is about to use unlawful deadly force against himself or a third person, or

2. When he reasonably believes it necessary and he reasonably believes that such other person is committing or about to commit a kidnapping, rape, or forcible sexual offense, or

3. When he reasonably believes that such other person has entered or is attempting to enter a dwelling place or has surreptitiously remained within a dwelling place without a license or privilege to do so, and that deadly force is

necessary to prevent the infliction of bodily injury by such other person upon himself or a third person who is present in the dwelling place. Further, a person who is in possession or control of a dwelling place or who is licensed or privileged to be therein is justified in using deadly force when he reasonably believes that deadly force is necessary to prevent or terminate the commission of criminal trespass by such other person who he reasonably believes has entered or is attempting to enter the dwelling place or has surreptitiously remained within the dwelling place without a license or privilege to do so and is committing or is likely to commit some other crime within the dwelling place. It must be noted, however, that a person may use deadly force under this latter set of circumstances only if he first demands that the person against whom such deadly force is to be used terminate the criminal trespass and that person fails to comply immediately with the demand. The only exception is if he reasonably believes that it would be dangerous to himself or to another to make such a demand.

In general, a person is not justified in using deadly force in defense of himself or another if he has provoked the other person to use such force, or he knows that the person against whom such deadly force is directed intentionally and unlawfully provoked the use of such force, or he knows that he or the third person he is defending can with complete safety retreat from the encounter, surrender property to a person asserting a colorable (valid or legal) claim of right to the property, or comply with the demand that he not do something which he is not otherwise obliged to do. It must be noted, however, that neither the person applying the deadly force nor the third person he is defending is required to retreat if he or the third person is in his dwelling house and was not the initial aggressor.

A recent case, *State v. Williams,* 433 A.2d 765 (Me. 1981) has held that you may threaten to use deadly force even in circumstances when you might not use the force itself, provided such a threat is reasonable under the circumstances.

Deadly force should be resorted to only when no lesser action will avoid the commission of the crime. The provisions allowing its use should not be used as an excuse to use it when unnecessary.

Maryland Law of Self-Defense

Source: George E. Tindal
          Attorney at Law
          Suite 301
          4 E. Franklin St.
          Baltimore, MD 21202

Mr. Tindal is associated with the law firm of Singleton, Dashiell & Robinson. He did his undergraduate work at Franklin and Marshall College in Lancaster, Pennsylvania, and spent his junior year at the University of Lancaster in Lancaster, England. Mr. Tindall received his law degree from the University of Maryland Law School in 1976.

The law of self-defense in Maryland states that deadly force may be used where the provocation is great and the violence extreme so as to justify the use of a deadly weapon. The character and extent of the assault are important considerations in determining whether the use of a deadly weapon to repel an assault is justified (Nixon v. State, 105A 2d. 243, 204 Maryland 475).

It is further stated that where one's home is about to be broken into or if a burglary is about to occur in one's home, that deadly force is excusable where the person using the force fears for his life while the burglary or breaking is in progress. The user of deadly force must reasonably believe and, in fact believe (subjectively) that he is in serious apparent and imminent and immediate danger of death or serious bodily harm. The individual belief of the user of deadly force must be such as would be believed of other reasonable and prudent persons in similar circumstances.

The law of homicide in Maryland states that homicide is excusable or justifiable for the protection of one's habitation or property. Generally, deadly force is allowed where it is necessary and used in good faith to prevent an attempted felony by force or by surprise. Where a felony is being committed in one's own home and elements of fear and/or surprise are apparent, no retreat is necessary. Nor is one required to give warning before using deadly force, where he is in serious imminent and immediate danger of his life.

Deadly force is allowed and indeed excused when it is used in the defense of another who bears a close association or family relationship to another. As a result, the defender may use the same degree and character of force as the one attacked could have used.

Under Maryland law, one may justifiably use deadly force in order to effectuate the arrest of a felon or prevent the escape of a felon. However, deadly force is allowed only where it is necessary and used in good faith.

My advice to one who keeps a gun at home for self-defense is to be sure that it is properly registered have a permit, and have the weapon in a safe, handy place in case a burglary or some other felony is about to occur on his property, while he is present. Before deadly force is used, he should satisfy himself that he is in imminent danger and is fearful of his person or that of others in his home.

Massachusetts Law of Self-Defense

Source: Karen L. MacNutt
         Attorney at Law
         Suite 902
         133 Federal Street
         Boston, MA 02110
         (617) 482-2621

Karen L. MacNutt is engaged in the general practice of law and is associated with the firm of Bowers & Bowers of Boston, Massachusetts. In addition to practicing in the State Courts, Attorney MacNutt is admitted to practice before the United States Supreme Court. She is a member of the Boston Bar Association and the Massachusetts Trial Lawyers Association. As a strong advocate of private gun ownership, Attorney MacNutt has been active in drafting anticrime legislation.

The Constitution of Massachusetts declares that all citizens have the unalienable right of "enjoying and defending their lives and liberties; and that of acquiring, possessing, and protecting property."

The question of whether or not deadly force may be used to defend lives or property is not governed by statute in Massachusetts. Instead, it has developed from the common law on a case-to-case basis. Each time a case involving the use of deadly force reaches the state's Supreme Judicial Court, the opinion written by the justices further develops the law. Because of this, the law governing the use of deadly force in Massachusetts could change at any time.

Deadly force as presently defined by state law is simply that degree of force likely to cause death or serious bodily injury. A deadly weapon is an object capable of inflicting death or serious bodily injury. Firearms are obviously deadly weapons. However, a bottle, a cigarette, and even a shod foot have also been held to be deadly weapons. It makes no difference if a victim was threatened with a real gun, a toy gun, or a club. If the victim was put in fear and believed his attacker had a deadly weapon, an assault with a deadly weapon has been committed. Thus, anyone who shows a gun in a manner which reasonably causes another to be placed in fear has committed an assault with a deadly weapon unless he was acting in self-defense. Even if a person was acting in self-defense, if he uses more force than is reasonably necessary to defend himself, he will no longer be deemed to be acting in self-defense but will then be held to be the aggressor.

In Massachusetts, firearms are treated differently from other deadly weapons in several important ways. One way is that a person must have a license to carry, transport, or even possess a handgun, rifle, or shotgun. Although the carrying of certain other weapons, such as a switch blade knife or sling shot, is made illegal, the carrying of a gun without a license carries a mandatory one-year jail sentence with no hope of parole. A second difference is that the firing of a gun within 500 feet of a dwelling in a nonemergency situation is a misdemeanor, thus warning shots are usually not advisable.

A person may use deadly force in Massachusetts to defend his own life if he "reasonably" fears that he is in immediate danger of death or serious bodily injury and has no "reasonable" means of escape or other way of preventing the harm. See *Commonwealth v. Crowley*, 46 N.E. 415 (1897); and *Commonwealth v. Kendrick*, 218 N.E.2d 408 (1966).

The question of whether or not the fear was "reasonable" is based upon the facts as known by the person being attacked. For example, a person attacked with a realistic-looking toy gun would have a reasonable fear of danger, although in reality the gun was harmless.

Although the question of whether or not a person had a "reasonable means of escape" will vary depending upon where an attack takes place, there is no absolute right in Massachusetts to use deadly force in one's own home. Massachusetts courts hold the minority position that a person attacked in his own home must retreat if he can do so safely, even if that means leaving the home. Only if there is no safe means of escape can a person use deadly force in his own home to defend his life. Because the case in which this rule was set involved a guest who attacked his host, it is not clear that the courts would have taken this same minority position if the case had involved a confrontation between a burglar and a legal occupant of the home. See *Commonwealth v. Shaffer*, 326 N.E.2d 880 (1975), *cf. Commonwealth v. Gagne*, 326 N.E.2d 907 (1975) as to duty to retreat in one's place of business.*

Deadly force may be used to defend another if the user of the deadly force believes:

---

*On December 24, 1981, the Massachusetts Legislature enacted a law designed to overrule the Shaffer decision.

The new law creates a defense for a person being prosecuted for using deadly force in a dwelling against another unlawfully in the building. The defense applies if the occupant was:

1. Inside the dwelling when the deadly force was used;
2. Acted in the reasonable belief the person unlawfully in the building was about to inflict great bodily injury or death to others lawfully in the dwelling, and
3. The occupant used reasonable means to defend himself.

There is no duty for an occupant to retreat from someone unlawfully in the building.

Although many parts of the statute are subject to interpretation, the first case brought under the new law before the Appeals Court was decided in 1984 (Commonwealth v. Gregory). The Court held that a person had no duty to avoid combat in his own home when facing an intruder. Thus the use of the words "reasonable means" does not require some need to avoid a confrontation if the other factors allowing the use of deadly force are present.

1. his intervention is necessary to protect the other person (that is the harm is imminent or ongoing), and
2. the person being defended would have been justified in using such force himself.

The relationship between the parties is a factor in determining whether or not the use of deadly force was reasonable. However, one may use deadly force to protect the life of a stranger if the above-referred two-pronged test is met. See *Commonwealth v. Martin,* 341 N.E.2d 885 (1976); *Commonwealth v. Monico,* 366 N.E.2d 1241 (1977).

The state of the law is unclear as to a person's ability to use deadly force to protect property. Where a crime has already taken place, one may not use deadly force to make a citizen's arrest if the crime only involved property. Thus, a home owner could not use a gun to stop someone on the street who had just burglarized his home. The courts have specifically refused to rule on whether or not deadly force may ever be used to protect property. *Commonwealth v. Klein,* 363 N.E.2d 1313 (1977). Considering the tenor of the Massachusetts courts, it is unlikely they would uphold the use of deadly force to protect property unless the crime were one such as burglary or arson where there is a significant risk of a violent confrontation or a placing of a life in danger.

Massachusetts recognizes the use of deadly force to accomplish a citizen's arrest under very narrow circumstances. Although the case in point is inconsistent, it would appear that a citizen must state his purpose before attempting a citizen's arrest. The arrest must be for a felony involving the use or threatened use of deadly force; and there must be a substantial risk that the person being arrested will cause serious bodily harm if his apprehension is delayed. Further, the citizen may not use deadly force to affect an arrest if there is the likelihood of injury to innocent persons. Such an arrest should probably not be attempted unless the crime has taken place in the presence of the arresting citizen. See *Commonwealth v. Klein* (id.).

Historically, Massachusetts courts and prosecutors have not been sympathetic to the victims of crimes; or to the use of deadly force to defend one's life, home, or business. In most instances, justice for such victims comes not from reliance on the law, but by the fairness of a jury. The choice of whether or not to use deadly force becomes a moral rather than a legal question, as usually deadly force is only justified when a life is in danger.

Michigan Law of Self-Defense

Source: Seymour Beitner
         Attorney at Law
         8137 W. Grand River
         Suite A
         Brighton, MI 48116
         (313) 229-8885

Mr. Beitner was admitted to practice in the State of Michigan in 1965. He currently practices before the federal and state courts following a general practice, and is on the National Rifle Association's list of attorneys available in the Michigan area.

The State of Michigan has long maintained a position that human life is not to be lightly disregarded, and the law will not permit it to be destroyed unless upon some most urgent necessity. When viewed properly, the right to use deadly force in self-defense is really a right to insure *protection* to life. The right of self-defense is a right afforded to peaceful members of society to deter wanton attack by criminals. While the use of deadly force to repel an attack may be a valid defense to prosecution in some cases, common sense dictates that in others it will not, and it is most difficult for an attorney to lay out a hard and fast rule which will guarantee immunity to an individual claiming self-defense under all circumstances. For this reason, the reader is cautioned that the law, like the wind, changes constantly. Its direction can be determined by the facts of the case, and no one should feel that he has been granted a "license" to use deadly force in Michigan without due regard for the circumstances of the situation.

Michigan law has consistently held that before the use of deadly force is condoned, it must appear that the party using it in his own defense was without fault, and was not the aggressor in bringing on the conflict. Further, there have been cases which have held that there is a distinction between what the circumstances *actually* were, from those as they *appeared* to be in the eyes of the person attempting to defend himself. The defender must have reasonably assumed that he was in imminent danger of losing his own life or suffering serious bodily injury, and there was no way open for him to retreat to a place of safety. This state has generally maintained that it is the duty of the defender to "retreat to the wall" wherever possible before utilizing deadly force, with the notable exception that deadly force may be utilized, with no retreat necessary, when one is *assaulted* in his own dwelling. Assuming that the definition of assault is the traditional definition of placing another in fear of injury, the Michigan courts have held that the exception to the retreat-to-the-wall doctrine extends the area within which one is not obligated to retreat beyond the mere physical structure utilized as an abode, to include any inhabited out-buildings upon the property.

Extreme resistance such as the use of deadly force is justified when serious bodily harm may result from a felonious attack, and the self-defender is not required, when hard-pressed, to draw fine distinctions as to the extent of the injury that a reckless and infuriated assailant may probably inflict. It becomes the duty of the self-defender to convince the authorities and, if prosecuted, the court or jury, that he in fact acted upon an honest belief arising from appearances which gave him reasonable grounds to believe that the danger was actual and imminent, although he may subsequently turn out to be totally mistaken. He must be able to convince the jury that he did everything he could to avoid a conflict, other than the exception noted in his own home.

Michigan, by court decision, has allowed the use of deadly force to prevent an assailant from forcibly entering the defender's home, even to the extent of taking the assailant's life. The courts have held that a defender need not retreat from his own dwelling even when attacked by somebody living within it, or his own spouse. The courts have drawn the line against trespassers, however, and have held consistently that no landowner can defend a trespass solely upon his land with the use of a dangerous weapon. Further, the unintended and/or accidental killing of an innocent bystander has been held not to be a felonious homicide if occasioned by conduct considered to be a legally proper self-defense; but it may be considered manslaughter if the self-defender's conduct under all of the circumstances was found to be reckless with regard to an innocent bystander.

A study of the Michigan cases further indicates that there is no clear and consistent requirement that the self-defender must "warn" an assailant before utilizing deadly force. It might well be considered by the authorities that an improper threat to use deadly force, coupled with an obvious and present means to execute the threat, would in fact by itself constitute a felonious assault on the part of the person who is attempting to defend himself without justification.

The key to almost all of the cases utilizing deadly force as an element of self-defense is that there must be a "perceived threat" to the defender, so it is difficult to clearly define the right of a defender to use deadly force to stop an intruder from *escaping*. This, of course, does not apply to a "peace officer," but seems to apply solely to the "citizen/defender." The question as to whether or not a homeowner has a right to use deadly force to prevent the *escape* of a burglar, rapist, assaulter, etc., can only be viewed in this state in terms of "perceived danger to the defender." While a jury might feel otherwise based on the facts, the law grants no protection to a homeowner who shoots someone "fleeing" the scene of a crime. There are some restrictions placed upon peace officers under the same circumstances, but it can generally be considered to be within the authority of a police officer to use deadly force to apprehend a fleeing felony suspect.

Michigan cases have held that deadly force *cannot* be used for the mere protection of personal property. It is only when that protection becomes involved with a simultaneous protection of one's life or safety that the use of deadly force is permitted.

In application and natural extension of the theories of self-defense, the right to use deadly force on the part of the citizen/defender, within his home, extends to the perceived danger of assault upon other occupants of that home by the intruder as well. It may well be reasoned under Michigan law that the citizen/defender armed with a deadly weapon to be used in his own defense may extend that use to those within the curtilage of his home and may act in *their* defense to save them from perceived injury. Once such deadly force was lawfully employed by the citizen/defender, the extreme results of its employment, namely injury or death, would be accepted as a natural consequence of the employment.

It should be specifically noted that the Michigan law expressly forbids the use of "spring-guns," which are casually defined as weapons set up in some form within a structure so as to cause them to be discharged when someone breaks in. Under such a circumstance, it is totally conceivable that a burglar could bring a legal action for damages arising out of any injury suffered by him as a result of being wounded by such a spring-gun, or other mechanical-type device utilizing deadly force to prevent a robbery. In short, the use of deadly force by a citizen/defender may well be condoned under the same circumstances where the mechanical discharge of an unattended weapon might not. The first instance may result in a medal for valor being awarded and the second a lawsuit for damages that may well have the burglar end up winning the *entire* home when he only intended to steal a small part of it.

In summation, I would quote to the reader the following Latin maxim: *"In jure omnia definitio periculosa est!"* Which, in translation, reads: "In law all definitions are perilous!"

Minnesota Law of Self-Defense

Source: David L. Ayers
         Attorney at Law
         301 Midwest Federal Building
         St. Paul, MN 55101
         (612) 224-4911

Mr. Ayers is a partner in the law firm of Ayers, Riehm and Wood. The firm is engaged in the general practice of law; however, Mr. Ayers' practice is restricted primarily to personal injury and criminal defense litigation. Mr. Ayers is a member of the Minnesota State and American Bar Associations, the Minnesota Trial Lawyers Association, the Association of Trial Lawyers of America, and the National Association of Criminal Defense Lawyers.

This section on the law of self-defense is based on the present statutory law and current judicial decisions by the Minnesota Supreme Court. The reader is cautioned that specific situations may give rise to issues that could result in legislative or judicial reform. Therefore, portions of the following discussion may be subject to modification and/or change.

Self-Defense Resulting in Death

The intentional taking of the life of another is justifiable and not a crime when the actor is resisting or preventing an offense which he *reasonably* believes exposes him, or another, to death or great bodily harm. Likewise, the intentional taking of the life of another is justifiable and not a crime when the actor is preventing the commission of a felony (e.g., burglary, robbery, or rape) *within* the actor's place of abode. However, in order for a killing to be justifiable for either of these reasons, three conditions must be met. First, the killing must have been done in the belief that it was necessary to avert death or great bodily harm. Second, the judgment of the actor as to the seriousness of the peril to which he or another was exposed must have been *reasonable* under the circumstances. Third, in light of the danger and alternative ways of avoiding the peril, the actor's decision to defend himself, or another, must have been *reasonable*.

Self-Defense Not Resulting in Death

The use of reasonable force is justifiable and not a crime when the actor is resisting, or aiding another who is resisting, an offense against the person (as distinguished from an offense against property). The use of *reasonable* force is justifiable as long as such an offense is being committed or the actor *reasonably* believes such an offense is being committed. It is lawful for a person who is being assaulted and who has *reasonable* grounds to believe that bodily injury is about to be inflicted upon him to stand his ground and defend himself from such attack, and in doing so he may use all force and means which he believes to be *reasonably* necessary to prevent the injury.

The kind and degree of force which a person may lawfully use in self-defense is limited by what a *reasonable* person in the same situation would believe to be necessary. Any use of force beyond that is regarded as excessive and unjustifiable.

Evidence: Burden of Proof

When the defense of self-defense is asserted, the individual has the burden of going forward with the evidence to support his claim of self-defense. However, the burden of proving the crime charged still remains with the prosecution. Further and most importantly, the prosecution is required to prove beyond a reasonable doubt that the individual did not act in self-defense.

Jury Question: Reasonableness

The word "reasonable" and its variations seem to permeate the entire law of self-defense. An individual who asserts this defense subjects the "reasonableness" of his actions to close scrutiny. Minnesota law does not set forth any guidelines for interpreting or defining the meaning of "reasonableness" in this context. Therefore, it is within the sound discretion of the jury or trier of fact to determine what is reasonable under the specific circumstances. If it is determined that the individual did not act reasonably, then the trier of fact may proceed to determine whether there is sufficient evidence to establish the elements of the crime charged.

Prior Warning/Threat

The law of Minnesota does not require an individual to issue a warning prior to using physical force, but one should not threaten to use physical force unless the individual is justified in using such force.

Reasonable Alternative—Retreat

One of the most difficult problems in the law of self-defense is determining whether the actor could have used another method to protect himself without resorting to the use of force. In this context, the axiom "the best defense is a good offense" has no application. The right to self-defense does not constitute a license to pursue. The legal excuse of self-defense is available only to those who act honestly and in good faith. This includes the duty to retreat or avoid the danger *if reasonably possible*. In the words of the Minnesota Supreme Court:

> Self-defense has not, by statute nor by judicial opinion, been distorted, by an unreasonable requirement of the duty to retreat, into self-destruction.

Mississippi Law of Self-Defense

Source: W. Glenn Watts
         Attorney at Law
         418 East Capitol St.
         P.O. Box 22783
         Jackson, MS 39205
         (601) 353-2641

Mr. Watts currently practices law in Jackson, Mississippi, where he is a member of the law firm of E. P. Lobrano, Jr., P.A. The firm has a general practice of law, with emphasis in the area of criminal law.

In the state of Mississippi, a person has the legal right to use deadly force to prevent certain criminal actions. The current law on self-defense is contained in the Mississippi Code of 1972, Title 97. The relevant section is Title 97-3-15, entitled "Justifiable Homicide."

A word of caution is in order in that this summary of the law in Mississippi does not take into consideration any and all of the factual variations, and legal subtleties relevant to a full understanding of this legal doctrine.

Generally, a person is justified in using deadly force in a variety of situations. The key words in our doctrine are "reasonable ground to apprehend," "good reason to believe," and "imminent danger." "Reasonable ground to apprehend" and "good reasons for believing" are used to indicate that a person must not only believe but have good reasons for believing based upon the overt acts of another that at the time of these actions he was in danger of suffering great bodily harm, or of being actually killed. These words indicate not necessarily real, but at least *apparently* real danger which is more than mere fear or apprehension. "Imminent danger" stresses the *present* nature of the threat to one's safety or life. While the danger must be in the present, it does not have to be immediate, or at the very moment of killing. A defendant does not have to wait until the very last moment, but may anticipate hostile acts and defend himself with the degree of force necessary to protect his life, property, and person.

"Great bodily harm" means "danger of loss of life or limb" or "enormous bodily harm." This has been interpreted to mean more than a fear of receiving blows sufficient to cause bruises, or have marks. While the mere fear of a simple assault would not justify the use of deadly force, if a person is assaulted in a violent manner by a much stronger and larger person, he can use deadly force to protect himself if he has good reasons for believing he is in danger of losing his life or suffering great bodily harm.

The key legal issue in using justifiable homicide as a defense to a charge of murder is whether a reasonable man under the circumstances would have believed that at the time he was in danger of suffering the loss of his life, or of great bodily harm at the hands of the deceased.

A person is justified not only in using deadly force to defend himself, but also to defend his spouse if he has good reason to believe that her life or chastity are in danger.

A person is also justified in using deadly force against unlawful entries into his home. And a person need not avoid danger by flight, provided he is at home, and neither the provoker or aggressor in the combat.

Generally, a person is justified in taking life in the defense of his habitation where it is actually or apparently necessary to do so in order to repel another person who attempts to enter in a forcible or violent manner for apparent purpose of committing a felony therein upon either person or property or of inflicting great bodily harm or of assaulting or offering personal violence to a person dwelling or being therein.

Ultimately, the question of whether a defendant acted in self-defense is one for the jury to determine. A defendant need not *prove* that he acted in justifiable self-defense, but only raise a reasonable doubt as to his being guilty of murder or manslaughter. Further, if the defendant or defendant's witnesses are the only eyewitnesses to a homicide, their version must be accepted as true, unless substantially contradicted in material particulars by a credible witness, or by physical facts or by facts of common knowledge.

Missouri Law of Self-Defense

Source: Steven K. Bogler
Attorney & Counselor at Law
c/o Bogler and York
818 Grand Avenue, Suite 700
Kansas City, MO 64106
(816) 842-9850

Steven K. Bogler is in the general private practice of law and is a 1977 graduate of the University of Missouri, Kansas City.

Missouri Statute Section 559.040 deals with those circumstances in which deadly physical force can be used by a non-aggressor to prevent certain criminal actions. Basically, this section states that one who is not an aggressor in an encounter is justified in using a reasonable amount of force against his adversary when he reasonably believes that he is in immediate danger of unlawful bodily harm from his adversary and that the use of such force is necessary to prevent his danger. Therefore, it would be reasonable to use non-deadly force against the adversary's non-deadly attack and reasonable to use deadly force against an *apparent* deadly attack (an attack threatening death or serious bodily harm), but it is never reasonable to use deadly force against non-deadly attacks.

Missouri law also states that an original aggressor can later assert the right of self-defense if he has retreated from his aggression and the aggressee is no longer in threat of attack.

The key word in this definition is the word *apparent*. One can only use deadly physical force if one reasonably believes that the other person is about to use unlawful deadly force (i.e. death or serious bodily harm). It is generally held that the party acts in lawful self-defense if he did not provoke the use of threat or force against himself by the aggressor; the party believed that he was in immediate danger of death or serious bodily harm; the party had reasonable cause for that belief; the party believed that it was necessary for him to act as he did to protect himself from such danger; and the party had a reasonable cause for that belief. Therefore, the aggressee is entitled to act upon appearances or what he had a reasonable cause to believe, based on the facts that presented themselves at the moment. The facts may reveal later that the aggressee was mistaken but the self-defense doctrine is based on the facts that were apparent to the aggressee.

Missouri law has held that the threat of physical violence, assault, or battery is the only provocation for using deadly force to stop an aggressor. Mere trespassing upon the property is not sufficient, although one may use force to prevent a trespass. One may not use deadly force unless the aggressor uses deadly force.

The Missouri Constitution recognizes every person's right to arm himself and go about his business and not avoid situations that might result in the eventual

212 Intruder in Your Home

use of deadly force. Missouri, however, has adopted the *retreat rule* by case law and that follows the doctrine that the aggressee is bound to retreat rather than take another's life, if he can do so safely, but if he cannot yield without endangering his own life he may use deadly force against his aggressor. Again, this rule may be modified by the appearances of the facts in question.

Missouri law allows you to use deadly force against apparent deadly force to protect those persons in your immediate surrounding or care including family, loved ones, or employees.

Missouri law has no requirement that you must warn someone before using deadly physical force. You can threaten to use such force only when you would be justified in using it, otherwise you become the aggressor and original trespasser has the self-defense doctrine working for him.

You can never use deadly physical force for the prevention of trespassing upon property alone. One can only use deadly physical force in the defense of a dwelling if parties are justified in using that force to protect themselves from an apparent threat of bodily injury or harm. I am often questioned by parties as to whether or not it is justifiable to kill someone who is breaking into their home. The common belief is that one is justified in shooting an intruder. However, if appearances are that the intruder is not about to use deadly force against the occupants then one would be guilty of manslaughter or murder. The same would hold true if a crime has been committed and the perpetrator is escaping. One cannot use deadly force to stop an intruder from escaping unless the party involved is still in danger of harm or has good reason to believe that the perpetrator is not withdrawing from the scene for good but rather is retreating and intends to come back and inflict continued harm on the party involved.

I personally believe that there is a lot of misinformation about the degree of force that can be used by a home owner to prevent an intruder from coming into the premises and I therefore recommend that guns not be kept in the home merely for the purpose of preventing intruders from entering same. However, I am sure my beliefs relating to the citizenry's ability to obtain and possess firearms is based directly on the number of senseless killings that occur each year due to one person's ability to obtain a firearm during a heated argument or a family squabble. My best advice would be that anyone who keeps a gun in the home for self-defense purposes should be properly trained in the use of this weapon and also understand his obligations to only use the weapon in the legal circumstances that warrant this use.

Montana Law of Self-Defense

Source: Jerrold L. Nye
         Nye Law Firm
         Suite 405, First Federal Bldg.
         2929 Third Avenue North
         Billings, MT 59101
         (406) 248-4816

Mr. Nye practices law in Billings, Montana, where he owns his own law firm. The firm primarily handles personal injury cases, but is also involved in general practice and criminal cases.

The use of self-defense in the protection of person and property is protected by statute in the State of Montana, Section 45-3-101, et. seq., Montana Statutes Annotated. The statutory protection is extensive and by the courts liberally construed. To date, for instance, the courts have not become embroiled in any debate as to whether a person has a duty to wound rather than kill an attacker. Neither have the courts gotten into an extensive debate as to the circumstances under which one must retreat or flee versus using force in self-protection. The prevailing attitude appears to be that if an individual unreasonably attacks or threatens to attack another person or unreasonably tries to break into an occupied structure, and he is met with deadly force and is killed or wounded, if the circumstances were such that self-defense would be justified and reasonable, then whatever happened to the attacker or perpetrator is justified.

By statute, one may use deadly force in defense of any occupied structure, not limited to a home, to prevent actual or attempted entry in a violent, riotous, or tumultuous manner if (a) the defender reasonably believes that deadly force is necessary to prevent assault upon or offer of personal violence to himself or another in the occupied structure, or (b) the defender believes the use of deadly force is necessary to prevent the commission of a forcible felony in the occupied structure.

A recent case involved an estranged husband who attempted to force entry through a locked door of the mobile home in which his wife was staying. Another occupant of the mobile home fired through the glass part of the door with a rifle, killing the husband. The action was held to be permissable self-defense.

Montana law does not require one to give a warning before using deadly force when it is legally justified, but I personally would strongly advise it if there is sufficient time and opportunity, unless the circumstances would only increase the danger to the defender. Nor is there any requirement that a person retreat before legally resorting to the use of such force. But again, if reasonable and possible, I would certainly recommend retreat. Otherwise, it could seem as if the defender is merely looking for an opportunity to injure or kill someone under color of law.

Montana law does not differentiate between the actual use of deadly force and a threat to use deadly force. You cannot threaten to use deadly force in a situation that does not actually permit you to use it. Montana takes the position that if you are permitted to use deadly force you may use it; otherwise, you may neither use it nor threaten to use it.

In Montana a defender may use deadly force to protect property only if it is necessary to prevent the commission of a forcible felony. This applies whether the property protected is within an occupied structure or not. A felony in Montana is $150 or more damage to or theft of property; so any threatened forcible taking of that amount of property or more would be sufficient grounds for the use of deadly force. However, within an occupied structure if the defender has reason to believe deadly force is necessary to protect his person, or that of another in the structure, we don't have to worry about property.

Nebraska Law of Self-Defense

Source: Peter J. Vaughn
         Attorney at Law
         500 Electric Building
         Omaha, NB 68102
         (402) 341-6000

Generally, under Nebraska law in order for a person to be justified or excused in using deadly force for the purpose of self-defense, the accused must not only have entertained the belief that his life was in danger or that he was in danger of suffering great bodily harm, but the belief must have been reasonable and in good faith. Use of deadly force in self-defense is grounded upon necessity; the right exists only in extremity where no other practical means exist to avoid death or great bodily harm apparent to the person resorting to it.

Two important terms to recognize are *necessary* and *reasonable*. The defense will not be allowed if there is no real or apparent necessity for the use of deadly force. Once the necessity for the use of such force has been established, the degree of force used is gauged by that which is reasonable or what a reasonable man would conclude in a sense of good faith.

The definition of deadly force as found in §1406 is:

"(3) Deadly force shall mean force which the actor uses with the purpose of causing or which he knows to create a substantial risk of causing death or serious bodily harm. Purposely firing a firearm in the direction of another person or at a vehicle in which another person is believed to be constitutes deadly force. A threat to cause death or serious bodily harm, by the production of a weapon or otherwise, so long as the actor's purpose is limited to creating an apprehension that he will use deadly force if necessary, shall not constitute deadly force."

The Nebraska Code provides under §28-1409, Use of Force for Self-Protection:

"(4) *The use of deadly force* shall *not be justifiable* under this section *unless the actor believes that such force is necessary to protect himself against death, serious bodily harm,* kidnapping or sexual intercourse compelled by force or threat, nor is it justifiable if:

(b) *The actor knows that he can avoid the necessity of using such force with complete safety by retreating or by surrendering possession of a thing to a person asserting a claim of right thereto* or by complying with a demand that he abstain from any action which he has no duty to take, (except that:)"

The statute does provide an exception to this section:

"(i) *The actor shall not be obliged to retreat from his dwelling or place of work, unless he was the initial aggressor or is assailed in his place of work by another person whose place of work the actor knows it to be.*"

For the protection of one's home, the use of deadly force is allowed under
§28-1411(1) (a):

"(a) To *prevent or terminate* an *unlawful entry* or other *trespass upon land* or
trespass against or the unlawful carrying away of tangible, movable property;
Provided, that such land or movable property is, or is believed by the actor to
be, in his possession or in the possession of another person for whose protection
he acts."

This statute does provide some limitations upon the use of force against a
trespasser.

"(3) The *use of force is justifiable under this section* only if *the actor first
requests the person against whom such force is used to desist from his interference with the property, unless* the actor believes that:

(a) Such *request would be useless;*

(b) *It would be dangerous to himself or another person* to make the request;
or

(c) *Substantial harm will be done to the physical condition of the property
which is sought to be protected before the request can effectively be made.*

(4) The *use of force to prevent or terminate a trespass is not justifiable under
this section if the actor knows that the exclusion of the trespasser will expose
him to substantial danger of serious bodily harm."*

The use of force for protection of home is made even more specific under
28-1411(6) (a):

"(6) The use of *deadly force is not justifiable under this section unless the
actor believes that:*

(a) The *person against whom the force is used is attempting to dispossess him
of dwelling otherwise than under a claim of right to its possession."*

There is record of two cases which discuss this issue. *Young v. State,* 74 Neb
346, 104 NW 867 (1905), where plaintiff was charged with murdering one
Samuel Winter. Winter and friend had been drinking and decided to go to
plaintiff's apartment, a box stall at the fairgrounds, to "do him up." Winter and
friend forced open the doors on the stall where accused was sleeping. Plaintiff
grabbed his revolver and shot in their direction, wounding one and killing the
other. In light of the facts, the Supreme Court held: "Where one is assailed in his
home (or domicile), or the home is attacked, he may use such means as are
necessary to repel the assailant from the house or prevent his forcible entry or
material injury to his home, even to the taking of life. But a homicide in such a
case would not be justifiable, unless the slayer, in the careful and proper use of
his faculties, bona fide believes, and has reasonable ground to believe, that the
killing is necessary to repel the assailant or prevent his forcible entry." *Id.,* at
869.

This same ruling was found in *Thompson v. State,* where the plaintiff was
charged with murder when he sought to keep his home from being broken into
by robbers. The court held: "The true rule undoubtedly is that a man may

defend his domicile, even to the extent of taking life, if it be actually or apparently necessary to do so in order to prevent the commission of any felony therein." *Id.*, at 63.

In 40 CJS, §110 at 976, the defense of property is discussed: "A person *may use such force as is reasonably necessary to protect his property,* real or *personal, in his possession,* and where the employment of such reasonable by him is resisted with means likely to produce death or to inflict great bodily harm on him, he is justified in killing."

The Nebraska Criminal Code provides protection of a third person under §28-1410.

"(1) Subject to the provisions of this section and of section 28-1414, *the use of force* upon or toward the person of another *is justifiable to protect a third person* when:

(a) The actor would be justified under section 28-1409 *in using such force to protect himself against the injury he believes to be threatened to the person whom he seeks to protect*;

(b) Under the *circumstances as the actor believes them to be,* the *person whom he seeks to protect would be justified in using such protective force*; and

(c) The actor *believes that his intervention is necessary for the protection of such other person.*"

Nebraska law does not allow one to threaten to use deadly force against someone unless that use is justifiable according to law. In *State v. Cowan*, the defendant threatened the use of deadly force against another who assaulted the defendant's friend. The defendant was not present during the altercation but upon arriving at the scene after the event happened, he got out of his car carrying a loaded .38 caliber revolver. The defendant pointed it at the assailant and told him not to leave the place, fired one shot in the air, and threatened to shoot off the assailant's kneecaps if he moved. The court held that nothing in the facts presented could possibly justify the actions of the defendant.

Nevada Law of Self-Defense

Source: Thomas M. Burns
         Attorney at Law
         2031 East Lake Mead Blvd.
         North Las Vegas, NV 89030
         (702) 649-4276

Nevada's law of self-defense is governed by Nevada Revised Statutes 200.120 through 200.200 which classifies self-defense as being one of the cases which fall within the category of justifiable homicide. Justifiable homicide, which is not punishable, also entails the defense of habitation, property, or person.

In order for the issue of justifiable homicide to arise, it is necessary that the deceased manifested intent or endeavored, by either surprise or violence, to commit a felony, or to enter the habitation of another for the purpose of assaulting or offering personal violence to any person inside. It is also a requisite that the defendant shows that his fear of the commission was reasonable and that the act was not one of revenge.

Justifiable homicide exists when a killing is committed which is in the defense of the defendant, his spouse, parents, children, or any person in his presence and there is reasonable basis for believing that the person slain planned to commit a felony and there is imminent danger that such a design would have been accomplished. The statutes further provide that justifiable homicide exists when one slays another while actually resisting an attempt by the slain to commit a felony upon the slayer or upon his home.

In Nevada, justifiable homicide also extends to situations where the slain has committed a felony and is fleeing from the premises and is within twenty miles of the premises. Since retreating could not possibly occur in this situation, the law is uncertain as to whether it is necessary for the third party to retreat. Possibly the requirement of retreat is not applicable to situations where one slays an assailant in defense of another or in defense of his dwelling.

However, in situations in which one kills another in defense of himself, the statutes require that the danger which exists be urgent and that in order to prevent receiving great bodily harm, the killing be absolutely necessary. It is also necessary that the person who was slain was the assailant or that the slayer had made a good faith endeavor to decline any further struggle before killing the slain. The questions which arise regarding self-defense are: (1) whether one who slays another who is merely an accomplice of an assailant will be able to assert the defense of self-defense; and (2) what is considered deadly force.

The law does not directly address either of these issues, so it is possible that one who slays another who is merely an accomplice, who did not actually attack the slayer, will not be able to claim self-defense. Since there is no definition of deadly force or statute authorizing the use of deadly force, a question could possibly arise regarding the reasonableness of the defendant's actions. However, this issue may be side-stepped by showing that the killing was absolutely necessary as required by the statutes.

Assuming the necessary requisites for self-defense or defense of another or defense of his dwelling are present, the person who is charged with homicide shall at the time of trial be fully acquitted and discharged of having committed the crime of murder.

New Hampshire Law of Self-Defense

Source: Martin J. Bender
         Attorney at Law
         RFD #1, Little Hill Road
         Webster, NH 03278
         (603) 648-2622

Mr. Bender practices law in Webster, New Hampshire. He has a general practice in a rural area with an emphasis on family law and criminal law.

The law in New Hampshire regarding the use of physical force in defense is found in the New Hampshire Criminal Code, specifically Chapter 627, "Justification." Force is divided into two categories—deadly force and non-deadly force. Before dealing with when force may be used, it will be helpful to explain what constitutes "deadly force."

"Deadly force" means any assault which a person commits with the intention (or which he or she knows creates a substantial risk) of causing death or serious injury. For example, firing a gun at someone is the use of deadly force.

"Nondeadly force" is an assault which doesn't constitute deadly force such as the use of one's fists. (As always, lawyers qualify such statements; Muhammad Ali's use of his fists may constitute deadly force.)

Under what circumstances can a person use deadly force in New Hampshire? If you reasonably believe that another person is about to use deadly force against you *or* a third person, you have the right to respond with deadly force. The right to use deadly force is extended against a burglar who is likely to use any "unlawful" force or against a person committing a kidnapping or a forcible sex offense.

Suppose a person threatens you with a knife on the street. Can you simply pull out a gun and shoot? New Hampshire law does *not* require that you give a warning first, but the law *does* require that you retreat if you can do so safely. Therefore, only when "your back is to the wall" can you justifiably use deadly force.

Suppose, however, that the assault takes place in your home. Unless you were the initial aggressor (that is, you started the fight) you no longer have the obligation to retreat. This rule applies regardless of whether you are defending yourself or a third person (who need not be related to you). Under New Hampshire law you have the right to use deadly force when the other person is "likely to use unlawful force in the commission of a felony against the actor . . ." However, unless you are positive that the other person is committing a felony (i.e., check with a lawyer before you shoot) it would be safer to respond with deadly force only when the other person is threatening deadly force.

As with most rules, though, there is an exception. What if the person who attacks you is not an intruder but a guest or even a cohabitant of your home? New Hampshire law is contrary to that of most states and reinstitutes the requirement that you retreat before using deadly force against your ex-friend.

How far can you go in defending your New Hampshire home and property? You have the right to use non-deadly force to the extent necessary to prevent a criminal trespass, but deadly force can *only* be used under the circumstances stated above; that is, if you or a third person are threatened with deadly force *or* if a burglar seems likely to use "unlawful" (not necessarily deadly) force against you. New Hampshire law also allows the use of deadly force if you reasonably believe it necessary to prevent arson by the trespasser. Therefore, there is no right to use deadly force against an intruder without first ascertaining the existence of a reasonable threat to your safety. It also follows that the use of a deadly trap (such as a spring gun) can never be justified.

As to a person unlawfully taking your property, the same rules apply. Use of non-deadly force is justified, but deadly force can only be used in defense of a person. The law places a higher value on lives than property.

What about the escaping burglar, rapist, etc.? The private citizen has a right to use non-deadly force to prevent an escape but may use deadly force only if the escapee is threatening the use of deadly force.

In summary, you have the right to use deadly force *only* when you or a third person is being threatened with what you reasonably believe to be deadly force or if you reasonably believe that you are being threatened with the use of force during the commission of a felony (such as burglary, rape, etc.). Anyone would be well advised to use deadly force only as a last resort. It would never be wise to shoot first and ask questions later. The consequences of harming an innocent person (or one whom you were not entitled to use deadly force against) are civil liability with resulting money damages as well as possible criminal liability.

New Jersey Law of Self-Defense

Source: Hubert Williams
         Attorney at Law
         Director, Newark Police Department
         31 Green St.
         Newark, NJ 07102
         (201) 733-6007

Mere breaking and entering, absent of any criminal intent, is trespass. The law is clear; there is no right to use deadly force against a trespasser. If an actor uses force to enter a home and has, at the time of entry, criminal intent, then his act would constitute the offense of burglary. Deadly force may be used against a burglar. However, there are caveats in the use of deadly force against a burglar. That is, if a burglar has committed a property offense and is in flight and there is no danger to the occupants, the cases tend to hold that the use of deadly force is excessive force.

The use of deadly force is justifiable if the actor reasonably believes that:

"The person against whom the force is used is attempting to commit or consummate arson, burglary, robbery or other criminal theft or property destruction; except that

(i) The person against whom it is employed has employed or threatened deadly force against or in the presence of the actor; or

(ii) The use of force other than deadly force to prevent the commission or the consummation of the crime would expose the actor or another in his presence to substantial danger of serious bodily harm." (NJSA 2C:3-2,4,5,6 and NJSA 2C:18-2,3.)

The use of deadly force is not justifiable under any of the provisions of the New Jersey Criminal Code as to the protection of personal property. However, if a person is protecting his property in his own home and conditions escalate to the point that his person becomes endangered to the extent of being killed or severely injured, then the use of deadly force is justified.

"A threat to cause death or serious bodily harm by the production of a weapon or otherwise, so long as the actor's purpose is limited to creating an apprehension that he will use deadly force if necessary, does not constitute deadly force."

The New Jersey Criminal Code is silent as to whether an actor must be warned before deadly force may be used against said actor. Therefore, the absence of mention of a warning gives rise to the conclusion that there is no warning requirement.

Deadly force may also be used to protect any other person in the dwelling of an owner. Further, there is no requirement that either the owner or the other person has an obligation to retreat. However, the owner may be required to retreat if the actor is also a member of the household.

New Mexico Law of Self-Defense

Source: Thomas E. Jones
Attorney at Law
Suite 1505
First National Bank Bldg., East
Albuquerque, NM 87108
(505) 265-5845

Thomas E. Jones has practiced law in Albuquerque, New Mexico for more than twenty years. While his chief interest is personal injury litigation and estate work, he has had a good deal of experience in the criminal law field and still practices criminal law when it is economically feasible to do so.

The law of self-defense in the State of New Mexico is contained in Chapter 30-2-7 N.M.S.A. 1978 Compilation, the case law decisions thereon, and, of recent, the Uniform Criminal Jury Instructions.

Simply stated, the law of justifiable homicide or self-defense states that the aggressor's life may be taken when necessary in the defense of a person's life, a person's family, or his property or in defending against any unlawful action directed against himself, his wife or family; and, in the lawful defense of himself or of another, when there is reasonable ground to believe that the design of the aggressor is to commit a felony or to do some great personal injury against the person or another, and there is imminent danger that the design will be accomplished; or when necessarily committed in attempting, by lawful ways and means, to apprehend any person for any felony committed in the defending person's presence, or in lawfully suppressing any riot, or in necessarily and lawfully keeping and preserving the peace.

The stating of the law is much easier than proving that one or more of those conditions existed at the time the alleged aggressor's life was taken. In order for the defending person to be allowed to raise the defense of self-defense, meaning that the court and/or jury will be allowed to consider this defense, evidence of certain elements must be present. The three elements that are essential are:

(1) That there was an appearance of immediate danger of death or great bodily harm to the defending person;

(2) That the defending person was in fact put in such fear; and,

(3) A reasonable person would have reacted in a similar manner. *State v. Martinez*, 95 N.M. 421, 622 P.2d 1041 (1981).

In essence, a defending person may act in self-defense if necessarily or reasonably defending against any unlawful action, felony or great personal injury. It is never considered reasonable to use deadly force against a non-deadly attack. A person may use a deadly force in self-defense only if defending himself against an attack which creates a substantial risk of death or great bodily harm.

The New Mexico courts have not had occasion to catalogue the unlawful actions which will allow a person to respond with deadly force. Accordingly, the type of felony which will allow a killing in self-defense has not been limited. Further, there has been no attempt to define the "unlawful act" which will allow the use of deadly force. But a deadly force cannot be used to repel a non-deadly threat. *Brown v. Martinez,* 68 N.M. 271, 361 P.2d 152 (1961). At the same time, the danger to the defending person need not be real but need only be apparent under the circumstances. The apparent harm must be imminent and under the circumstances must be such as to excite the fears of a reasonable person.

The New Mexico Law regards an attack upon a dwelling house, especially in the nighttime, as the equivalent to an assault on an individual's person. New Mexico has reaffirmed the proposition that a man's house is his castle. Wanton slaying is not countenanced, but the security of life is considered the most vital interest of society, and so the law of habitation and the resistance to the commission of a felony thereon gives the householder the right to kill the aggressor if such killing was necessary or apparently necessary to prevent or repel the felonious aggression. *State v. Couch,* 52 N.M. 127, 193 P.2d 405 (1946).

Of course, if the danger is no longer present, the defending party no longer has a right to use deadly force. *State v. Garcia,* 83 N.M. 51, 487 P.2d 1356 (1971). But, a householder is not obliged to retreat, even though that person may do so safely.

A person may use a deadly force in defending another person, but only if he reasonably believes the other person to be in danger of death or great bodily harm. The New Mexico law does not require the intervening person to know the actual facts but only to act as a reasonable person under the circumstances having reasonable grounds to believe an unlawful design exists in the aggressor. *Territory v. Baker,* 4 N.M. (Gild.) 236, 13 P.31 (1887). A defending person is not guilty of homicide if he unintentionally kills an innocent third person in self-defense.

It is apparent from the foregoing that the standard is one of necessity and reasonableness as to the use of deadly force. It is further apparent that the apprehension of the harm is necessarily subjective. This being the situation, despite what has been set forth above, prudence dictates that caution should always be exercised. What might be a life threatening experience to one person might be entirely different to another.

New York Law of Self-Defense

Source: Frank R. Webster
         Attorney at Law
         720 Crossroads Bldg.
         2 State St.
         Rochester, NY 14614
    Mr. Webster is a partner in the law firm of Webster & Chase, P.C. The firm is
involved in the practice of general law, and Mr. Webster personally specializes
in criminal law.

The following is a brief summary regarding the use of deadly physical force in defense of oneself, defense of another, and defense of property, all of which have been codified in the New York State Penal Law under the generic heading of "Justification." (See Article 35, Penal Law of the State of New York.) This summary is not intended to be a comprehensive or exhaustive commentary on the subject.

In the State of New York, the use of *deadly physical force* is justified where a person reasonably believes another person is using or is about to use deadly physical force. Deadly physical force is defined as "physical force which under the circumstances in which it is used is readily capable of causing death or other serious physical injury." (Penal Law §10.00[1].) Any person who uses deadly physical force in his personal defense must not only believe he is in danger, but he must in fact have reasonable ground for that belief. The question is not only "What did that person believe?", but also "What did he have a right to believe?"

Deadly physical force may also be used in a variety of situations, e.g. where the user reasonably believes that another person is committing or attempting to commit a kidnapping, forcible rape, forcible sodomy, or robbery. It may also be used where the user reasonably believes that another person is committing or attempting to commit a burglary of his dwelling and when he reasonably believes it to be necessary to prevent or terminate the commission or attempted commission of such burglary. [But see the final paragraph of this entry.]

In addition, deadly force is justified if a person reasonably believes such to be necessary to prevent or terminate the commission or attempted commission of arson. This applies only with regard to "premises," which includes buildings and any real property. Deadly force is not justified in defense of personal property alone.

Before using deadly force, there is a duty to retreat if the user knows he can retreat with complete safety to himself and others. However, there is *no* duty to retreat where the user is in his own dwelling and is not the initial aggressor. Nor is there a duty to retreat where the user reasonably believes a kidnapping, forcible rape, forcible sodomy, or robbery is being committed or where he reasonably believes it necessary to prevent or terminate a burglary of his dwelling. There is no requirement under New York State Law that you must warn someone before using deadly physical force.

Where there is a commission or attempted commission of the crimes specified earlier (i.e., kidnapping, etc.), once the menacing person has ceased the criminal activity or appears to be departing, the use of deadly physical force would not be justified. In the event of a burglary of a person's dwelling, the statute speaks of force necessary to prevent or terminate the commission or attempted commission of such burglary and, therefore, if it appears the menacing person has ceased his unlawful activity and is departing, then deadly physical force would not be justified.

The following are representative examples of the application of New York State Law. In the late night hours, an individual discovers a burglar in his home. The homeowner has a weapon, and he kills the intruder.

A shopkeeper's place of business has been burglarized several times. He sits in his shop during the nighttime hours with a shotgun. An intruder enters and is killed by the shopkeeper.

There is no criminal responsibility for the conduct in either case, since the intruder was, in fact, a burglar, although he had no weapon. Either killing is justified, assuming deadly physical force was necessary to terminate the burglary and the homeowner or shopkeeper believed himself to be in danger.

In the past five years, New York State police agencies have arrested fewer persons using deadly physical force under circumstances showing "justification." But if an arrest is made, the case is usually referred to a Grand Jury with no consequences to the person exercising his rights to defend himself.

The reader must remember that a burglary that justifies the use of deadly force is not breaking and entering a building or dwelling to commit larceny. Rather it is breaking and entering a building or dwelling to commit any heinous crimes such as kidnapping, rape, sodomy, robbery, or arson.

North Carolina Law of Self-Defense

Source: Eben Turner Rawls, III
         Attorney at Law
         720 E. 4th St.
         Charlotte, NC 28202
         (704) 373-6830

Mr. Rawls practices law in Charlotte, North Carolina, where he is an Assistant Public Defender for North Carolina's Twenty-sixth Judicial District.

The following discussion is only a brief synopsis and general outline of North Carolina law on self-defense, defense against sexual assault, defense of family, defense of property, and defense of habitation. It is not intended to cover all fact situations. Every case involving self-defense is different and often turns on what at first blush appears to be a minute or subtle fact. This is expecially true in cases involving self-defense, because so much turns on what was reasonably in the mind of the person claiming self-defense or defense of habitation.

The State of North Carolina recognizes the legal doctrine of self-defense. A person, therefore, may sometimes not be guilty of a crime (s)he has been charged with even if (s)he did the act charged and knew what (s)he was doing. In North Carolina self-defense, defense from sexual assault, defense of family, defense of persons other than family, and defense of habitation may, under certain circumstances, justify and excuse assault, assault with deadly force, and homicide.

Generally, a person may use force against another when the amount of force (s)he uses appears reasonably necessary to protect himself or herself from another person's assault, even when the other person's assault is not deadly. In *State of North Carolina v. Anderson,* 230 N.C. 54, (1949), then North Carolina Supreme Court Justice (later Senator) Sam Ervin summarized the North Carolina law of self-defense:

> The law does not compel any man to submit in meekness to indignities or violence to his person merely because such indignities or violence stop short of threatening him with death or great bodily harm. If one is without fault in provoking, or engaging in, or continuing a difficulty with another, he is privileged by the law of self-defense to use such force against the other as is actually or reasonably necessary under the circumstances to protect himself from bodily injury *or offensive contact* at the hands of the other, even though he is not thereby put in actual or apparent danger of death or great bodily harm (emphasis added).

Thus, in North Carolina a person has the right to protect himself or herself from actual or apparent bodily injury and actual or apparent offensive physical contact, even though (s)he were not put in actual or apparent danger of death or great bodily harm. In order to exercise the right of self-defense, however, the law of North Carolina requires several prerequisites. The person exercising self-defense cannot use more force than appears reasonably necessary to repel an assault, that is, the force used cannot be excessive. Usually one cannot use a gun to repel an attack with bare hands, but in determining whether force is excessive, judges and juries consider all the circumstances including sex, size, age, and strength of the assailant as compared to the person exercising self-defense as well as the fierceness of the assault, whether or not the assailant possessed or appeared to possess a weapon, and the reputation of the assailant for danger and violence. The person exercising self-defense cannot provoke or initiate the altercation, that is, (s)he cannot be the aggressor. In North Carolina, words may be enough to initiate or provoke an altercation.

A person may use deadly force and kill an assailant in self-defense if (s)he is without fault in bringing on the altercation and if it is necessary or appears necessary to kill in order to prevent death or great bodily harm to himself or herself. The same restrictions mentioned earlier apply to the use of deadly force in self-defense. A person cannot generally claim self-defense if (s)he provoked the attack unless, after (s)he initiated an altercation, (s)he withdraws and lets the other person know that (s)he is withdrawing. Thus, even if a person initiates a fight, self-defense may be available if the original aggressor attempts to abandon the fight and gives the other person or persons notice that (s)he is abandoning. If the other person or persons thereafter continue the affray, one is privileged to use deadly force if threatened or apparently threatened with death or great bodily harm.

Some North Carolina cases hold that a person is required to retreat as far as (s)he can before resorting to deadly force to repel an attack. However, a person is not required to retreat if an attack is made on his or her own premises, or if the attack is made suddenly with intent to kill, or if the person is a law enforcement officer in the lawful performance of his or her duty. Generally, if a non-felonious assault is made upon a person, (s)he is required to retreat but may repel "force by force and give blow for blow" and after "retreating to the wall," may use deadly force if necessary in self-defense. When using deadly force to repel an assault, a person cannot use excessive force. As mentioned earlier, in determining whether deadly force is excessive, North Carolina courts consider all of the circumstances of the altercation.

North Carolina has no requirement that a warning must be given prior to using deadly force in self-defense. A warning can be a two-edged sword: It may frighten an assailant, but at the same time it may also escalate the assailant's use of deadly force.

In North Carolina a person may act in self-defense and even use deadly force to defend himself or herself from a sexual assault. Sexual assaults include rape, attempted rape, any forcible crime against nature, or attempted forcible crime against nature. Once again there are several important restrictions. It must appear to the person and (s)he must believe it necessary to use deadly force or kill in order to save oneself from or prevent a sexual assault. Consistent with the other rules of self-defense, the person claiming defense from a sexual assault cannot be the aggressor. This means that a person who voluntarily and without provocation enters an encounter is considered the aggressor unless thereafter (s)he attempts to abandon the encounter and gives notice that (s) he is doing so. Finally, one cannot use excessive force in repelling a sexual assault. Force is considered excessive if it is more force than reasonably appears necessary to repel the sexual assault.

A person may use deadly force and kill in the defense of his or her family when it reasonably appears to be necessary to prevent the infliction of death or great bodily harm to one or more members of his or her family. The right of the person to defend the family member is no less than the right of that family member to defend himself. When using deadly force that results in death, it is not required that the killing must have in fact been necessary, only that the person exercising defense of family, under the circumstances, reasonably believed that deadly force was necessary to save a family member from death or great bodily harm. The restrictions mentioned earlier prescribing excessive force apply. Moreover, defense of a family member is a legal excuse or justification only if the person claiming the defense was not the aggressor. If (s)he enters the fight for any purpose other than the lawful one of defending a family member, (s)he is considered the aggressor unless (s)he thereafter attempted to abandon the affray and gave notice that (s)he was doing so.

One may generally use force to protect one's own property or property of someone (s)he is acting for, but (s)he may never use more force than the minimum amount that is reasonably necessary to protect the property. One may not use deadly force to protect personal property unless one's life appears to be in danger.

One may use deadly force in defense of habitation only to prevent a forcible entry into the habitation under such circumstances that the occupant reasonably apprehends death or great bodily harm to himself or other occupants at the hands of the intruder/assailant OR believes the intruder/assailant intends to commit a felony. Felonies include burglary, larceny, rape, kidnapping, robbery, sexual offenses, and assaults with a deadly weapon inflicting serious injury.

Under North Carolina case law, once entry is gained by the assailant, the usual rules of self-defense or defense of family replace the rules governing defense of habitation with the exception that there is no duty to retreat. The rule of thumb in North Carolina has been that at least part of the intruder's body must be inside the habitation before the deadly force can be used. However, there is case-law authority that the property holder in exercising the right of defense of habitation may open the door of the house to shoot the assailant outside if apparently or actually necessary for self-protection or protection of family. The law does not require the householder to wait until the intruder attacks if there is real or apparent danger to oneself or family. Once again, the householder will not be excused if (s)he employs excessive force, whether in defending one's habitation or person.

The law in North Carolina does not directly address the question of using deadly force if the assailant/intruder were leaving after committing a felony such as rape or robbery. It would appear, however, that if the assailant were out of the house in the yard and there were no longer imminent danger of death or great bodily harm, self-defense or defense of habitation would no longer be available, and one would not be justified in using deadly force to prevent escape. If, however, the intruder/assailant remained in close proximity and there was a reasonable apprehension of death or great bodily harm or the commission of another felony, one would be justified in the use of deadly force. One's claim of self-defense would be weakened or strengthened by the intruder's distance away from the dwelling or business and the location of the wounds on the intruder's body. For example, a gunshot wound or wounds in the intruder's back several hundred yards away from one's house, without any other evidence, would not be a strong defense.

Anytime one uses deadly force, especially a firearm, extreme care should be exercised. Often unforeseen consequences result from the careless or reckless use of firearms. In North Carolina, district attorneys usually will not prosecute clear cases of self-defense where the evidence is overwhelming and the facts are undisputed. Generally, however, the facts are disputed or at least are not clear and district attorneys will often let judges and juries decide whether one was justified in the use of deadly force in his or her defense. This is especially true in cases where homicide resulted from the use of deadly force. This is sometimes a cop out, because the district attorney will be able to "pass the buck" at re-election time by saying it was the judge or jury that decided the case. This means that criminal charges will be brought against the person claiming self-defense or defense of habitation and he or she must stand trial. In a criminal trial there is always some uncertainty as to what a jury will or will not do. Moreover, one is subjected to the not inconsiderable monetary and psychological pressures of being a criminal defendant.

North Dakota Law of Self-Defense

Source: Thomas J. Aljets
         Attorney at Law
         1405 Main St.
         Carrington, ND 58421
         (701) 652-3280

Mr. Aljets currently practices law in Carrington, North Dakota, where he is a member of the law firm of Heinley & Aljets. He is a former assistant professor of law at the University of North Dakota and is currently the group reporter for the Speedy Trial Planning Group for the District of North Dakota.

Under certain circumstances a person in North Dakota is justified in using force upon another person to defend himself, another person, a premises, or property. The statutory law on self-defense, defense of others, and defense of premises and property is set forth in Chapter 12.1-05 of the North Dakota Century Code.

A person is justified in using force upon another person to defend himself against imminent unlawful bodily injury, sexual assault, or detention, unless he is the initial aggressor, has intentionally provoked the activity, or has entered into mutual combat. The primary question to be resolved is whether the person using the force did so in good faith believing himself to be in such imminent danger of bodily injury, sexual assault, or detention that he was justified in using force to protect himself.

A person is justified in using force to protect another person if the person defended would be justified in defending himself.

Force may also be used to terminate an unlawful entry or other trespass in or upon premises or to prevent an unlawful carrying away or damaging of property. The person contemplating the use of force to protect premises or property must first request the violator to desist from the interference. Such request is not necessary, however, if the request would be useless or dangerous or if substantial damage would be done to the property before the request could be made. Note that this premises or property need not be owned by the person seeking to use force against the violator.

The force that may be used in each of these circumstances is limited to that force which is necessary and appropriate. Force which creates a substantial risk of causing death or serious bodily injury (referred to as deadly force) may be used in very limited situations. Deadly force may be used in self-defense or in defense of others to protect against death, serious bodily injury, or the commission of a felony involving violence. Even in these situations, deadly force is to be avoided if retreat is an alternative, except that one is never required to retreat from his dwelling or place of work. One may also use deadly force to prevent commission of arson, burglary, robbery, or a felony involving violence in his dwelling or place of work if use of some lesser force would expose anyone to substantial danger of serious bodily injury.

One can see from this very abbreviated discussion of North Dakota's statutory law that even minimal interference with your person or property justifies the use of some force. The key question is generally whether the force used was greater than the circumstances warranted. Therefore, although you might use force to stop someone from breaking into your home, this force cannot be such force as creates a substantial risk of causing death or serious bodily injury unless some further act occurs; which act would lead to death or serious bodily injury to yourself or another if not stopped or which act amounts to commission of a felony involving violence.

If you are otherwise justified in using deadly force against another, no warning is required to be given before using such deadly force, nor are you required to retreat within your home or from your place of work. Further, you are allowed to use deadly force to protect others within your home against death, serious bodily injury, or the commission of a felony involving violence.

Since the use of deadly force is limited to necessary protection from death, serious bodily injury, or the commission of a felony involving violence, deadly force is not justified to protect personal property when life 'or limb is not endangered, nor is deadly force justified to stop a violator from escaping after commission of an act which would in itself justify deadly force. Deadly force is for protection only.

Deadly force consists of an act which creates risk of causing death or serious bodily injury. The mere threat of the use of deadly force does not constitute deadly force, and, therefore, one may threaten to use deadly force even in those situations where the use of deadly force is not justified.

Two warnings are issued to anyone in the State of North Dakota who would force in self-defense, the defense of others, or the defense of premises or property:

(1) If, while justified in using force against another, you recklessly or negligently injure an innocent bystander, you will find yourself criminally liable. The law does not provide justification when a third party is injured.

(2) The legal justifications of self-defense, defense of others, and defense of premises or property do not impair possible civil actions. If you injure or kill another in defense, you might find yourself civilly liable, even though not criminally liable.

Ohio Law of Self-Defense

Source: Matthew C. Giannini
          Attorney at Law
          204 Stambaugh Bldg.
          Youngstown, OH 44503
          (216) 744-5151

Mr. Giannini has a general practice of law in Youngstown, Ohio. He is also an assistant professor of forensic medicine at Northeastern Ohio University College of Medicine.

The law in Ohio relative to the self-defense of an individual's habitation is solely based upon common law. The right of the occupant of the habitation to use deadly force to repel the assailant is limited to those circumstances involving either an intent to perpetrate a felony or to inflict on the occupants a personal injury resulting in loss of life or great bodily harm. In addition, the threat of danger must be imminent and probable. This theory is applicable when preventing an intrusion as well as when attempting to terminate an intrusion which has actually occurred.

Ohio has adopted the "true man" doctrine which in effect holds that an individual does not have to retreat from the assailant even if a path of retreat exists. This theory is applicable when the threat of assault is felonious and produces imminent danger of death or great bodily harm. Where the threat of death or great bodily harm is compelling and imminent, the requirement to give a warning is waived. In both situations the key element is that the threat of loss of life or great bodily harm must be apparent or real. The mere entrance into the habitation by an assailant does not obviate the need of a warning.

The threat of actual or apparent death or great bodily harm does not have to be directed against the actual individual who subsequently repels the initial threat. In fact, the individuals may combine their efforts to repel the threat. (*Goins v. State*, 46 OS 457, 21 NE 476). In addition, persons of close relationship have a right to use force in certain situations to repel the acts of the aggressor in defending the habitation.

The right to threaten deadly force is dependent upon the circumstances present at the particular time. If great bodily harm or death is real or apparent, then the right of the individual to make a reciprocal threat is authorized and permitted. If, however, the individual is not being threatened in any of the aforementioned ways, he may not make any provocative remarks. If the individual makes any life-threatening statements, then the individual can be viewed as the aggressor and therefore become totally responsible if any violence should subsequently result (*State v. Powell*, 10 Dec Rep 38).

Presently, the law is devoid in the area concerning an individual's right to use deadly force once the perpetrator has completed his felonious action. Based upon the definition of self-defense, however, the individual has a right to use reciprocal force only when there is an imminent and apparent threat of death or great bodily harm. Once the threat has ceased it would therefore be logical to conclude that the individual is then precluded from pursuing reciprocal action.

Presently, Ohio authorizes the use of deadly force only in defending an individual's habitation. The right to use force in the defense of personal property is not authorized unless the property is attached to the person.

An individual who keeps a firearm within the confines of his home may afford himself the necessary protection he may need in certain situations; however, he may use the weapon at a time when the situation does not warrant such action with the result being homicide instead of self-defense.

Oklahoma Law of Self-Defense

Source: Richard M. Healy
         Attorney at Law
         Triad Center, Suite 310
         501 N.W. Expressway
         Oklahoma City, OK 73118

When Oklahoma became a state, thus necessitating the enactment of statutes and codes, the state borrowed heavily from the states abutting it, predominantly Kansas, to assist in enacting the Oklahoma Statutes. In that regard, the Oklahoma Statutes maintained a certain "Wild West" ambiance about them. The applicable statute is Title 21 Oklahoma Statutes, §643, which reads in pertinent part:

> To use or attempt to offer to use force or violence upon or toward the person of another is not unlawful in the following cases:
>
> When necessarily committed by any person in arresting one who has committed any felony, and delivering him to a public officer competent to receive him in custody.
>
> When committed either by the party about to be injured, or by any other person in his aid or defense, in preventing or attempting to prevent an offense against his person or any trespass or other unlawful interference with real or personal property in his lawful possession; provided that the force or violence used is not more than sufficient to prevent such offense.

One may, therefore, utilize such force as is necessary, under the circumstances, to defend himself. The reasonableness and necessity of the force used is a question for the trier of fact, the jury. As a practical matter, the district attorney is unlikely to bring criminal charges against a truly innocent victim of an attack who gains the advantage by force reasonably calculated to terminate the difficulty.

Once the attacker has ceased his assault, the victim may not continue using force upon the attacker and must, certainly, cease utilizing whatever weapon was reasonable and necessary to terminate the difficulty. One may not continue in the affray, continue beating the attacker, and then invoke the claim of self-defense.

By implication Oklahoma law would permit the use of deadly force if the "victim" reasonably believed that his own life or safety was in immediate danger. Each case will, of course, stand on its own facts and it will be up to a jury, if charges are brought, to determine whether or not the "victim" acted reasonably under all circumstances.

If the person assaulted is in a place where he has a right to be and the danger is not of his own seeking or willfully provoked by him, he is not required to flee from it, but may resist it with adequate and reasonable force until he is safe. Bear in mind that the person assaulted must: A. Be in a place where he has the right to be; and, B. He cannot be the instigator of the assault. Thus if a person is on land belonging to another or in a restaurant or tavern where he has been previously asked to leave by the innkeeper, he is not in a place where he has a right to be. Secondly, the assaulted person must be innocent of provoking the incident before he can shield himself legally with the claim of self-defense.

There is no duty to retreat if one is threatened with bodily harm or assaulted. Even if one is trespassing he has a right of self-defense within reasonable bounds to repel a dangerous, unlawful attack after he has availed himself of every reasonable means of retreat. Therefore, even if the attack is unlawful a trespasser, under Oklahoma law, does have a duty to retreat. Generally, any duty to retreat under Oklahoma law seems to be confined to a trespasser.

Under Oklahoma law one may go to the defense of another and, in an appropriate situation, can use deadly force. However, the right to defend the victim is coexistant with the victim's right of self-defense. Thus if the victim was the aggressor or lacked the right to use force, deadly or otherwise, on the putative aggressor, the person coming to the victim's aid would therefore lack the right to use force. Legally, the defender stands in the same shoes as the victim. Even where the defender is unaware that the victim was in actuality the first aggressor, he may still be held liable and may not be permitted to shield himself with the claim of self-defense.

A person may use such force as is reasonable and necessary under the circumstances to protect his property, both personal and real. Whether or not one would be entitled to use deadly force to protect property would depend upon the circumstances. One may be justified in using deadly force against a purse snatcher who is taking it off the person carrying the purse whereas it may not be justified in a case where the purse is being stolen from a chair in a restaurant.

Finally, under Oklahoma law one may use deadly force "in arresting one who has committed any felony, and delivering him to a public officer competent to receive him in custody." Therefore in a situation where a rape, burglary, or robbery is being attempted, the law would probably justify the use of deadly force. Even where the crimes have been completed, deadly force may be legal in attempting to apprehend or stop the fleeing felon.

Oregon Law of Self-Defense

Source: Charles L. Best
   Deputy District Attorney
   600 County Court House
   Portland, OR 97204

Mr. Best is a Senior Deputy District Attorney for Multnomah County where he is assigned to the Major Violator Unit.

The law of self-defense in Oregon is codified in Oregon Revised Statutes 161.209 through 161.255. Generally, a person is justified in using physical force upon another person when defending himself or a third person from what he reasonably believes to be the use or imminent use of unlawful physical force. He may use that degree of force which he reasonably believes to be necessary to protect himself or a third person (ORS 161.209).

The statute reflects the common law rule that one may meet force with equal force when defending against the use of unlawful physical force. The amount of force used in defense of persons would be evaluated under a reasonable person standard. While the statute does not require use of unlawful physical force first before one is justified in using force in defense, it does require that the defender reasonably believe the use of unlawful force is imminent.

ORS 161.215 specifically limits the use of physical force in defense of a person. It provides that a person is not justified in using physical force on another person if:

1. He provokes another person into using unlawful physical force and has the intent to cause physical injury or death to that person.

2. He is the initial aggressor, except when as the initial aggressor, he withdraws from the encounter and effectively communicates his intent to do so, but the other person continues or threatens to continue the use of unlawful force.

3. The physical force involved is the product of a combat by agreement (ORS 161.215).

The use of deadly physical force in defense of oneself or a third person is limited to situations in which a person reasonably believes that the other person is:

1. Committing or attempting to commit a felony in which force is used or imminently threatened.

2. Committing or attempting to commit a burglary in a dwelling.

3. Using or about to use unlawful deadly physical force against a person.

Oregon law clearly allows the occupant of a dwelling or motel room to use deadly force against a person committing a burglary. The statute also says deadly force may be used against a person attempting to commit a burglary. Caution should be observed here, as what constitutes an attempted burglary is obviously subject to factual interpretation. One would not be able to shoot a trespasser in a yard nor someone who had already left the residence after completing the crime. It also appears that a store owner being robbed at gun point could shoot to kill the robber even if only an implied threat to use the gun were present.

Oregon law is silent on whether or not a person must retreat before using force or deadly physical force. However, it should be noted that he statutes require a "reasonable belief" that the force is necessary.

Likewise there is no specific duty to warn before using physical force to defend people or a residence. This too would be tempered by the "reasonable belief" standard.

When defending premises such as a business, one is justified in using physical force when and to the extent that it is reasonably believed necessary to prevent or terminate a criminal trespass. A person may only use deadly physical force in defense of nonresidential premises when he reasonably believes it necessary to prevent the commission of an arson or a felony by force and violence by the trespasser. This again clearly justifies the use of deadly physical force in an armed robbery or a similar situation. In the crime of arson, a number of questions could arise, however. If an arsonist was about to throw a fire-bomb, would you have to yell at the suspect or could you shoot first and ask questions later? This situation could pose a difficult question as to what would constitute "reasonable belief" about what action was necessary.

Physical force is also available in defense of personal property when and to the extent a person believes it necessary to prevent or terminate the commission or attempted commission of theft or criminal mischief of property. The use of deadly physical force is specifically excluded by statute in defense of personal property. This is obviously subject to the exceptions already mentioned where deadly physical force is justified and personal property is the object of a robbery, burglary, etc.

When confronted with preventing an escape or making an arrest, a private citizen may only use the amount of physical force reasonably believed necessary to make an arrest or prevent an escape. The use of deadly physical force is specifically ruled out in preventing an escape or making an arrest unless a person reasonably believes it is necessary to defend himself or a third person from what he reasonably believes to be the use or imminent use of deadly physical force. Therefore, deadly physical force can only be used in defense of a person and not in the apprehension of the suspect.

A person may be authorized to use physical force by a peace officer when assisting the officer in making an arrest or preventing an escape. The use of force is limited to that amount of force a person reasonably believes necessary to carry out the officer's directions. A person may even be authorized to use deadly force by a peace officer to assist in making an arrest or preventing an escape. However, this is limited solely to situations where the officer has directed a person to use deadly force or the person reasonably believes it necessary to protect himself or others from the imminent use of deadly physical force. When a person is using deadly physical force at the direction of a peace officer, this is justified unless the person knows the peace officer himself is not authorized to use such force under the circumstances. Here, there is a change from the reasonable belief standard; unless a person actually knows that the officer is not authorized to use deadly force, a person's use of deadly physical force at a peace officer's direction is justified.

Finally, there is nothing in Oregon statutes or common law that prevents a person from threatening an aggressor with physical force or deadly physical force in situations where the use of that force would not be justified.

Pennsylvania Law of Self-Defense

Source: William J. Fulton
         Attorney at Law
         407 N. Front St.
         Harrisburg, PA 17108
         (717) 238-7151

Mr. Fulton received his B.A. degree from Gettysburg College in 1974. He graduated from the University of Pittsburgh School of Law in 1977 and was admitted to practice before the State Supreme Court that same year. Formerly an assistant public defender for Dauphin County, Mr. Fulton is now an associate of the firm of Graf, Knupp & Andrews.

At common law, one confronted with the imminent threat of deadly force was justified in defending himself in a like manner. Pennsylvania courts have held that the general principles of justification enacted by the legislature are essentially "a codification of the common law of self-defense."[1] An analysis of the law in regard to the use of deadly force against home intrusion is, therefore, dependent upon statutory enactments and judicial interpretations. For the most part, the applicable law is found in 18 Pa.C.S.A. §502 through §507.

Under Pennsylvania law it is unclear whether deadly force can be employed to stop someone from breaking into a dwelling house. The resort to deadly force is clearly justified, however, where entry has been effected by the intruder. A 1980 amendment to 18 Pa.C.S.A. §507, popularly known in the media as the "Homeowner's Right to Shoot the Intruder" Act, provides that:

(i) The use of deadly force is justifiable under this section if: (A) there has been an entry into the actor's dwelling; (B) the actor neither believes nor has reason to believe that the entry is lawful; and (C) the actor neither believes nor has reason to believe that the force would be adequate to terminate the entry.

(ii) If the conditions of justification provided in subparagraph (i) have not been met, the use of deadly force is not justifiable under this section unless the actor believes that: (A) the person against whom the force is used is attempting to disposses him of his dwelling otherwise than under a claim of right to its possession; or (B) such force is necessary to prevent the commission of a felony in the dwelling. 18 Pa.C.S.A. §507(c) (4) (i) *et seq.*

Arguably, under the latter subsection, a homeowner need not wait until a felonious entry has been effected before turning to lethal force. If, however, his belief that a felony was about to occur later proves to have been unreasonable under the circumstances, then the resident who uses pre-emptive deadly force may face criminal responsibility for his hasty action.

The question was formerly controlled by 19 Pa.C.S.A. §505 which required a homeowner to reasonably believe that his life was in danger before resorting to deadly force. One commentator has suggested that the recent amendment extends the right to use deadly force to the protection of property in the home in addition to the protection of life. The same writer notes that accurate application and interpretation of the new statute will have to await court decisions.[2]

Statutory law, in particular the section quoted above, makes no provision requiring one to give a warning prior to using deadly force against an intruder. However, other statutes and appellate cases impose such a duty in other factual contexts. 18 Pa.C.S.A. §507(c) (1), which relates to the use of nondeadly force to prevent interference with property, provides that a request to desist from interference must first be made except where the request to do so would be useless or dangerous. Failure to issue a warning, where such action would be a reasonable alternative to using deadly force, has been held to legally vitiate a subsequent claim of self-defense.[3] Given the current lack of authority interpreting the 1980 amendment regarding home intruders, it is practical to advise Pennsylvania homeowners to first issue a warning before shooting a burglar if such warning would provide a safe and reasonable alternative to the immediate resort to deadly force.

Under both common and statutory law, there is no duty to retreat when inside one's home or place of business. 18 Pa.C.S.A. §505(b) (2) (ii) (A). There is a duty to retreat, however, where one is attacked by a co-occupant and safe retreat is possible. The yard of a house is not part of the dwelling house for the purpose of self-defense.[4]

One may use deadly force to protect others in the home provided that the applicable prerequisites to valid self-defense are present. The issue is controlled by 18 Pa.C.S.A. §506. If the third person could lawfully avail himself of deadly force in self-protection, then one coming to that person's aid has the same rights and options.

If one is not entitled to use deadly force, then he cannot threaten to use it either. To do so may constitute the crime of Assault by Physical Menace: A person is guilty of assault if he attempts by physical menace to put another in fear of imminent serious bodily injury. 18 Pa.C.S.A. §2701(a) (3).

In Pennsylvania, a private citizen is not entitled to use deadly force to detain or capture a fleeing felon. Deadly force is generally a legally available alternative where one believes it necessary to prevent death or serious bodily injury to himself or another. If the crime has been completed and the homeowner/victim is no longer in danger, then he should not resort to deadly force to prevent the criminal's escape. Individual facts and circumstances would play heavily in any given analysis. In Harrisburg, Pennsylvania, recently, a storekeeper shot an armed robber in the back as the felon fled down the street. The storekeeper was never criminally charged. On the other hand, a jury in Allegheny County, Pennsylvania, recently convicted a physician of voluntary manslaughter after he shot a youthful burglar as he fled through a side yard following a nighttime intrusion into his home. In many instances, the decision of whether to prosecute in such a case is delicately vested in the discretion of the police and district attorney.

As noted earlier, the recent amendment to the Pennsylvania law of justification vis-à-vis self-defense appears to extend the right to use deadly force to protection of property in the home.

The law of self-defense as it applies to the defense of the home must be understood in light of the general rules of justification. Like most other jurisdictions, Pennsylvania requires that the individual who chooses to resort to deadly force cannot be at fault in provoking or continuing a given confrontation. In addition, it is generally required that one must believe or have reason to believe that there is a bona fide threat of death or serious bodily injury before employing deadly force. While the legislature has chosen to relax the latter requirement in the home intruder situation, care should be exercised to avoid the use of lethal force in situations not reasonably requiring it. This is especially true in Pennsylvania, where the courts have not had opportunity to apply and interpret the law which will most often control the issue of whether a homeowner was within his rights to confront an intruder with deadly force.

1. *Commonwealth v. Walley,* 466 Pa. 363, 353 A.2d 396 (1976).
2. Jarvis, *Pennsylvania Crimes Code and Criminal Law,* George T. Bisel Co., Phila. 1981 Supplement, p. 39.
3. *Commonwealth v. Black,* 474 Pa. 74, 376 A.2d 627 (1977).
4. *Commonwealth v. Marcocelli,* 27 Chester Co. L.R. 8 (1978).

Rhode Island Law of Self-Defense

Source: William J. Conley
Assistant Public Defender
Providence County Courthouse
Providence, RI 02903

In the state of Rhode Island, the use of deadly force against an intruder in a person's home is governed by R.I.G.L. §11-8-8 which states: "In the event that any person shall die or shall sustain a personal injury in any way or for any cause while in the commission of any criminal offense enumerated in §§11-8-2 through 11-8-6, inclusive, it shall be presumed as a matter of law in any civil or criminal proceeding, that the owner, tenant or occupier of the place wherein the offense was committed, acted in self-defense at the time and in the place where the death of the person or the injury to the person was inflicted, caused, or sustained; provided, however, that said presumption shall be rebuttable."

The mentioned statutes prohibit the breaking and entering of a dwelling (11-8-2); the breaking and entering of a dwelling while possessing instruments for setting fires (11-8-2.1); entering a building or ship with the intent to commit murder, sexual assault, robbery or larceny (11-8-4); breaking and entering any building not included in R.I.G.L. (11-8-2 through 11-8-4) with the intent to commit any felony or misdemeanor (11-8-5); breaking and entering a business place, public building, or ship in the daytime (11-8-5.1); and breaking and entering, or entering during the nighttime any enclosure with the intent to steal poultry (11-8-6).

Consequently, if any person is charged with a criminal homicide and produces some evidence that he or she acted in self-defense pursuant to R.I.G.L. 11-8-8, then the prosecution must prove behind a reasonable doubt that the intruder was not committing one of the crimes enumerated in R.I.G.L. 11-8-2 through 11-8-6.

There is no requirement under the statute to retreat as far as possible inside a home before using deadly force, nor is there any requirement to give a warning, nor does there appear to be any criminal responsibility for a mere threat to use deadly force, even if one is not entitled to actually use such force.

In these situations where the facts do not fall within R.I.G.L. 11-8-8, the Rhode Island Supreme Court has noted that other jurisdictions have not required a person to retreat from attack when it occurs within the occupant's dwelling, but it has expressly deferred any consideration of such a situation until such time it is squarely confronted with the issue (*State v. Guillemet*, 430 A2d 1066 [1981]).

Otherwise, Rhode Island law does require one who is assaulted outside of his dwelling to retreat before employing deadly force in his own defense if an avenue of escape is available, but one may stand his ground and not retreat to employ less than deadly force. Deadly force may be used in self-defense outside of the home when there is a reasonable apprehension of death or great bodily harm and there is no avenue of escape available (*State v. Guillemet, supra*).

A third party comes to the aid and defense of another at his own peril and has only the same self-defense rights as the person whom he or she seeks to aid. The "rescuing" party may use deadly force in defense of another, only if the party whom he or she seeks to aid could use deadly force. *State v. Small,* 410 A2d 1336 (1980); *State v. Gelina,* 417 A2d 1381 (1980).

This brief and general summary does not provide all the information needed to answer questions regarding all specific circumstances. As long as all other legal requirements are met for owning a gun, a gun can be kept in the home for purposes of self-defense, but as can be seen, use of the gun, even in the home, does not automatically establish such use as self-defense.

South Carolina Law of Self-Defense

Source: William T. Toal
         Attorney at Law
         1108 Blanding St.
         Columbia, SC 29202
         (803) 252-9700

The following discussion of the South Carolina Law of Self-Defense is taken primarily from an article written by Mr. Toal for the *South Carolina Law Review*.

"To make out a plea of self-defense in South Carolina four things must be shown: First, the person must have thought the action necessary to prevent bodily harm or death; second, a person of ordinary reason and firmness in similar circumstances must think the action necessary; third, the person must have been without fault in bringing on the difficulty; and fourth, the person must have attempted to retreat prior to using force calculated to bring about death or great bodily harm." Except, "One who is on his own premises need not retreat. This applies to one who is in his own home or within his curtilage, or in his place of business, or on his own property outside the curtilage, or is a guest in the home of another. The immunity from retreat for one on his own premises is founded on the premise that a person confronted in his home should not be required to abandon his home to the attacker or be liable for the consequences if he remains.

"To establish the right to self-defense the defendant must show that he thought his actions necessary to prevent bodily harm or death. The necessity may be either real or apparent. Evidence of threats previously communicated by the deceased are admissible to show the defendant's belief of impending danger. A prior threat alone is insufficient unless accompanied by a demonstration of an immediate intention to execute that threat. Mere knowledge of previous misconduct is insufficient to show a brief in the necessity to act. If this necessity is shown, the defendant must also show that a man ordinarily constituted, or a man having an ordinary amount of two of the following characteristics would have believed it necessary to act if similarly situated: courage, firmness, judgment, prudence, discretion, and reason.

"A person claiming the right of self-defense must be without fault in bringing on the difficulty. This means that the defendant must not have been the aggressor nor have provoked the difficulty himself. Thus the use of language reasonably calculated to bring on difficulty deprives the defendant of the plea. This is true even if the language is directed toward someone under the care of the person who is provoked into attack rather than at him personally. The right of self-defense is not lost when the opprobrious words are used in reply to a similar attack.

"'[A] man's house is his castle . . .' Out of the underlying reason for this ancient maxim, rules have been formulated giving a person the right to use force in expelling unwanted persons from his home under some circumstances. The landmark case in this area, *State v. Bradley*, wisely divides the law of habitation into four situations: First, when the occupant is the slayer and stands on the right to protect his habitation, apart from the plea of self-defense; second, when the occupant is also the slayer and stands upon his right of self-defense claiming immunity not from the right to protect his habitat, but from the law of retreat; third, when the occupant is the slain and the homicide occurred while he was in the exercise of his right to protect his habitation; and fourth, when the occupant is also the slain and the homicide occurred while he was attempting to eject a trespasser from a part of the premises outside of his habitation.

"In the first situation the owner relies on the right of protection within the house to keep aggressors out. Thus when a man is assaulted in his home he may use such force as is necessary to protect himself or a member of his family from injury and combine such force as is reasonably necessary to eject the assailant, even to the extent of taking life. A guest in the home of the owner has the same opportunity to defend the habitation 'as if he were under his own roof or within his own doors.' The right to defense of habitation ceases as soon as the danger has passed.

"In the third and fourth situations the person slain is the owner of the premises. If the owner in using force is protecting his habitation, then the slayer is not without fault in bringing on the incident and cannot rely on the justification of self-defense. If, however, the ejection is wrongful under the principles previously discussed, the person being ejected is without fault in bringing on the incident and can rely on a plea of self-defense providing the other elements are established.

"Although a person is initially without fault in bringing on a difficulty, he may be at fault, and thus lose the right of self-defense, by responding with a disproportionate amount of force. The amount of force justified is not limited to the degree or quantity of the opposing force but rather can be that amount reasonably necessary for self-protection."

While a person may use deadly force to stop someone from breaking into his home, depending on the reasonableness of his actions, he cannot use deadly force simply to protect property. It should be emphasized, however, that the law is fairly clear that there must be an element of danger to the defender before he can use deadly force. I would not advise someone to immediately resort to the use of deadly force if the use of lesser and more reasonable force would have prevented the criminal act.

South Dakota Law of Self-Defense

Source: Jon E. Arneson
         Attorney at Law
         101 S. Main Ave., Suite 404
         Sioux Falls, SD 57102
         (605) 335-0083

There are several statutes in South Dakota that implicitly recognize a right to use deadly force in certain circumstances. However, South Dakota Supreme Court decisions indicate that the underlying condition for use of deadly force is that it appear reasonably necessary to prevent a particular victimization, although the requirement of reasonableness is not expressly incorporated within some of the statutes.

Two statutes, SDCL 22-16-34 and SDCL 22-16-35, specifically define two types of justifiable homicide. Since homicide obviously implies the use of deadly force, it is clear that the former statute permits a person to use deadly force to resist any felony attempted upon him, upon a dwelling house in which he is present or in a dwelling house in which he is present. Therefore, it is logical to assume that a person inside a home may use deadly force to prevent intrusion, since an attempted intrusion could be classified as an attempted burglary, which in turn could be classified as an attempted felony "upon or in any dwelling house," unless that phrase is interpreted very, very narrowly.

Although SDCL 22-16-34 contains no specific limitation on the use of deadly force in the felonious situations it covers, the case law does not sanction its use absent reasonable belief that it is necessary to prevent commission of the crime.

The second justifiable homicide statute, SDCL 22-16-35, allows the use of deadly force in defense of one's person, spouse, parent, child, master or mistress (in this context meaning employer of a servant), or servant against the commission of a felony or from the infliction of great personal injury. The statute does contain the qualification that the person using the deadly force in defense must have an actual and reasonably founded belief that a design to commit the felony or to inflict great personal injury existed and that the commission or infliction was imminent. Again, the South Dakota Supreme Court has added the second condition that the force used must be limited to that which appears reasonably necessary to prevent the felony or the injury. However, the Court's decisions plainly indicate that the person who uses the deadly force in defense is not required to make fine distinctions between the type or amount of force necessary.

Another area in which the use of deadly force might be justified is in the pursuit of a felon for purpose of arrest. SDCL 22-18-3 provides that a person may use or attempt or offer to use force or violence upon another person who has committed a felony when it is necessary to effect an arrest. It should be noted, however, that the statute is different from the aforementioned preventative statutes. The purpose of SDCL 22-18-3 is to facilitate apprehension so that a felon can be delivered to a public officer authorized to take custody. In effect, deadly force is not authorized per se. Presumably, the statute does not contemplate an intentional killing. But, the statute may permit the use of deadly force in a manner not intended to cause death.

Our general statute covering the use of force in defense is SDCL 22-18-4, which provides that one may use or attempt or offer to use force or violence upon another to prevent or attempt to prevent that other person from committing an offense against the person defending or a third party. The statute also authorizes a person to use or attempt or offer to use force or violence upon another to prevent a trespass or any other unlawful interference with real or personal property in his possession. There is a proviso, however, that the force or violence used be confined to that which is sufficient to prevent the offense. Obviously, the qualification is tantamount to a requirement that the force used appear reasonably necessary under the circumstances. The statute is not an automatic prohibition against the use of deadly force. However, it is clear that not all situations covered by SDCL 22-18-4 have been incorporated in the justifiable homicide statutes. Therefore, it is questionable whether deadly force can be used in defending all third persons and all types of property.

In short, it is difficult to assess precisely how restricted the use of deadly force in South Dakota is. Certainly, the vestiges of common law affect the exact application of the statutes to various factual situations. At a minimum, the use of any deadly force is conditioned, generally, on existence of circumstances which reasonably lead to the belief that the deadly force is necessary to prevent the offense.

Although there are no clearly defined rules whether a warning is a condition precedent to the use of deadly force, statutes and Court decisions do not suggest that a warning is necessary. However, if a warning is, in itself, adequate to prevent an offense, the use of actual force may not be justified.

Also, there is no precise position on retreat vis-à-vis use of deadly force. Certainly, the statutes make no reference to retreat. The pattern jury instructions used in South Dakota indicate that deadly force may be used without first attempting retreat in all of the aforementioned situations except when a person is being assaulted only with hands or fists and has no reason to believe that he will suffer great bodily harm or that the person assaulting him intends to inflict great bodily harm or worse. Basically, a person can stand one's ground and may even pursue, if that conduct appears reasonably necessary to eliminate the danger.

Threatening to use deadly force when it is not authorized by statute or case law is, technically, an assault. However, from a practical standpoint, if a threat or offer to use deadly force is made in the course of preventing some kind of attack and the circumstances would not actually justify the use of deadly force, it is highly unlikely that the person making the threat would be prosecuted.

Tennessee Law of Self-Defense

Source: Richard K. Mabee
         Attorney at Law
         1229 Volunteer State Life Bldg.
         Chattanooga, TN 37402

The following information is taken from the Tennessee Pattern Jury Instructions and, therefore, presents the instructions that have been given to juries on this subject.

Defense of Home or Habitation

"When an assault or an attempted forcible entry is made against a home or habitation under such circumstances that would create in the mind of a lawful occupant a well-founded and reasonable belief that he is in present and imminent danger of death or great bodily harm at the hands of the attacker or that the attacker intends to commit a felony therein, then a lawful occupant of a dwelling can use such reasonable force as is necessary, including deadly force, to prevent the intrusion."

[A person has the right to protect his own house and family, and to preserve peace and good order in his own house, and he has the right to use reasonable force to eject therefrom those who are drunken, disorderly, and dangerous. If while engaged in his duty, he is beset or menaced, he is entitled not only to the right of self-defense, but he may use such force as may be necessary to protect himself and family and to eject the intruder from his house.]

"A person is under no duty to retreat in his own home, even if he can safely do so, but may stand his ground and use reasonable force to prevent or stop an invasion of his home or habitation.

"In determining whether the defendant's use of force in defending his home or habitation was reasonable, you may consider not only his actual use of force but also all the facts and circumstances leading up to it. Also, it is proper for you to consider the relative size and strength of the parties, and whether and how they were armed."

Defense of Property

"Generally, a person has the right to use reasonable force in defense of his property or property that he has a legal right to protect. However, such person must have had a reasonable belief that the force he used against the intruder was immediately necessary to prevent the interference with his property. Whether the belief of the defendant was reasonable and whether the amount of force used was reasonable are questions that the jury must determine, based on all the facts and circumstances in the case.

"Generally, in the absence of the use of force by an intruder, a person is not justified in the infliction of great bodily injury on such intruder, or the use of force to an extent that would endanger life. On the other hand, when the owner of property, while exercising reasonable force in its defense, meets with such acts of the aggressor as endanger such owner's life, then the owner may inflict great bodily harm or even kill in self-defense to protect his person, as distinguished from protecting his property."

Defense of Another

"A person interfering in a dispute, affray, or fight on behalf of another simply steps into the latter's shoes. He may lawfully do in another's defense only what that person could have done, and no more. He stands on the same plane, is entitled to the same rights, and is subject to the same conditions, limitations, and responsibilities as the person defended. And his act must receive the same construction as the act of the person defended would receive if the (killing) (assault) had been committed by that person.

"Thus, a person is not entitled to the plea of defense of another unless a plea of self-defense would have been available to the person on whose behalf he intervened. In other words, a person can do whatever the person for whom he intervened could have done in his own self-defense.

"For the defendant's contention that he acted in defense of another to be successful, the proof must have shown that the person for whom he intervened was assaulted in such a way as to induce in that person's mind a genuine and well-founded belief that he was in actual and imminent danger of death or great bodily harm. Whether the person on whose behalf he intervened could have acted in self-defense, as the defendant claims, is a question for you (the jury) to decide."

Texas Law of Self-Defense

Source: Bradford E. Yock
         Attorney at Law
         202 Travis, Suite 408
         Old Cotton Exchange Bldg.
         Houston, TX 77002
         (713) 224-8093

Mr. Yock, a sole practitioner, practices law in Houston, Texas, where his practice consists of exclusively criminal cases.

Images of western-style gunfights spring forth when one mentions "self-defense" and "Texas" in the same breath. The statutory law of self-defense, which may be found in Sections 9.01 through 9.63 of Vernon's Annotated Penal Code, conveys a less romantic picture of the right of self-defense than one would find represented in the popular media. The law of self-defense essentially is concerned with one's right to use physical force against another person.

Initially, one at least must reasonably believe that the force one is going to use is immediately necessary to protect himself against another's use or attempted use of unlawful force. Additionally, if one is using deadly force to protect his home, he must reasonably believe that the force is immediately necessary to prevent the other's imminent commission of certain specified crimes, e.g. burglary.

Before using deadly force one must also believe that either one's home cannot be protected by other means than deadly force, or the mere use of non-deadly force would allow the intruder to pose a substantial risk of death or serious bodily injury.

Of course, this discussion is not complete without a word of caution to those who would rely upon the above discussion as the final word. The law of self-defense is far too complex to be explained in a few short paragraphs. The information set forth here is only intended as a guide and should not be followed mechanically.

Another key restriction on the use of deadly force is the duty to retreat before using deadly force. One has the duty to retreat, even in one's own home, if a reasonable person in that situation would have retreated and the intent is to defend oneself rather than to repel an intruder.

However, Texas law is unclear whether one must ever retreat before using deadly force in the defense of the home. There is clearly no absolute requirement of warning or notice to the intruder, before using deadly force, if its use is otherwise justified.

The use of deadly force in defense of a third person is lawful if one has a reasonable belief that the acts threatened against the third person would justify the use of deadly force to protect oneself. Further, one must reasonably believe that the use of deadly force is immediately necessary to protect the third person.

One may threaten to use deadly force, only if he is entitled to use it. It should be remembered that "deadly force" includes any force that is intended to cause or in the manner it's use may cause death or serious bodily injury. A firearm is only one type of deadly weapon.

The code only allows for the use of deadly force, when it is reasonably thought to be immediately necessary to prevent escape following the commission of specified crimes: burglary, robbery, aggravated robbery, or theft during the nighttime. No other crimes are included.

Among other significant points of general interest in the law of self-defense is the notion that the use of force or deadly force is not lawful simply because one is provoked by verbal insults. The lawful use of force against another is also affected, when there exists a special legal relationship such as; a law enforcement officer making an arrest, between a parent and child.

There are also special rules governing the use of force in situations where a person's life is in danger, e.g. suicide attempts. The law of self-defense restricts the use of any device that operates in your absence to deter intruders.

No discussion of the law of self-defense is complete without a reference to civil liability. Even though one accused of a crime might be found not guilty because he was found to have acted in self-defense, he may still be liable for civil damages. Therefore, for those who maintain guns or other deadly weapons the best advice is to err on the side of caution.

Utah Law of Self-Defense

Source: John W. Call
Attorney at Law
211 East Broadway
Salt Lake City, UT 84111
(801) 532-7937

Use of legal force in Utah is currently governed by §76-2-401 et. seq., Utah Code Annotated. These provisions outline justification which will exclude criminal responsibility. There are separate provisions for different instances where force can be used.

A person is justified in using deadly force in defense of his habitation only if (1) the entry or attempted entry is "violent and tumultuous" *and* he "reasonably believes" that the entry will result in personal violence to anyone therein and that deadly force is necessary to prevent it, or (2) he "reasonably believes" that the entry will result in the commission of a felony *and* that deadly force is necessary to prevent it.

In the most recent decision concerning the foregoing provision, the Utah Supreme Court held that a defendant who killed an intruder who refused to leave the defendant's sister's home (where the defendant was staying) was entitled to raise this defense.

There are no requirements in the defense of habitation section that one give a warning to the intruder or retreat further within his habitation before using deadly force, assuming he otherwise has the right to use such force.

A threat to use deadly force where use of such force is not proper could constitute a criminal offense. In fact, Utah law defines the threat to use a "dangerous weapon" in a fight or quarrel as a Class B misdemeanor. However, in one's own home, a threat to use deadly force could arguably be seen as use of lesser force. Such lesser force is allowed by the statute in instances where deadly force is not proper.

Where the act has already been committed, it would appear that one would *not* be justified in using deadly force to prevent the criminal from escaping. The statute allows use of such force only to prevent violence or a crime. In the words of a neighboring state's supreme court construing a similar statute, "the right is limited to prevention; it does not extend to punishment for an act already committed." Utah frequently follows the decisions of neighboring states.

I should include mention that Utah law specifically allows all persons not otherwise prohibited from owning firearms (convicts, mental incompetents, etc.) the right to keep loaded weapons at their place of business or residence and unloaded (empty chamber) in their vehicles. This right extends to temporary residences and camps.

As for my advice to a Utah resident who keeps a gun at home for self-defense,

I would first say be familiar enough with the weapon to use it properly. In Utah it is no defense to a homicide charge to say the wrong person was killed. Accordingly, make sure the weapon is not so powerful that overpenetration would be a serious problem. I would tell my client that if he reasonably felt in danger to not hesitate thereafter in use of a weapon, for, as a great jurist of the past once said, "the law does not demand detached reflection in the face of an upraised knife."

Vermont Law of Self-Defense

Source: Peter F. Langrock, Esq.
         Attorney at Law
         15 South Pleasant St.
         Middlebury, VT 05753

In Vermont, a person may use deadly force when he, a member of his household, or another person is threatened with death or great bodily harm. An actual threat of such danger is not required, only a reasonable belief that such danger exists. What constitutes a reasonable belief in death or great bodily harm varies with the circumstances. This discussion provides an overview of some aspects of Vermont law regarding the use of deadly force.

1) An individual may use deadly force to prevent another from breaking into his home when he reasonably believes that the purpose of breaking in is to inflict death or great bodily harm to him or his family (perhaps inhabitants). (*State v. Patterson,* 45 Vt. 308). A person may not use deadly force upon someone breaking in when he reasonably believes the trespasser does not intend to inflict death or great bodily harm, but only intends to abscond with or injure property. (*Id*). A determination of what a reasonable person would believe is the intent of a trespasser would involve the type of invasion, the manner of entering, the physical appearance of the trespasser, and his belief as to the intruder's knowledge of his whereabouts.

2) Vermont law has no requirement that a warning be given before resorting to deadly force.

3) There is a general duty to retreat if that opportunity appears to the person attacked to be reasonably available and sufficient for safety (*State v. Albano,* 92 Vt. 51). This general duty applies even when one is threatened at home (*State v. Tubbs,* 101 Vt. 5). The presence of an intruder in one's home, as opposed to some other locations, may, however, significantly affect the reasonable availability and sufficiency of retreating in response to the invasion. An occupant may not be required to retreat from the presence of an intruder to another room if such retreat would not effectively remove the threat of death or great bodily harm.

4) Vermont statutory law permits an individual to use deadly force in the just and necessary defense of himself, his spouse, parent, child, sibling, master, servant, guardian, or ward (V.S.A.T. 13 §2305[1]). In addition, Vermont law permits the use of deadly force to prevent murder or forcible (violent) rape, burglary, or robbery (V.S.A.T. 13 §2305[2]). Thus, a host could use deadly force to protect a guest from an attempted murder or attempted forcible rape or an attempted forcible robbery.

5) Since a person is only entitled to use deadly force when in reasonable apprehension of death or great bodily harm to himself or others, a threat to use

deadly force when not in such reasonable apprehension will not be sanctioned, and may constitute an assault.

6) After a felony has been committed and the perpetrator is escaping, the person attacked may not use deadly force if he no longer reasonably believes himself to be in danger of death or great bodily harm (*State v. Roberts,* 63 Vt. 139). He may, however, use deadly force if an escaping attacker still poses a reasonable threat of death or great bodily harm. The proximity of the escaping attacker, the manner of escape, and the nature of the attack are some of the circumstances relevant in determining the reasonableness of a continued belief in death or great bodily harm from the attacker(s).

(Author's note: Mr. Frank Conrad of Ludlow, Vermont, also researched the Vermont law of self-defense. Although his information wasn't used because of time and space limitations, his efforts are certainly appreciated.)

Virginia Law of Self-Defense

Source: James S. Sease
Attorney at Law
7 East Franklin St.
Richmond, VA 23219

Virginia law states: "Killing in self-defense may be either justifiable or excusable homicide. Justifiable homicide in self-defense occurs where a person, without any fault on his part in provoking the difficulty, kills another under reasonable apprehension of death or great bodily harm to himself. Excusable homicide in self-defense occurs where the accused, although in some fault in the first instance in provoking the difficulty, when attacked retreats as far as possible, announces his desire for peace, and kills his adversary from a reasonably apparent necessity to preserve his own life or save himself from great bodily harm. But bare fear that a person intends to inflict serious bodily injury on the accused, however well-grounded, unaccompanied by any overt act indicating such intention, will not warrant killing such person."

"A defendant may always act upon reasonable appearance of danger, and whether the danger is reasonably apparent is always to be determined from the viewpoint of the defendant at the time he acted."

One of the essential elements in the right to self-defense is *reasonable* grounds to believe (as well as an actual belief) that the danger is imminent. The circumstances must be such that a reasonably prudent person would believe the danger actually existed even if that belief was later proved to be false.

A simple fear that a person intends to attack you is not sufficient justification for the use of deadly force. There must be some overt act, on the person's part, indicative of imminent danger. Mere words without an overt act are not enough to justify the use of deadly force. Thus, if someone is standing outside your home shouting that he is going to kill you, you would not be entitled to defend yourself with deadly force unless the person actually began to smash his way into your home, shoot at you, etc.

In general, Virginia law does not allow a defender to use excessive force to protect himself. The force employed must be reasonably necessary for that purpose. Furthermore, the law does not allow a person to provoke an attack, slay his assailant, and then claim that he acted in self-defense.

One may use deadly force against an intruder if his dwelling is assailed with intent to take life or to inflict great bodily harm. An individual in his own home may also use deadly force to prevent an intruder from committing a felony therein, but only if there is no other way of preventing the felony.

The retreat rule, mentioned previously, does not apply to one who is assaulted in his own home. To the contrary, one who is without fault and is attacked in his own home is entitled to stand his ground and defend himself.

An individual does not have a right to use deadly force merely to protect property. One does have a right to use force in order to protect his property, but that force must not be excessive, on the theory that human life is more important than material goods. Nor does one have the right to use deadly force against a simple trespasser, such as a person who is merely walking across your property.

There is no requirement in Virginia that a person defending himself in his home has to give a warning before resorting to the use of deadly force—when he is entitled to use that force. If you do decide to issue a warning, you should be careful about threatening the use of deadly force. If you were to issue a threat or warning that was provocative, it could be construed to be "fighting words." This could make you the aggressor and justify the use of force against you. Of course, this would not apply if you were facing an intruder in your home in the middle of the night. The problem would be more likely to arise if you were in a situation that did not entitle you to use the force that you were threatening another with.

An individual is entitled to use deadly force to protect others in his home as he would himself. This right extends to strangers as well as to other family members. But the defender stands in the shoes of the third party he is protecting; i.e., whether or not the third party was the original aggressor and is himself entitled to the use of deadly force for self-defense.

Washington Law of Self-Defense

Source: William J. Sorcinelli
        Attorney & Counselor at Law
        N. 917 Adams, Suite 102
        Spokane, WA 99201
        (509) 328-9295

Mr. Sorcinelli is a sole practitioner in Spokane, Washington, where he engages in the general practice of law with emphasis in the litigation of personal injury and criminal law cases.

In Washington, the use, attempt, or offer to use force upon or toward the person of another is statutorily declared *not* unlawful in certain circumstances. RCW 9A.16.020 (2) allows force to be used whenever its use is necessary to arrest and then deliver one who has committed a felony to a public officer competent to receive him into custody.

The next section, RCW 9A.16.020 (3), allows a party to lawfully use force in preventing or attempting to prevent an offense against his person, a malicious trespass, or other malicious interference with real or personal property lawfully in his possession. This statute allows the use of force to the extent necessary to prevent such an offense, but it is silent as to any distinction between "deadly" force and other "reasonable" force.

Washington court developed law has restricted the amount of force that may be used in self-defense by requiring the person claiming justification of his force to produce some evidence tending to prove that such force was reasonably necessary, as viewed by one standing in his shoes. Under the conditions appearing to him at that time, a person may use the same degree of force that a reasonably prudent person would consider necessary to protect himself or another. (No direct relationship such as husband-wife or brother-sister need exist before one can protect another person.) This subjective standard seems to require that no reasonably effective alternative appeared to exist at the time.

Washington, along with several other western states, does not extend the "reasonably effective alternative" to require one to retreat or give warning before using deadly force against a party committing or appearing to commit a felony or some great personal injury upon the defender or his dwelling. A homeowner in his dwelling or, for that matter, in a place where he has a lawful right to be does not have to retreat or run, but may stand his ground and defend himself even to the extent of taking a human life.

When such a confrontation occurs in the defender's dwelling, Washington law does not appear to require that the defender be in imminent personal danger before resorting to the use of force. Nor does a warning need to be given unless the circumstances of the individual case would lead a reasonable man to believe that he or his family were in no danger from the intruder. This apparent right to defend a dwelling would most likely not extend to personal property alone without a trespass into the dwelling with the resulting danger to its occupants.

Persons committing a certain class of crime—felonies committed by violence and surprise—are open game to the defenders of such crimes. These crimes have been identified by Washington court cases as murder, robbery, burglary, arson, and breaking into a dwelling with the intent to rob and rape. This open season on felons appears to stem from the feeling that one committing or attempting to commit such a crime is not deserving of a warning or an opportunity to "shoot first" during the commission of the crime.

A felon who is fleeing from the commission of a felony is committing a felony in his attempt to escape from the scene of the crime. If the felon were leaving a room in a victim's dwelling after committing one of the above mentioned crimes, and the person reasonably felt that he or she were still in danger or felt that the felon might do further bodily harm to someone else in the dwelling, the use of deadly force would most likely be sanctioned in the state of Washington. It is extremely doubtful that a rape victim would be held "not justified" in taking the life of her rapist, just because he had begun to leave the scene of the crime. Of course, the reasonableness of the amount of force used would become more difficult to ascertain as the rapist moved farther and farther away from his victim.

One who intends to use a gun to protect his home would be well advised to learn the appropriate uses of the weapon and its limitation. He should also be aware of his own limitations, whether they be physical or moral, for once the lead starts traveling at 3,000 feet per second, the decisions relative to its justification cannot be altered.

For a complete legal opinion of the rights and obligations relative to self-defense in Washington, any lay person should contact his legal counsel for a breakdown of the rights and obligations as they relate to him personally at that time. Self-defense is such a fertile field for litigation and legislation, that these rights and obligations change almost daily.

West Virginia Law of Self-Defense

Source: Gregory E. Elliott
          Hanna and Elliott, Attorneys at Law
          1510 Kanawha Boulevard, East
          P.O. Box 2311
          Charleston, WV

Mr. Elliott is engaged in the general practice of law in Charleston, West Virginia. Prior to entering private practice, Mr. Elliott was an Assistant Attorney General for the State of West Virginia, during which time he handled many criminal appeals for the State of West Virginia.

In the state of West Virginia, a person has the legal right to use deadly physical force to prevent certain criminal actions. The current law on the subject has evolved on a case-by-case basis and it is important to note that this brief synopsis cannot be applied rigidly to all fact situations because there nearly always is an exception to any given rule. The application of the rule of self-defense depends on the facts and circumstances of each individual case.

A person may be justified in using deadly force in some situations. The key word in the application of the rule of self-defense is the word "reasonable." Usually, the defense of one's person or property is considered to be a permissible defense.

In West Virginia, "when one without fault himself is attacked by another in such a manner, or under such circumstances, as to furnish reasonable grounds for apprehending a design to take away his life, or do him some great bodily harm, and there is reasonable ground to believe, and does believe such danger is imminent, he may act upon such appearance, and without retreating, kill his assailant, if he has reasonable grounds to believe, and does believe, that such killing is necessary to avoid the apparent danger; and the killing, under such circumstances, is excusable, although it may afterwards turn out that the appearances were false, and there was in fact neither design to do him serious injury, nor danger that it would be done; but of all this the jury must judge, from the evidence and circumstances of the case." (*State v. Evans*; 33 W. Va. 417, 10 SE 792 [1890]).

An individual who has been assaulted has the right to use such force as he deems necessary to repel the attack (*State v. Reppert,* 132 W. Va. 675, 52 SE2d 820 [1949]). The essential element in order to justify using a deadly weapon in one's own defense is that an individual have "reasonable grounds" that the killing was necessary to preserve his own life or protect him from great bodily harm (*State v. Cain,* 20 W. Va. 679 [1882]).

If the accused individual has reason to believe the killing was warranted, and a reasonably prudent person would also believe the killing was warranted, and a reasonably prudent person would also believe the killing was necessary given the circumstances of the case, a valid defense may exist (*State v. Preece,* 116 W. Va. 176, 179 SE 524 [1935]). The facts and circumstances of each individual case are a question of fact which is subject to a jury's determination. The jury makes the final determination with regard to whether the killing was actually done in self-defense.

Some type of "overt act" is necessary at the time the fatal act is committed and an "overt act" is defined as any act which in the mind of a reasonably prudent person shows a present intent that the attacker means to kill that person, or do him serious bodily harm (*State v. Thornill,* 111 W. Va. 258, 161 SE 431 [1931]). Words or threats unaccompanied by an overt act do not constitute reasonable grounds for a homicide under the law of self-defense (*State v. Crawford,* 66 W. Va. 114, 66 SE 110 [1909]).

A plea of self-defense is not applicable when there is no imminent danger, or if the accused purposely brought on the shooting himself (*State v. Curry,* 112 W. Va. 549, 165 SE 810 [1932]).

If an attack is made with both a murderous intent and a deadly weapon, there being a sufficient overt act, the person being attacked being without fault, is under no duty to retreat and may stand his ground, and if need be, take the life of his attacker (*State v. Clark,* 51 W. Va. 457, 41 SE 204 [1902]).

One who is attacked in a public street, being without fault himself, is not bound to retreat, and may repel the assault with whatever means he deems necessary to protect his own life or save himself from great bodily harm (*State v. Donahue,* 79 W. Va. 260, 90 SE 834 [1884]).

A retreat is not necessary if you are attacked in your own home by an intruder, if it reasonably appears necessary for the protection of his home (*State v. Clark,* 51 W. Va. 457, 41 SE 204 [1902]).

The right to stand one's ground in defense of his property, without retreating, also extends to one's place of business, however this defense is permissible only within the bounds of necessity (*State v. Laura,* 93 W. Va. 250, 116 SE 251 [1923]). The use of a deadly weapon against an attacker does not usually extend to the taking of a life. The taking of another's life is viewed as being a last resort, and the person being attacked, must reasonably believe that the attacker will cause death or serious bodily harm to him or his family. If the wrongful act taking place on the property is a felony, then the intruder may be killed, if there is no other way to protect the property.

Extreme caution needs to be used however, for if the killing is outside the bounds of necessity, a person may be guilty of second degree murder or manslaughter. There may be a right to resist an intruder, but not to take his life. The facts and circumstances of each individual case are subject to a final analysis by a jury.

The right of self-defense may be exercised in behalf of a mother, wife, brother, or stranger, provided one would lawfully be entitled to the defense himself, upon being threatened with death or great bodily harm (*State v. Foley,* 131 W. Va. 326, 47 SE2d 40 [1948]).

The law is silent as to whether or not you must warn someone before using deadly force. It is advisable that one would threaten to use deadly force only when you would be justified in using it.

If an assailant has committed an assault, and is still present in the immediate proximity, the plea of self-defense may be justified, depending upon the facts and circumstances of the individual case.

Anytime the plea of self-defense is invoked, and the use of a firearm is involved, *extreme care* and *caution* should be used. If an individual was not justified in using deadly force, or if an innocent bystander was injured, the person responsible would be subject to both criminal and civil liability for his negligence. In West Virginia, any felony committed with the use of a firearm carries, upon conviction, an automatic sentence of three years in the State Penitentiary.

Wisconsin Law of Self-Defense

Source: Joseph M. Recka
         Attorney at Law
         414 E. Walnut St.
         Suite 101
         Green Bay, WI 54301

Wisconsin Statute 939.48 states that "...[One]... may not intentionally use force which is intended or likely to cause death or great bodily harm unless he reasonably believes that such force is necessary to prevent imminent death or great bodily harm to himself." ("Great bodily harm" would include rape.) It is very important to note the word "reasonably" in the preceeding statute. Even though you may have believed that the use of deadly force was absolutely necessary, if a court finds that your belief was not reasonable, you would not be entitled to a claim of self-defense.

The courts have also held that when one is entitled to use force that force must not be excessive. Wisconsin Jury Instructions #800 state that "the amount of force used must be no more than a person of ordinary intelligence and prudence would have believed necessary and not excessive under the circumstances." A person who shoots an inebriated neighbor who has lost his house keys and is climbing through the window of what the neighbor thought was his own house might be in for a hard time.

Wisconsin law is silent as to whether someone is required to give a warning before resorting to deadly force. I would hesitate to advise someone to issue a warning to an intruder with a flashlight in one hand and a gun in the other. On the other hand, in some cases a warning might alleviate the need for deadly force. A person who shoots an unarmed twelve-year-old burglar without giving a warning may be in for a lot of grief.

While a person is generally required to retreat as far as possible before resorting to deadly force for purposes of self-defense, this retreat rule does not apply when one is attacked in his own home. The attack must be by someone who does not live in the home, and the defender must not have been the original aggressor. However, the fact that retreat was feasible may be taken into account in determining whether the person reasonably believed that the amount of force used was necessary.

One is generally allowed to protect others in his home from criminal attack under the same rules that are applied to the defense of oneself. Wisconsin Statute 939.48 (4) allows a person to protect a third person if that force is necessary for the protection of the third person.

Wisconsin law does not allow a person to resort to deadly force in an attempt to protect personal property. You may use force, but that force must not be excessive. Wisconsin Statute 939.49 (1) states, "It is not reasonable to intentionally use force intended or likely to cause death or great bodily harm for the *sole* purpose of defense of one's property."

Wisconsin Supreme Court decisions interpreting the right to self-defense are few. The decisions available are generally from criminal cases where the right to self-defense has been denied. One situation where the claim of self-defense was rejected involved a person who returned to a tavern after a fight and killed his adversary with a shotgun. In another case an armed gunman told his victim, "this is a stickup." At that point the victim attacked the gunman and was shot to death. The gunman attempted to claim self-defense, but it was properly rejected.

The decision to prosecute someone who has used deadly force rests with the district attorney. His opinion of how the community views the particular situation and his knowledge of the feelings of the local judges will decide what the repercussions are for a person who exercises his right to self-defense. Basically, the decision to prosecute rests on the facts of each individual case.

The grief and suffering that may afflict a party who uses a firearm or even displays one with the threat of using it can be dismaying. Under Wisconsin law, one may not threaten the use of a firearm unless he is in a situation that legally entitles him to use it.

One client we represented, a slightly built sixty-year-old disabled veteran, lived in a furnished room in a home for transients. After he complained to the landlord about a loud party, one of the party goers, a twenty-eight-year-old recently released convict, forcibly entered the man's room. Our sixty-year-old client backed into a corner and finally took a twenty-five caliber automatic out of his dresser. When he pointed it at the intruder, the fellow left and called the police who promptly responded to the call and arrested the sixty-year-old man.

Rather than fight the case, which we wanted to do, the sixty-year-old pleaded guilty to disorderly conduct and let the police confiscate his gun. Few cases are going to be as clear-cut as that one was. As a result, before you decide to exercise your privilege of self-defense and resort to the use of deadly force, you should carefully consider how the case will look to the police and to a jury.

Wyoming Law of Self-Defense

Source: Laurence P. Van Court
         Attorney at Law
         The Teton Bldg.
         1807 Capitol Ave.
         Cheyenne, WY 82001
         (307) 635-2881

Mr. Van Court is an attorney in Cheyenne, Wyoming. His general practice has a heavy emphasis in criminal defense work. He also holds a third degree of black belt in karate; teaching, lecturing, and demonstrating self-defense in the Cheyenne area.

Wyoming's civil and criminal law of self-defense can be stated only in general rules of conduct, which must be applied to the varied set of facts and circumstances of the particular case, and based on a general concept of reasonableness.

In defense of one's self, the facts and circumstances surrounding an attack by another person must reasonably place the victim in fear of bodily harm at the hands of the attacker. The fear of bodily harm must have a reasonable basis in fact.

The question of self-defense does not arise unless and until someone objects, by civil or criminal means, to the use of civil defense by the victim. At this point, the facts and circumstances of the event must be made available to the court or jury in order to show that the victim, now turned "defendant," observed and discerned the situation, reasonably concluded that he or she was in danger of bodily harm, and reacted with just enough force to repel or neutralize the attack. In a criminal matter, raising the issue of self-defense does not shift the burden of proof to the defendant, and a jury must be so instructed.

In the use of force for self-defense, only so much force can be used as will repel the aggressor or neutralize his attack to relieve the risk of harm. If excessive force is used by the victim, or if the victim refuses to allow his attacker to abandon the attack, the victim may become the aggressor.

The concept of "reasonably being in fear" indicates that the victim need not retreat all the way to the wall before applying a defense. Nor must the victim seek every possible avenue of escape before defending with force. Both retreat or escape must be reasonably available.

When the victim is on his "home ground," his residence or place of business, reasonable force may be used against an intruder to prevent damage to the property or the occupants, but, again, only so much force as is reasonable under the circumstances.

A person may lawfully arm himself in anticipation of a dangerous attack. When the victim employs a weapon in self-defense, the problem of seriously injuring or killing the attacker arises, and it must appear at trial that the victim reasonably believed he or she was in great peril of death or serious bodily harm, that the injury or killing was justified as a necessary and reasonable means of avoiding the threatened harm, and that the facts and circumstances surrounding the event must be such as to afford the belief of great peril.

A person asserting the justification of defense of another who is in peril steps into the shoes of the person defended: defense of another takes its form and content from defense of self. The defender must side with the victim of aggression, not the initiator of the attack, and the victim must be in immediate danger of unlawful bodily harm. The defender's use of force must be reasonable and necessary to relieve the risk of harm to the victim.

When two people have elected to fight, under Wyoming law, both parties are considered aggressors; the law does not allow anyone to take sides and aid one of the two to overcome the other.

When parties voluntarily engage in mutual combat, each combatant is liable in civil damages to the others in the fight. The fact that entering the fight was voluntary is not a defense to an action by other combatants.

The initiator of an attack may become a defender and may employ self-defense when he has attempted to abandon his attack, withdraw, or retreat from the event, and is not permitted to do so. At the point where the attacker attempts to retreat and is not allowed by the other party to do so, he may exercise the right of self-defense by use of only such force as will relieve the risk of harm.

The battered spouse (woman) syndrome has been raised as a form of self-defense in several states. The Wyoming Supreme Court, in April of 1981, indicated that research on the subject was still in its infancy and that acceptance or recognition of the phenomenon is limited. In the particular case the high court had before it, the state of the art had not been adequately demonstrated to the trial court.

The reader must be aware that to this point I have made no delineation of the circumstances of attack in which self-defense may be utilized. Wyoming law has based its premise on the "unlawful" attack. This seems to take in a lot more territory than the casual reader might expect because of the broad spectrum of crime and human behavior where violence arises. Rape or attempted sexual assault would constitute an unlawful attack and give cause for self-defense by the victim. The reasonableness of the amount of force used to repel the rapist will, as in all cases, be determined in retrospect by the trier of fact.

Notes

Chapter 2

1. Don B. Kates, Jr., ed., *Restricting Handguns: The Liberal Skeptics Speak Out.* Croton-on-Hudson, N.Y.: North River Press, Inc., 1979, p. 156.
2. Ibid., pp. 154-55.
3. E. B. Mann, "Can Crime Be Curbed?" *Field & Stream,* December 1979, p. 17.
4. Kates, p. 151.

Chapter 11

1. F. Lee Bailey and Henry B. Rothblatt, *Crimes of Violence: Homicide and Assault.* Rochester: The Lawyers Co-operative Publishing Co., 1973, p. 402.
2. Ibid.

Bibliography

Anderson, Ronald A. *Wharton's Criminal Law and Procedure,* Vol. I. Rochester: The Lawyers Co-operative Publishing Co., 1957.

Bailey, F. Lee, and Rothblatt, Henry B. *Crimes of Violence: Homicide and Assault.* Rochester: The Lawyers Co-operative Publishing Co., 1973.

Kates, Don B., Jr., ed. *Restricting Handguns: The Liberal Skeptics Speak Out.* Croton-on-Hudson, N.Y.: North River Press, Inc., 1979.

Mann, E. B. "Can Crime Be Curbed?" *Field & Stream,* December 1979, pp. 16-17.

———— "We Challenge Goliath," *Field & Stream,* October 1975, pp. 116-122.

U.S. Federal Bureau of Investigation, *Uniform Crime Reports,* 1980.

U.S. Treasury Department, Bureau of Alcohol, Tobacco and Firearms, *Federal Regulation of Firearms and Ammunition,* 1979.

Index

OTHER STEIN AND DAY BOOKS

			U.S.	Canada
	8056-0	**THE BOOK OF GHOST STORIES** Peter Haining	3.95	NCR
	8012-9	**CASEBOOK OF A PSYCHIC DETECTIVE** Dixie Yeterian	2.95	2.95
	8044-7	**FIFTY TRUE MYSTERIES OF THE SEA** John Canning. ed.	3.95	NCR
	8094-3	**THE SIN EATER** Elizabeth Walter	2.95	NCR
	8047-1 (Occult)	**STAR SIGNS FOR LOVERS** Liz Greene	3.95	NCR
	8018-8	**THIS HOUSE IS HAUNTED** Guy Lyon Playfair	3.50	NCR
	8025-0	**YOUR PERSONALITY AND THE PLANETS** Michel Gauquelin	3.50	NE

OTHER STEIN AND DAY BOOKS YOU'LL ENJOY:

			U.S.	Canada
8064-1	**ASSASSINATION DAY** Kenneth Royce		3.95	NCR
8042-0	**C.L.A.W.** Richard Graves		3.50	3.95
8013-7	**DIRTY TRICKS** Chapman Pincher		3.50	NCR
8019-6	**THE DUNKIRK DIRECTIVE** Donald Richmond		3.50	NE
8084-6	**FALLS THE SHADOW** Emanual Litvinoff		3.95	NCR
8066-8	**THE GAZA INTERCEPT** E. Howard Hunt		3.50	3.50
8032-3	**MAN ON A SHORT LEASH** Kenneth Royce		2.95	NCR
8080-3	**THE RED DOVE** Derek Lambert		3.95	NCR
8028-5	**THE RUN TO MORNING** Jack Higgins		3.50	3.50
8052-8	**SIEGE** Edwin Corley		3.95	3.95

Buy them at your local bookstore or use this convenient coupon for ordering:

STEIN AND DAY/Publishers
Scarborough House, Briarcliff Manor, NY 10510
DEPT. SC

Please send me the books I have checked above. I am enclosing $ _____ .
(Please add .75 per book to cover postage and handling.) Send check or money order—*no* cash or C.O.D.s. Prices and numbers are subject to change without notice.

Name _____

Address _____

City _____ State _____ Zip _____

Allow 4-6 weeks for delivery.

MILITARY BOOKS FROM STEIN AND DAY

			U.S.	Canada
	8035-8	**ALL THE DROWNED SAILORS** Raymond B. Lech	3.95	4.50
	8015-3	**DEATH OF A DIVISION** Charles Whiting	2.95	2.95
	8109-9	**THE GLORY OF THE SOLOMONS** Edwin Hoyt	3.95	4.95
	8100-1	**A HISTORY OF BLITZKREIG** Bryan Perrett	3.95	NCR
	8039-0	**HOW WE LOST THE VIETNAM WAR** Nguyen Cao Ky	3.50	3.95
	8027-7	**MASSACRE AT MALMEDY** Charles Whiting	2.95	3.50
	8045-5	**ROMMEL'S DESERT WAR** Samuel W. Mitcham, Jr.	3.50	3.95
	8105-2	**SALERNO** Eric Morris	3.95	4.95
	8033-1	**SECRETS OF THE SS** Glenn B. Infield	3.50	3.95
	8093-5	**SUBMARINES AT WAR** Edwin P. Hoyt	3.95	4.95
	8037-4	**THE WEEK FRANCE FELL** Noel Barber	3.95	4.50
	8057-9	**THE WORLD AT WAR** Mark Arnold-Forster	3.95	NCR